D1372003

Hebrew

PHRASEBOOK & DICTIONARY

Acknowledgments
Associate Publisher Mina Patria
Managing Editor Brigitte Ellemor
Editor Kate Mathews
Series Designer Mark Adams
Managing Layout Designer Chris Girdler
Layout Designer Carol Jackson
Production Support Larissa Frost
Language Writers Justin Ben-Adam (Rudelson), Ilana Wistinetzki

Thanks
Ben Handicott, James Hardy, Annelies Mertens, Naomi Parker, Trent
Paton, Piers Pickard, Raphael Richards, Jacqui Saunders, Branislava
Vladisavljevic, Wendy Wright

Published by Lonely Planet Publications Pty Ltd
ABN 36 005 607 983

3rd Edition – March 2013
ISBN 978 1 74179 138 9
Text © Lonely Planet 2013
Cover Image Covered market, Old City, Jerusalem, Israel. Walter
Bibikow / AWL Images ©

Printed in China   10 9 8 7 6 5 4 3

Contact lonelyplanet.com/contact

MIX
Paper from
responsible sources
FSC™ C02174

acknowledgments

This 3rd edition of Lonely Planet's *Hebrew phrasebook* is based on the previous edition by the Lonely Planet Language Products team and authors Justin Ben-Adam (Rudelson) and Ilana Wistinetzki.

about the authors

Justin Ben-Adam (Rudelson), formerly Justin Jon Rudelson, was born in Beverley Hills, California. He is also the author of Lonely Planet's *Central Asia phrasebook*. He holds a doctorate in Social Anthropology from Harvard University, and speaks more than 20 languages.

Much of Rudelson's work has pursued bridging relations between Israel and China. This is appropriate, since Xinjiang, China, where Rudelson has done extensive work with the Uyghur Muslims, lies halfway between Beijing and Jerusalem. He introduced Israeli irrigation systems to the deserts of China, helped retrieve the remains of an Israeli tourist from the Xinjiang–Tibet border, initiated research missions of Chinese desert scientists to Israel, and brought about the first Hebrew language courses ever taught in China, at Beijing University. His greatest accomplishment and joy is the bridge of love he has built with his wife, Chelle.

While working in China in 1985, Rudelson met Ilana Wistinetzki, the only Israeli student in China, while she was studying at Beijing University. They shared the same hope for bridging China–Israel relations, and both rode their bicycles though the streets of China singing Hebrew songs at the top of their lungs. As fate would have it, Ilana later went on to teach Beijing University's Hebrew courses. Over the years they have kept in touch, sharing wild tales of Israel's oft-times bizarre waltz with China. Their co-authorship of this book is yet another chapter in this unfolding saga.

Ilana Wistinetzki was born in Tel Aviv and grew up in Givataim. At age 27 she exchanged the Mediterranean spell with the charms of Paris, where she went to study Chinese. She has been a student of Chinese ever since.

from the authors

In his odyssey with the Hebrew language, which began at age 20, Justin gives his greatest thanks to Rabbi Michael Paley, his rebbi while he was an undergraduate at Dartmouth College. Rabbi Paley filled him with the desire to learn the language of his wandering ancestors and with the joy of Jewish learning, even when all he could do during worship services was to rock back and forth in his chair, smile and hum.

In Israel, Justin's tremendous love goes to Monette, Christian, Moshe and Keren Seboun, who gave him a home in the Holy Land and welcomed him from his wanderings abroad with hearts filled with love and understanding. He gives his thanks to those who helped him recover the Hebrew language lost during the Jewish Diaspora to his ancestors. These include Ulpan Akiva in Netanya, Dana Stern, and especially Ronit Feingold. He gives his huge khibukim to the entire Feingold family of Nataf, including Haim, Ronit, Daniel, Tal and Irit. They invigorated his love of Hebrew during his stay in New Orleans and in Israel taught him that his destiny is to be a citizen of the world. May melakh rats forever!

Justin's contribution to this book is dedicated to his wife, Chelle 'Che' Rudelson, who is the love of his existence.

The opportunity to work with Justin, whom Ilana Wistinetzki first met in Beijing in 1985, was her greatest motivation to embark on this project. But her part in this very book could not have been accomplished without the help of very dear and close friends. Peter, her charming prince who, not least, cracked off-handedly the mysteries and vagaries of the software; Talya, who always remembered the words she didn't; her brother Yoram and nephew Idan, who updated her on idioms; Susan her enthusiastic student and friend who, together with Noa, provided a list of dishes; and, last but not least, Cristina in Paris, who needs to refresh her Hebrew vocabulary.

She dedicates this book in memory of her father, Johanan Wistinetzki, whose love for languages was second only to his love of music.

from the publisher

Thanks to the Lonely Planet Language Products team who produced the 2nd edition of the *Hebrew phrasebook*, on which this one is based: Mimoon AbuAta, Joanne Adams, Julian Chapple, Peter D'Onghia, Patrick Marris, Renée Otmar, Sally Steward, Danny Tedeschi and Vicki Webb.

CONTENTS

INTRODUCTION   הקדמה

Hebrew is one of the world's oldest languages, and is the principal language of the State of Israel. Although the modern Hebrew language was developed over the past century, it's spoken and written in much the same way as the ancient Hebrew language of the Bible more than 3000 years ago. Hebrew is a Semitic language related to Arabic. It was spoken during the migration of the ancient Hebrews into the Land of Canaan (the Holy Land) and by the Israelites during the Old Testament period. The language declined and then ceased to be spoken around 250 BC. At this time, Aramaic, the lingua franca of the Middle East, which was spoken by Jesus of Nazareth, gained supremacy. Unlike the spoken language, written Hebrew has continuously served as the language of religious, scholarly and interpersonal communication within and among Jewish communities throughout the world.

Israelis attribute great respect to a single individual for Hebrew's revitalisation – Eliezer Ben-Yehuda. In the late 19th century, Jewish spoken communication throughout the world was divided between the Ladino language of Sephardic Jews living in North Africa, Spain, the Middle East and Turkey (a Sephardic Jew is a person from the Oriental Jewish community), and the Yiddish language of Ashkenazi Jews (European Jews) living in Northern and Eastern Europe. Although the two languages were both written in the Hebrew alphabet, they were mutually unintelligible, with Ladino resembling Spanish and Yiddish being related to German.

In an attempt to unify Jews around the world by bridging this barrier, Ben-Yehuda and others devoted their lives to reviving Hebrew as a spoken language. They introduced thousands of modern words based on biblical Hebrew, and their efforts proved a great success. Spoken Hebrew gained popularity among Jewish settlers in Palestine, and became one of the the official languages of

Israel, along with Arabic, on its independence in 1948. Today, more than five million people speak Hebrew. Several years ago, Ben-Yehuda's grave was desecrated by graffiti written in Hebrew. While the nation was outraged, his family declared the graffiti proved Ben-Yehuda's ultimate victory, for it was written in Hebrew and not in the Yiddish or Ladino languages.

Modern Hebrew is a combination of Biblical Hebrew blended with the religious and scholarly Hebrew used in written communication for nearly 2000 years. Over the past two or three generations, thousands of new words have been created to accommodate science, technology, politics and literature. Many words and expressions have developed through borrowings from Arabic. But the revitalised Modern Hebrew language is so true to that used in the Bible, that readers of modern Israeli newspapers, books and journals are able to read Biblical Hebrew fluently.

The Hebrew alphabet has 22 letters, with five of these letters changing their form when at the end of a word. The script is written from right to left, which some attribute to the ease of chiseling a stone from right to left by right-handed people. The structure of the language is fairly easy to understand, because each word is made up of a root consisting of three consonants. A word changes its meaning by changing the vowels associated with that word, or by adding prefixes and suffixes to the word.

The Hebrew vowel system that uses small dots and dashes inside, above and below consonants (nikud) isn't used in daily practice in Israel, and isn't used in this book. This system was developed in about the 8th century AD, and is still used today in prayer books, poetry, texts for foreigners and children's books. Vowels are a difficult feature of Hebrew, because they're omitted from words written on posters, street signs, newspapers and books. If you can make out that a sign reading 'BNK' is about a 'bank', there's no need to add the 'a'. By sounding out billboards and street signs, you'll gradually get the hang of it.

Although many Israelis speak English, nearly all Israelis speak Hebrew. Most immigrants to Israel learn Hebrew quickly in an intensive language centre called ulpan, where tourists can also study. Although Hebrew is the common language, the linguistic diversity of Israel is extremely broad. Each Israeli city or town represents one of the various waves of immigration to Israel. In a single town, you might find people from Poland, Morocco and Argentina, and in another emigrants from Ethiopia, Russia and Uzbekistan. So if you speak languages other than English, such as French, Russian, Spanish or Chinese, you might seek out these immigrant communities to learn of their history.

Most Israelis will be pleased to speak with you in Hebrew, but if you can't get your meaning across with words, the Israelis are masters of gesture and body language. Most Israelis openly discuss personal matters, but there are also many touchy subjects you'll need to be sensitive about. It's important to acknowledge that the Arab–Israeli conflict has been a tragedy on all sides. The issues involved in the lives of Muslim and Christian Arabs of Israeli citizenship, and of Palestinians living in the West Bank and Gaza Strip, are extremely complex. Jerusalem itself, with its mixture of traditional Arab and orthodox Jewish neighbourhoods, and their tense coexistence with secular modernist parts of the city, seems to reflect all the sensitive issues in Israel. This said, Israelis love to debate Israeli and international affairs. So don't be surprised if total strangers engage you in heated discussion while you wait for a bus or for a shawarma (doner kebab) at a falafel stand.

ABBREVIATIONS USED IN THIS BOOK

מפתח קיצורים בשיחון

f	feminine
lit	literal
m	masculine
pl	plural
pol	polite
sg	singular

HOW TO USE THIS PHRASEBOOK

איך להשתמש בשיחון

You *Can* Speak Another Language

It's true – anyone can speak another language. Don't worry if you haven't studied languages before, or that you studied a language at school for years and can't remember any of it. It doesn't even matter if you failed English grammar. After all, that's never affected your ability to speak English! And this is the key to picking up a language in another country. You just need to start speaking. Once you start, you'll be amazed at how many prompts you'll get to help you build on those first words. You'll hear people speaking, pick up sounds from TV, catch a word or two you know from the local radio – all these things help to build your understanding.

Since Hebrew is a gendered language, and since the phrases in this book are intended to be used in everyday situations, we have devised a system whereby the same phrase can be properly used by a female speaker and a male speaker. The masculine and feminine forms are sometimes presented by giving the feminine suffix in brackets after the masculine form.

to speak	medaber (m)
	medaberet (f)
presented in this book as	medaber(et)

For words in which the masculine and feminine forms differ in the use of vowels, the whole word is provided for both genders.

I need assistance.   ani tsarikh (tsrikha) ezra

On some occasions, especially when the pronoun 'you' is involved and there's a risk of confusion, two full sentences are quoted.

Do you have a cigarette?
   yesh lekha sigariya? (m)
   yesh lakh sigariya? (f)

You'll notice that sometimes the masculine and feminine forms in the Hebrew script are identical; this is one of the benefits of having a script without embedded vowels. For example, the consonants for lekha and lakh are identical, and the speaker/reader is required to choose the appropriate form, depending on the context.

Plunge In

There's just one thing you need to start speaking another language – courage. Your biggest hurdle is overcoming the fear of saying aloud what may seem to you to be just a bunch of sounds. There are a number of ways to do this.

Firstly, think of some Hebrew words or phrases you are familiar with, such as 'shalom' or 'kibbutz'. From these basic beginnings you can start making sentences. Don't worry that you're not getting a whole sentence right first time. People will understand if you stick to the key word. And you'll find that, once you're in the country, it won't take long to remember the complete sentence.

The best way to start overcoming your fear is to memorise a few key words. These are the words you know you'll be saying again and again, like 'hello', 'thank you' and 'how much?' Here's an important hint though – right from the beginning, learn at least one phrase that will be useful but not essential. Such as 'good morning' or 'good afternoon', 'see you later' or even a conversational piece like 'lovely day, isn't it?' or 'it's cold today' (people everywhere love to talk about the weather). Having this extra phrase (just start with one, if you like, and learn to say it really well) will help you move away from the basics, and when you get a reply and a smile, it'll also boost your confidence. You'll find that people you speak to will like it, too. They'll appreciate that you've tried to learn more of the language than just the usual essential words.

Ways to Remember

There are several ways to learn a language. Most people find they learn from a variety of these, although people usually have

INTRODUCTION

a preferred way to remember. Some like to see the written word and remember the sound from what they see. Some like to just hear it spoken in context (if this is you, try talking to yourself in Hebrew). Others, especially the more mathematically inclined, like to analyse the grammar of a language and piece together words according to the rules of the grammar. Those who are visually inclined like to associate the written word, and even sounds, with some visual stimulus, such as from illustrations, TV and general things they see in the street. As you learn, you'll discover what works best for you – be aware of what made you really remember a particular word, and keep using that method.

Kicking Off

Chances are you'll want to learn some of the language before you go. So you won't be hearing it around you. The first thing to do is to memorise those essential phrases and words. Check out the basics (page 57) ... and don't forget that extra phrase (see Plunge In!). Try the sections on Greetings or First Encounters in the chapter on Meeting People (pages 57 and 58) for a phrase you'd like to use. Write down some of these words and phrases and stick them up around the place – on the fridge, by the bed, on your computer, as a bookmark – somewhere where you'll see them often. Try putting some words in context – the 'How much is it?' note, for instance, could go in your wallet.

Building the Picture

We include a grammar chapter in our books for two main reasons. Firstly, some people have an aptitude for grammar and find understanding it a key tool in their learning. If you're such a person, then the grammar chapter in this phrasebook will help you build a picture of the language, since it works through all the basics.

The second reason for the grammar chapter is that it gives answers to questions you might raise as you hear or memorise some key phrases. You may find a particular word is always used when there is a question – check out Questions in the Grammar chapter. You don't have to read the grammar chapter from start to finish, nor do you need to memorise a grammatical point. It will simply present itself to you in the course of your learning. Key grammatical points are repeated throughout the book.

Any Questions?

Try to learn the main question words (see page 51). As you read through different situations, you'll see these words used in the example sentences, and this will help you remember them. So if you want to hire a bicycle, turn to the Bicycles section in Getting Around (use the Contents or Index to find it quickly). You'll see the words for 'where' and 'bicycle' a number of times in this book. When you come across the sentence 'Where can I hire a bicycle?', you'll recognise the key words which will help you remember the whole phrase. If there's no category for what you want, try the dictionary (the question words are repeated there too, with examples), and memorise the phrase 'How do you say ...?' (page 72).

I've Got a Flat Tyre

Doesn't seem like the phrase you're going to need? Well, in fact it could be very useful, as are all the phrases in this book, provided you have the courage to mix and match them. We have given specific examples within each section. But the key words remain the same even when the situation changes. So while you may not be planning on any cycling during your trip, the first part of the phrase 'I've got ...' could refer to anything else, and there are plenty of words in the dictionary that, we hope, will fit your needs. So whether it's 'a ticket', 'a visa' or 'a condom', you'll be able to put the words together to convey your meaning.

INTRODUCTION

Finally

Don't be concerned if you feel you can't memorise words. On the inside front and back covers are the most essential words and phrases you'll need. You could also try tagging a few pages for other key phrases, or use the notes pages to write your own reminders.

The Hebrew alphabet has only 22 letters – all of them consonants. Hebrew does have a vowel system, nikud, but it isn't
embedded in the alphabet. These vowels consist of fixed symbols,
dots and strokes, and a few combinations of both, to represent
the five traditional vowels of 'a, e, i, o, u'. The Hebrew vowel
system is mobile – the symbols, dots and strokes can be added
above, under and inside the printed word – but it can also be
omitted. Nowadays children are taught to read and write without the help of nikud.

The nikud system has not been used in this book. Instead,
an English-based transliteration system has been provided to
help you use Hebrew in everyday situations. It should also be
helpful should you decide to undertake an indepth study of
the Hebrew language.

Most consonants used in the transliteration system sound the
same as in English. Some words may seem difficult to pronounce at
first, as consonants aren't always followed by a vowel, and words like
kvutsa, efshar, ashkelon and meshalshel may take some practice.

VOWELS

תנועות

In the system of transliteration provided here, there are five major
vowels and a two-vowel cluster, or diphthong.

a   as the 'a' in 'after'
e   as the 'e' in 'egg'
i   as the 'i' in 'mistake'
o   as the 'o' in 'north'
u   as the 'u' in 'flute'

Diphthongs

ei   as the 'ay' in 'day'

PRONUNCIATION

HEBREW ALPHABET

א	aleph	a guttural consonant gone mute. Today what we actually hear is the sound of its vowel.
ב	bet	as the 'b' in 'bold'
ב	vet	as the 'v' as in 'vast'
ג	gimel	as the 'g' in 'game'
ד	dalet	as the 'd' in 'door'
ה	heh	as the 'h' in 'hope'
ו	vav	as the 'v' in 'voice'; ו vav also serves as a marker for the vowels o and u
ז	zain	as the 'z' in 'zebra'
ח	khet	the 'ch' sound in 'Bach'. This sound is identical to that of the letter כ khaf.
ט	tet	as the 't' in top
כ	kaf	as the 'k' in 'king'
כ	khaf	sounds like the 'ch' in 'Bach'
ל	lamed	as the 'l' in 'love'
מ	mem	as the 'm' in 'mother'
נ	nun	as the 'n' in 'nature'
ס	samekh	as the 's' in 'soul'
ע	ayin	this letter is a glottal stop, and sounds like the catch in the throat made between the words in the exclamation 'uh-oh' or in place of the 't' in Cockney 'bottle'. Most Ashkenazi Jews don't articulate this letter, but in Sephardic Jews' speech it's very much alive.
פ	pe	as the 'p' in 'peace'
פ	fe	as the 'f' in 'fabulous'
צ	tsadi	as the 'ts' in 'its'
ק	kof	as the 'k' in 'king'
ר	resh	a guttural 'r' as in the French 'Paris'
ש	shin	as the 'sh' in 'shape'
ש	sin	as the 's' in 'soul'
ת	tav	as the 't' in 'table'

HEBREW ALPHABET

When certain letters appear at the end of a word, they take a different form, but keep the same sound:

ך	khaf	as the 'ch' in the German 'Bach'
ם	mem	as the 'm' in 'mother'
ן	nun	as the 'n' in 'nature'
ף	feh	as the 'f' in 'fabulous'
ץ	tsadi	as the 'ts' in 'its'

PRONUNCIATION

CONSONANTS   עיצורים

The Hebrew language contains all the consonant sounds of English, except the letter 'w'. When a foreign word with the 'w' sound needs to be transcribed into Hebrew, two vav letters are used.

In early times, the Hebrew alphabet didn't provide for sounds such as the 'ch' in 'check', the 'g' in 'George' and the 'j' in 'Rio de Janeiro'. Today these sounds are created by adding the symbol '' after tsadi, gimel and zayin respectively.

Some consonants may include a vowel 'inside' the letter – this vowel is represented by a dot, and is called dagesh. The dagesh has a phonetic impact on three consonants – the ב bet, כ kaf and פ pe. Without the dagesh, these consonants are pronounced vet, khaf and fe. When you encounter these letters in a word, you can't be sure of their pronunciation, unless they appear at the end of a word, when they'll always be soft, without a dagesh.

ch	as the 'ch' in 'cheese'
kh	as the 'ch' in German 'Bach'
g	as the 'g' in 'goose'
r	as in the French 'Paris'
ts	as the 'ts' in 'bits'
y	as the 'y' in 'yellow'

PRONUNCIATION

PRONUNCIATION HINTS

איך להגות נכון

The letter ה heh is aspirated, as in the 'h' in 'hot'. This 'h' sound is vastly different from the 'kh' sound of ח khet and כ khaf. Some Israelis often pronounce ה heh with a tremendous burst of air, while many pronounce it like the 'h' in 'hotel'.

Both letters ח khet and כ khaf are pronounced as the guttural 'ch' sound in the German 'Bach'.

It can take a while to get used to the transliteration system. At first, you'll probably be inclined to pronounce more (teacher) as in 'more red wine' and nose (topic) as in 'my nose is bleeding'. But these words each have two syllables and should be said as mo-re and no-se respectively. Also, when two vowels follow each other but are part of different syllables, they're separated by the symbol ' ". Thus, me'il (overcoat) is pronounced me-il and not 'meil', and me'al (above) should be read as me-al and not as 'meal'.

Stress

In Hebrew, stress is usually on the last syllable (as in Israel), or on the second last (as in Yerushalaim). In words borrowed from other languages, stress is usually placed on the first syllable (as in telephone). For some homonyms, differences in meaning are conveyed by stress.

BIra	beer
biRA	capital

When a syllable which ends with a consonant is followed by one that begins with a vowel, the symbol ' " is used to separate the syllables. Thus, lir'ot is 'to see', while lirot means 'to shoot'. Mad'ei means 'science (of)' but madei is 'uniform (of)'.

GRAMMAR

Although the grammar of Hebrew differs in structure from English, it's fairly easy to grasp. Each verb and most nouns are systematically based on a root consisting (in most cases) of three consonants, upon which all variations in meanings are based. However, there are a few aspects of Hebrew grammar that are difficult at first. For example, there are two genders – masculine and feminine. Furthermore, while there are only three major tenses of verbs, verbs fall within one of seven different forms of conjugation. The following description of Hebrew grammar is intended to serve as a basic guide to help you understand the sentences in this phrasebook, and cover most major points of grammar.

WORD ORDER
סדר המילים במשפטם

In the basic Modern Hebrew sentence, the subject comes before the verb. As in English, word order is Subject-Verb-Object.

Subject-Verb-Object	Joseph eats falafel.	yosef okhel falafel
Subject-Adjective	Joseph's fat.	yosef shamen
Subject-Adverb	Joseph's here.	yosef po

In present tense sentences which do not contain a verb (and are therefore called nominal sentences) but in which the noun is followed by an adjective, Hebrew commonly omits the verb 'to be' between the noun and the adjective. In these sentences, the adjective agrees in number and gender with the subject. One can say that the mere act of naming the subject, be it a personal pronoun, a proper name, or an object, is the evidence of the existence of that subject.

The coat is on the chair.   hame'il al hakise
(lit: the-coat on the-chair)

She is a teacher.   hi mora
(lit: she teacher)

| The students are hungry. | hastudentim re'evim
(lit: the-students hungry) |
| Dina is tired. | dina ayefa
(lit: Dina tired) |

ARTICLES

הא הידיעה

The definite article 'the' in Hebrew is ha in both the singular and plural and for both masculine and feminine genders. The article ha can precede nouns, adjectives and verbs. The placement of ha affects the meaning of a sentence.

good student (f)	studentit tova (lit: student-f good)
the good student (f)	ha-studentit ha-tova (lit: the-student the-good)
the student is good (f)	ha-studentit tova (lit: the-student good)
tasty felafel	falafel ta'im (felafel tasty)
the tasty felafel	ha-falafel ha-ta'im (lit: the-felafel the-tasty)
the felafel is tasty	ha-falafel ta'im (lit: the-felafel tasty)

When the definite article ha is preceded by either the preposition le ('to' and 'for') or the preposition be ('at', 'in' or 'by means of'), they're consolidated into one article. This article consists of the consonant of the preposition together with the vowel a of the definite article, to form la and ba.

| He goes to an ulpan. | hu holekh le-ulpan
(lit: he goes to-ulpan) |
| He goes to the ulpan. | hu holekh la-ulpan
(lit: he goes to-the-ulpan) |

GRAMMAR

He eats at a restaurant.	hu okhel be-mis'ada
	(lit: he eats at-restaurant)
He eats at the restaurant.	hu okhel ba-mis'ada
	(lit: he eats at-the-restaurant)

Although there are no words in Hebrew for the indefinite articles 'a', and 'an', they're indicated by the absence of ha in front of the noun.

He writes a letter.	hu kotev mikhtav
	(lit: he write letter)
He writes letters.	hu kotev mikhtavim
	(lit: he write letters)

PREPOSITIONS   מילות יחס

Most verbs in Hebrew are followed by prepositions. Their function is to indicate the relationship that binds the verb with the noun that follows it. Most prepositions are composed of one letter and are directly attached to the word they precede without a visible separation. (This is also the strategy that has been adopted in the transliteration of the words and phrases throughout the phrasebook.) Some other prepositions are independent words that are separated from the verb which precedes them and the noun that follows them. However, in the following examples, and for the sake of demonstration only, the prepositions are marked by a hyphen. The most common prepositions in spoken Hebrew are le-, be-, mi- (min) and et.

> The preposition le- expresses 'to' and 'for'

The pronunciation of le- may vary and become li- or la-, depending on the vowel in the first syllable of the word it precedes.

We go to the match today.	anakhnu holkhim la-miskhak hayom (lit: we go to-the-match today)
Are you (m, sg) going to Tiberias?	ata nose'a li-tveria? (lit: you-m travel to-Tiberius)
The cappucino is for David.	ha-cappucino le-david (lit: the-capuccino for-David)
The letter for John is here.	ha-mikhtav le-john po (lit: the-letter for-John here)

The preposition be- expresses either 'at', 'in' or 'by means of'.
The pronunciation of be- varies similarly to that of le-.

She sits in a Mercedes.	hi yoshevet be-mercedes (lit: she sits in-Mercedes)
We met at the opera.	nifgashnu ba-opera (lit: we-met at-the-opera)
They (m) speak on the phone.	hem medabrim ba-telefon (lit: they-m speak by-telephone)
They (f) are speaking Hebrew.	hen medabrot be-Ivrit (lit: they-f are-speaking by-means-of-Hebrew)

This last sentence suggests that they can speak a number of languages but at present, they use Hebrew to express themselves.

I (f) write with a Parker pen.	ani kotevet be-et Parker (lit: I-f write by-pen Parker)
Are you (f) going by foot?	At holekhet ba-regel? (lit: you-f go by-foot?)

GRAMMAR

In English, these four actions require three different prepositions – 'on', 'with' and 'by', or no preposition at all. In Hebrew they are all expressed by be-, 'by means of'.

> The preposition mi- signifies origin (from).
> It can also be expressed as min.

Are koalas from Australia?
ha-koalot me-australia?
(lit: the-koalas from-Australia?)

This is a physicist (f) from China.
zot fisika'it mi-sin
(lit: this physicist-f from-China)

He is coming from the kibbutz.
hu ba me-ha-hakibuts
(lit: he comes from-the-kibbutz)

The professor leaves the bank.
ha-professor yotse me-ha-bank
(lit: the-professor leaves from-the-bank)

The particle et is a special Hebrew feature that doesn't have an equivalent in English. The particle et links the verb of the sentence and its direct object, when it is definite. When the object is not definite, the particle et isn't used.

Peter reads a book.
peter kore sefer
(lit: Peter read book)

Peter reads the book.
peter kore et ha-sefer
(lit: Peter read et the-book)

Etti drinks champagne.
etti shota shampaniya
(lit: Ettie drinks champagne)

Etti drinks the champagne from France.
etti shota et ha-shampaniya mi-tsorfat
(lit: Ettie drinks et the-champagne from-France)

GRAMMAR

The definite object can also be a proper name.

Young (people) like Tel Aviv.	tse'irim ohavim et tel aviv
	(lit: young-people love et
	tel aviv)
Robert loved Clara.	robert ahav et clara
	(lit: Robert loved et Clara)

However, in Hebrew names of languages and subjects of study are considered indefinite.

Ilana studied Chinese in Paris.	ilana lamda sinit be-paris
	(lit: Ilana studied Chinese
	in-Paris)
He teaches philosophy at the	hu melamed filosofia ba-
university.	universita
	(lit: he teaches philosophy
	at-the-university)

NOUNS
Gender

שמות עצם

Hebrew nouns are classified as either feminine or masculine, even though this gender division often isn't related to the 'maleness' or 'femaleness' of the object. For example, 'sun' is feminine and 'moon' is masculine, the opposite of the case in French.

In general, the distinction between masculine nouns and feminine ones, when they don't belong to the 'irregular elite', is pretty straightforward. Feminine nouns often end with the open syllable -a, or with the consonant -t. Those ending in -a are stressed on the last syllable, as with glida, mita, ashpa, gluya and magevet, while the stress of nouns ending in -t, as in mekhonit, akhot, ta'ut is on the second last syllable. The names of towns, cities and countries are always feminine.

Masculine nouns usually end with a closed consonant sound – yeled, sefer, sakin, ba'it. Verbs and adjectives take the same gender as the noun they modify. If you remember these rules, you're likely to identify nouns correctly and make few mistakes.

Plurals

Masculine nouns are pluralised by adding the suffix -im to the noun, which usually undergoes some pronunciation modifications – sefer becomes sfarim, ba'it becomes batim, and yeled becomes yeladim. Yet, there are some irregular masculine nouns which take the feminine suffix when plural – shulkhan (table) becomes shulkhan-ot (tables) and kise (chair) becomes kis'-ot (chairs). This, however, doesn't affect their gender, and when an adjective is attached to the noun, it agrees with the original gender of the noun, regardless of its plural suffix.

beautiful table	shulkhan yafe
beautiful tables	shulkhan-ot yaf-im

The plural of the feminine noun is achieved by dropping the -a sound of the last syllable, and replacing it with the suffix -ot. Mita becomes mit-ot, glida becomes glid-ot, and gluya becomes gluy-ot. When a feminine noun ends with t, the t usually becomes yot in the plural. Thus mekhonit becomes mekhoni-yot, akhot becomes akha-yot, and ta'ut becomes ta'u-yot.

Exceptions to these rules have to be memorised, and Israelis will be sure to correct you when you use the wrong form. Since many immigrant Israelis are still in the process of learning Hebrew, it becomes second nature to correct anyone who's also learning Hebrew. Don't feel self-conscious when this happens to you – children of immigrants frequently correct their parents, as do friends.

'GET OFF MY BALDNESS'

khaval al hazman   חבל על הזמן
all-purpose expression which describes an extreme situation,
whether positive or negative
(lit: waste of time)

sababa   סבבה
great/cool

akhla   אחלה
great/cool
The tone is all important.

ptsatsa/ptsatsot/pitsuts   פצצה/פצצות/פיצוץ
excellent; beyond description; great!
The word chosen depends on the intensity of your feelings at
the time.
(lit: a bomb; bombs; an explosion)

mashehu mashehu   משהו משהו
used when something defies description and words fail
(lit: something something)

ba li hase'if   בא לי הסעיף
when something annoying happens and you lose your temper
(lit: the clause came to me – namely the 'nerves' clause of the
military health chart. When soldiers 'lose their nerves' in duty,
they're likely to be discharged.)

tered li mehakarakhat   תרד לי מהקרחת
when somebody's nagging you and you want to get rid of
them, fast
(lit: get off my baldness)

khapes oti basivuv   חפש אותי בסיבוב
when someone's pestering you to do something you don't
care about, and you want to tell them to get lost
(lit: go and look for me in the street corner)

GRAMMAR

'GET OFF MY BALDNESS'

lama ma   למה מה
used when someone asks you to do something you think is
preposterous
(lit: why what)

katan ala'i   קטן עלי
when someone apologetically asks for a favour they feel
may be demanding and difficult, and you're more than
happy to oblige
(lit: it is small on me, meaning 'I can do so much more')

al hapanim   על הפנים
when you feel a situation is hopeless, and you're surrounded
by gloom
(lit: on the face)

neshama   נשמה
what you call somebody you think is wonderful, sweet,
goodhearted, generous and lovable
(lit: soul)

yal'la bye   יאללה ביי
a cool way of saying 'goodbye'
Yal'la comes from an Arabic term of encouragement meaning
'let's ...', and English 'bye'.

ba'asa   באסה
used when you're bored and dispirited

akhi   אחי
when you meet someone you really like, a cool person like
you, you call them akhi, 'my brother'

kif   כיף
used when you meet a friend and you both express your
pleasure with a hearty handshake. When your friend extends
their hand, you give them yours and say kif.

ADJECTIVES   שם תואר

Adjectives come after nouns, and take the same gender and number as the noun they follow.

a good movie	seret tov
a good pizza	pitsa tova
good musicians	musika'im tovim

Forming Nouns

Some nouns can be formed from adjectives, often by adding a variation of -ut to the ending.

sweet	matok	sweetness	metikut
fast	mahir	swiftness	mehirut

Comparatives

To say that something is more beautiful, better, faster, smarter and so on, the word yoter (more) is placed either before or after the adjective.

yoter na'im or na'im yoter   more pleasant

To say someone or something is 'more stylish than' and so on, yoter is placed before the adjective, followed either by mi- or me'asher, and then the object of comparison.

She's younger than Yarden.	hi yoter tse'ira mi-yarden (lit: she more young than-Yarden)
In Tel Aviv, it's warmer than in Safed.	be tel aviv, kham yoter me'asher bitsfat (lit: in Tel Aviv hot more than in-Safed)

The preposition mi- (which also means 'from' when preceding the name of a location), when combined with a personal pronoun, is conjugated according to standard suffixes.

GRAMMAR

than/from me	mimeni	than/from us	mimenu/me'itanu
than/from you (m, sg)	mimkha	than/from you (m, pl)	mikem
than/from you (f, sg)	mimekh	than/from you (f, pl)	miken
than/from him	mimenu	than/from them (m)	mehem
than/from her	mimena	than/from them (f)	mehen

Cristina is taller than me.	cristina yoter gvoha mimeni
	(lit: Cristina more tall than-me)
Hamit is smarter than you.	hamit yoter inteligenti mimkha
	(lit: Hamit more intelligent than-you)

To express that two things are the same, as in 'He is as big as me', the word kmo is used.

The student is as stupid as a wall.	hastudent tipesh kmo kir
	(lit: the-student stupid like wall)
Ayala is as beautiful as a flower.	ayala yafa kmo perakh
	(lit: Ayala beautiful like flower)

As with the preposition mi-, when combined with personal pronouns, kmo can also be conjugated following the standard suffixes.

Singular: kamoni, kamokha, kamokh, kamoha, kamohu

Plural: kamonu, kmokhem, kmokhen, kmohem, kmohen.

| My brother is as handsome as you. | akhi khatikh kamokha |
| Rachel is as old as her. | rakhel zkena kamoha |

Superlatives

To say that something is 'the most' or someone is 'the fattest' or the 'most famous', the word beyoter (the most) is placed after the adjective.

This is the most boring professor in the university.	ze haprofessor hamesha'amem beyoter ba'universita
Dana International is the best singer in Israel.	dana internashenal hi hazameret hatova beyoter beisrael

However, if the beyoter is the more 'educated' form of speech, there is a more colloquial and popular form, using the slang expression hakhi placed in front of the adjective.

She's the best in the world.	hi hakhi tova ba'olam
This is the most 'in' pub in Jaffa.	ze hapub hakhi in beyafo
The food in this restaurant is the most delicious in Jerusalem.	ha'okhel bamis'ada hazot hakhi ta'im birushala'im

Quantity

a lot of ...	hamon ...
black coffee	kafe shakhor
beautiful students (f)	studentiyot yafot
many ...	harbe ...
books	sfarim
friends	khaverim
a little ...	ktsat ...
romantic	romanti
sugar in the tea	sukar ba-te
a few ...	me'at ...
clementines (tangerines)	klementinot

all the ...	kol ha ...
buses	otobusim
TVs	televizyot

how many ...?	kama ...?
Israelis	israelim
zebras	zebrot

PRONOUNS   כינויי גוף
Subject Pronouns

As exceptions to the rule, first-person pronouns don't distinguish between genders. We can tell them apart only by the form of the noun or adjective that follow. Ani, 'I', isn't modified according to whether the speaker is male or female, as in ani bil or ani hilaree. The same goes for anakhnu, 'we'.

We are Israelis.   anakhnu israeliyot (f)
                            anakhnu israelim (m)

However, a single male in a female crowd is sufficient to make the whole crowd take the masculine form. At least theoretically. Sorry girls.

I	ani	we	anakhnu
you (m)	ata	you (pl)	atem
you (f)	at	you (f, pl)	aten
he	hu	they	hem
she	hi	they (f)	hen

There's no equivalent for the pronoun 'it'. Instead, the third-person pronoun is used.

GRAMMAR

VERBS

הפועל

Hebrew verbs have three major tenses – past, present and future. There's also an imperative form (used for requests or orders), and an infinitive form (to ...). Hebrew verbs have two special characteristics.

Firstly, they're based on a root, shoresh, mainly composed of three consonants, though in some rare cases it may include four letters. The image of the root is appropriate – underground and hidden from the naked eye. Nevertheless, it's the root that breathes life into the whole tree. Similarly, the grammatical root sustains the whole structure of the Hebrew language, giving it logic and form.

Secondly, each verb falls within one of seven patterns of conjugation, called binyanim (constructions), which provide verbs with their actual meanings.

Verb Roots

In Hebrew, all verbs and many adjectives and nouns are based on patterns of consonants known as 'roots'. These roots form a structure or skeleton upon which verbs of related meanings are constructed. The roots impose an extremely logical system of conjugation patterns for verbs to follow. Taken alone, the root isn't a word (it can be distinguished from any three-letter word by the dots that are interposed between its three letters) and doesn't have a meaning by itself. The meaning is obtained when the root is conjugated according to one of the seven conjugation patterns that give nuances of meaning to the verb root. For example, the three-letter root L.M.D may acquire the following meanings when conjugated:

lomed	he studies
melamed	he teaches
nilmad	it is being studied/taught
mitlamed	he is becoming specialised

KEY VERBS

All verbs are listed in their present-tense, third person singular forms.

afraid	mefakhed
ask (a question)	sho'el
begin	matkhil
buy	kone
call (by phone)	metsaltsel
cost	ole
do	ose
drink	shote
eat	okhel
explain	masbir
find	motse
forget	shokhe'akh
receive	mekabel
give	noten
go	holekh
have to	tsarikh
look for	mekhapes
pay	meshalem
put	sam
read	kore
receive	mekabel
return	khozer
say	omer
see	ro'e
sell	mokher
send	shole'akh
start	matkhil
take	loke'akh
tell	mesaper
walk	metayel
write	kotev

In this example, all four forms produce meaningful words that are related to studying and teaching. For most roots, the different conjugation patterns will produce associated meanings. However, there are some roots for which different conjugation patterns create unrelated meanings. Take the root S.P.R, for example:

mesaper	he tells a story
	he cuts somebody's hair
nispar	it's being counted
mistaper	he's having a haircut
mesupar	it's being told

Using the same root to form nouns, we get:

sapar	a barber
sipur	a story
mispar	a number
safran	a librarian

There's no doubt a reason for the cohabitation of these three unrelated meanings within one root, but it isn't evident to the average Hebrew speaker. When homonyms appear in printed texts, the context determines the meaning and pronunciation of a word.

Theoretically, every root can be conjugated in all seven patterns. Yet, not all of these patterns are expected to yield meaningful verbs. In fact, most roots are conjugated in part of the binyanim only.

Verb Patterns – Binyanim

Though based on logical patterns, the verb binyan system is fairly complex, owing to the existence of two categories of verbs – regular verbs, shlemim (complete), and irregular verbs. While the conjugation of shlemim is easy and adheres to the basic rules of the binyan, irregular verbs require modifications of the rules. Irregular verbs have roots which are made up of one or more of eight letters – the five guttural consonants (alef, he, khet, ayin, resh), and yod, vav, nun. When they appear in certain positions in the root, and in some conjugation patterns, these letters do not follow the regular behaviour of their binyan.

Every verb follows one of seven verb patterns. To label these patterns, Hebrew uses the letters Pe, Ayin and Lamed, which, when put together, form the word po'al (verb). These conjugation patterns are grouped in three sets of grammatical pairs, each containing an active form and a passive form. There are four active binyanim and three passive ones.

Active	Passive
Pa'AL	niF'AL
hiF'IL	huF'AL
Pi'EL	Pu'AL
hit Pa'EL	

In the first pattern, Pa'AL, (aka Kal, namely 'easy', since it's considered the simplest pattern among the seven verb patterns) the three letter root G.N.V becomes GaNaV in the past tense and means '(he) stole'. The passive of this binyan, niF'AL, is formed by adding the syllable ni in front of G.N.V root and changing the vowels of the three letters, to get niGNaV 'was stolen'.

For the active pattern, hiF'IL, the root S.B.R in the past tense, hiSBiR, means '(he) explained'. The same root in the passive pattern huF'AL, becomes huSBaR (was explained).

The active pattern Pi'EL of KHiLeK (he handed out) becomes KHuLaK in the passive Pu'AL pattern, to mean 'was handed out'. The final binyan, hitPa'EL, is an active pattern which comprises three verbal relationships – reciprocal, reflexive and passive.

Reciprical
(they) corresponded   hitKaTVu
(they) saw each other   hitRA'U

Reflexive
(he) got drunk   hiSHtaKeR
(he) dressed himself   hitLaBeSH

Passive
For some roots it acts as the passive form for the active Pi'EL

(he) cooked   BiSHeL
(it got) cooked   hitBaSHeL

The Infinitive

The Hebrew infinitive corresponds to English 'to ...', as in
'I want **to** ...' and 'It's difficult **to** ...'. All infinitives in Hebrew
are prefixed by le- (or its modified forms, li- or la-) such as
le'EHoV (to love), liRKoD (to dance), and laAMoD (to stand
up). The most frequent use of the infinitive is in phrases when
two verbs, related to one subject, follow each other, the first often
being a verb expressing motion or an ability. In such cases, the
first verb is conjugated and the second is in the infinitive.

I can speak four languages.	ani yode'a ledaber arba safot
	(lit: I can speak four languages)
Who wants to go to	mi rotse lalekhet lasherutim?
the toilet?	(lit: who wants to-go to-toilet)

The infinitive never changes form, regardless of the tense used,
or the gender or number of the people you're speaking to. The
infinitive is also used when making a command.

Present Tense

The present tense is similar to that of English 'I eat' and 'I am eating'. There are singular and plural forms in the present tense for both masculine and feminine. Thus, I (f), you (f) and she all use the same form of the verb.

> I/you/she study/   ani/at/hi lomedet ivrit
>   studies Hebrew.

Likewise, we (m), you (m) and they (m) all use the same form of verb.

> We/you/they are   anakhnu/atem/hem
>   dancing Tango.   rokdim tango

The same goes for the use of masculine singular and feminine plural. The multiple function of each verb form requires us to specify who is performing the action. Thus medabrot batelefon (f, pl), 'speaking on the phone', is an incomplete sentence. Who's on the phone? Is it us? You? Them?

Present			
		lirkod 'to dance'	
I (m)	no suffix	I dance	ani roked
I (f)	-t	I dance	ani rokedet
you (m, sg)	no suffix	you dance	ata roked
you (f, sg)	-t	you dance	at rokedet
he	no suffix	he dances	hu roked
she	-t	she dances	hi rokedet
we (m)	-im	we dance	anakhnu rokdim
we (f)	-ot	we dance	anakhnu rokdot
you (m, pl)	-im	you dance	atem rokdim
you (f, pl)	-ot	you dance	aten rokdot
they (m)	-im	they dance	hem rokdim
they (f)	-ot	they dance	hen rokdot

The basic form for all conjugations is the masculine form of the verb in third-person singular. Various suffixes are then added to create the other forms of the verb. This occurs not only for the present tense, but for past and future tenses as well. All present tense verbs employ the same suffixes used for nouns and adjectives to mark gender and number. The suffix -im is added to create masculine plural forms, -a or -t are added to feminine singular forms, and -ot is added to feminine plural forms.

Past Tense

The Hebrew past tense covers four past tenses found in English – 'I ate', 'I have eaten', 'I was eating' and 'I had eaten'. Each verb has nine forms when conjugated in the past tense. These correspond to nine of the 10 Hebrew personal pronouns – the third-person plural feminine and masculine share the same form.

A verb in the past tense can be viewed as having two components. The first is the verbal stem, which marks the past tense and is derived from the third person masculine singular of the past tense, with some phonetic modifications. The second component is a suffix which indicates the person who performed the action. Luckily, these suffixes are identical for all verbs, regular and irregular alike, and for all binyanim. They are easy to remember since, with the exception of the third person (singular and plural), they're associated with the pronoun of each person of the conjugation.

GRAMMAR

Past			
to tell (a story) LeSaPeR			
I told	ani siparti	we told	anakhnu siparnu
you (m) told	ata siparta	you (m) told	atem sipartem
you (f) told	at sipart	you (f) told	aten siparten
he told	hu siper	they (m/f) told	hem/hen sipru
she told	hi sipra		

The form of the verb in the past tense includes the subject. Hence, karati (I read) is a complete sentence including subject and verb – kara + ti (read + I). One could also say ani karati and it would be grammatically correct, but the addition of the pronoun ani burdens the sentence with redundancy. It can be useful, however for emphasis. If somebody asks you, in disbelief, at karat? (have *you* read?), you can answer emphatically, ani karati (*I* have read). The exception is the third person singular and plural, that always require a pronoun.

he studied	hu lamad
she studied	hi lamda
they (m/f) studied	hem (hen) lamdu

Future Tense

The future tense in Hebrew is similar to the future tense in English. For every verb there are eight forms in the future tense. There are five for the singular, but only three for the plural – first, second and third person, without a distinction between the masculine and feminine forms.

The verb in the future tense has two elements – a subject pronoun prefix (and suffix for some) and the future-tense verb stem. As with the past tense, the prefixes and the suffixes are

Future			
		leDaBeR 'to speak'	
I	a-	I will speak	adaber
you (m, sg)	t-	you will speak	tedaber
you (f, sg)	t...i	you will speak	tedabri
he	y-	he will speak	yedaber
she	t-	she will speak	tedaber
we	n-	we will speak	nedaber
you (pl)	t...u	you will speak	tedabru
they	y...u	they will speak	yedabru

GRAMMAR

identical for all the roots and for all the binyanim. What is comprised inbetween the two, however, may vary largely.

IMPERATIVES
ציווי

Modern Hebrew has both negative and positive imperative tenses. Positive requests use the imperative tense. The form of the imperative verb depends on the conjugation pattern (binyan) of the verb and there are only three forms for it. When a command is made to a male, the verb takes no suffix, but if made to a female, the verb takes the suffix -i. When a command is made to more than one person, male or female, the suffix -u is added to the verb.

Imperative form of the verb lavo, 'to come'		
Come here! (m, sg)	no suffix	bo hena
Come here! (f, sg)	-i	bo-i hena
Come here! (m/f, pl)	-u	bo-u hena

While most verbs aren't often used in the imperative, many are quite common in colloquial speech.

kakh et ze	(lit: take this)
sa maher	(lit: drive fast)
shvi besheket	(lit: sit (f, sg) quietly)
simu lev	watch out (lit: put (m, pl) heart)
ten li yad	(lit: give to-me hand)
zuz mipo	(lit: move from here)

Negative Imperatives

There are two types of negative imperatives. Firstly, there are fixed requests, addressed to an anonymous public, as in 'Do not park on this side of the street'. This form of imperative is made by prefixing the negative particle lo to the infinitive form of the verb.

GRAMMAR

Do not speak during the concert!	lo ledaber bizman hakontsert! (lit: not to-speak in-time of-the-concert)
Careful, don't run!	zehirut, lo laruts! (lit: careful not to-run)
Electricity. Do not touch!	khashmal lo laga'at! (lit: electricity no to-touch)

The second type of negative imperative is a request or order addressed to a particular individual in a particular situation, as in 'Don't drink any more!', or 'Don't walk, run!' This form is created by putting the negative particle al before the future tense of the verb.

Don't speak English! (m)	al tedaber anglit! (lit: don't speak-m English)
Don't drink all the vodka!	al tishti et kol havodka! (lit: don't drink et all the-vodka)
Don't smoke in the house!	al te'ashnu baba'it! (lit: don't smoke in-the-house)

TO BE   להיות

Sentences in English which require a form of the verb 'to be' don't always need this verb in Hebrew. Instead, they're made up of simple noun–adjective constructions.

| They are strange. | hem muzarim
(lit: they strange) |
| Haifa is beautiful. | haifa yafa
(lit: Haifa beautiful) |

However, in sentences where the subject or object are made up of more than a single word or comprise a clause, a third person pronoun (which agrees with the gender and number of the subject) may be placed between the subject and the predicate.

My father is an excellent lawyer.	avi hu orekh-din metsuyan (lit: my-father hu lawyer excellent)
The opera singer that sang all night is my friend.	zameret haopera sheshara kol halaila hi khavera sheli (lit: singer the-opera that-sang all the-night hi friend mine)

TO HAVE   יש

To express 'to have', the verbal construction yesh le- is used, literally meaning 'there is to (someone or something)'.

I have a dog   yesh li kelev
                                (lit: there-is to-me dog)

To Have			
I have	yesh li	we have	yesh lanu
you (m) have	yesh lekha	you (m, pl) have	yesh lakhem
you (f) have	yesh lakh	you (f, pl) have	yesh lakhen
he has	yesh lo	they (m) have	yesh lahem
she has	yesh la	they (f) have	yesh lahen

Yesh is never conjugated, but the particle le- is, when the possessor is expressed by means of a personal pronoun and not by a proper name.

Sentences using proper names such as 'Dana has a Volvo' are written with the le- placed before the name.

ledana yesh Volvo   (lit: to-Dana there-is Volvo)

To express that something is lacking, the construction ein le-, meaning literally 'there is/are not to (someone or something)', is used.

He doesn't have a girlfriend.   ein lo khavera
                                (lit: there-is-not to-him girlfriend)

GRAMMAR

We don't have time on the weekend.	ein la-nu zman baweekend (lit: there-is-not to-us time on-weekend)
I have a few dollars.	yesh li dolarim me'atim. (lit: there-is to-me dollars a-few)
Israelis also have lots of problems.	gam laisraelim yesh harbe be'ayot (lit: also to-Israelis there-are many problems)

In the past and future tenses, the past and future forms of the verb 'to be', liheyot, replace yesh. In both tenses, the form of the verb should be in agreement with the gender and number of the possessed object. Thus, only three forms are used – masculine singular, feminine singular and also plural. The past-tense forms are haya, hayta and hayu, and future tense forms are yiheye, tiheye and iheyu.

| I had a nice car. | hayta li mekhonit yafa (lit: had to-me car nice) |

Mekhonit (car) is a feminine noun in Hebrew, and therefore determines the form of the past tense. Changing the possessor to he, we (masculine or feminine) and so on, will merely result in the change of the conjugated particle le-.

He had a nice car.	hayta lo mekhonit yafa
She had a nice car.	hayta la mekhonit yafa
They (m) had a nice car.	hayta lahem mekhonit yafa
They (f) had a nice car.	hayta lahen mekhonit yafa

| They had a supermarket in Tel Aviv. | haya lahem supermarket betel-aviv (lit: had to-them supermarket in-Tel Aviv) |

GRAMMAR

We will have a pleasant Sabbath.	tiheye lanu shabbat ne'ima (lit: will-be to-us Sabbath pleasant)
You (m) will have many stories.	yiheyu lakhem harbe sipurim (lit: will-be to-you-m many stories)

Both expressions, yesh and ein, can be used independently without the preposition le. Yesh (there is/are) and ein (there isn't/aren't), when used in impersonal sentences, express general truths or facts.

There's a blender on the table.	yesh blender al hashulkhan (lit: there-is blender on the-table)
There are Chinese restaurants in Israel.	yesh mis'adot siniyot beisrael (lit: there-are restaurants Chinese in-Israel)
There isn't any good wine in the supermarket.	ein ya'in tov basupermarket (lit: there-isn't wine good at-the-supermarket)
There aren't any cows in the kibbutz.	ein parot bakibbutz (lit: there-aren't cows in-the-kibbutz)

MODALS   תאור אופן
Must; Need To; Have To

To express 'must', 'need to' and 'have to', the participle tsarikh is used in its present-tense form, followed either by a noun or the infinitive. Tsarikh has four forms, each indicating gender and number. They can be easily identified, since they take the regular suffixes for feminine and plural.

tsarikh (m, sg)	tsrikhim (m, pl)
tsrikha (f, sg)	tsrikhot (f, pl)

He needs a sports car.	hu tsarikh mekhonit sport
She has to get up early.	hi tsrikha lakum mukdam
We (m) need a TV.	anakhnu tsrikhim televizia
You (f) must get on the bus.	aten tsrikhot la'alot la-otobus

To express 'must', 'need to' and 'have to' in the past or future tenses, the participle tsarikh is preceded by an appropriate conjugation of the verb 'to be'.

I (m) needed to buy coffee.	ha'iti tsarikh liknot kafe
She needed an elegant dress.	hi hayta tsrikha simla elegantit
You (m/pl) needed a jeep.	ha'item tsrikhim jeep
You (f/pl) had to buy a film.	ha'iten tsrikhot liknot film

I will have to go to Haifa.	eheye tsarikh linso'a lehaifa
I (f) will need a ticket.	eheye tsrikha kartis
They (m) will need help.	hem iheyu tsrikhim ezra
You (f, pl) will have to speak Hebrew.	aten tiheyu tsrikhot ledaber Ivrit

Can; To Be Able

The notion of 'can' or 'to be able' is expressed by the verb yakhol. The past and future tenses of this verb follow an irregular conjugation.

Past – Can			
I could	yakholti	we could	yakholnu
you could (m, sg)	yakholta	you (m) could	yekhaltem
you could (f, sg)	yakholt	you (f) could	yekhalten
he could	hu yakhal	they (m/f) could	hem/hen
she could	hi yakhla		yakhlu

GRAMMAR

Present – Can

can (m, sg)	yakhol
can (f, sg)	yekhola
can (m, pl)	yekholim
can (f, pl)	yekholot

Future – Can

I will be able	ukhal
you will be able (m, sg)	tukhal
you will be able (f, sg)	tukhli
he will be able	hu yukhal
she will be able	hi tukhal
we will be able	nukhal
you will be able	atem/aten tukhlu
they will be able	hem/hen yukhlu

She can eat a lot.	hi yekhola le'ekhol harbe (lit: she can to-eat a-lot)
I could tour Eilat.	yakholti letayel be'eilat (lit: I-could to-tour in-Eilat)
You (f, sg) will be able to speak Hebrew well.	tukhli ledaber ivrit heytev (lit: you-will-be-able to-speak Hebrew well)

TO LIKE   לחבב ולאהוב

There are two ways frequently used to express 'to like'. Israelis commonly use the verb le'ehov (to love), as in ani ohev le'ekhol falafel beshabat (I like eating falafel on Saturday), or hem me'od ohavim glida (They love ice cream very much). The same verb serves to express love relationships.

David loves Natasha but Natasha loves Andre.	david ohev et natasha aval natasha ohevet et andre

GRAMMAR

Another way to express 'to like' is to use the expression:

motse khen be'einei ...
(lit: it-finds grace in-somebody's-eyes)

When the object of liking is a noun, it precedes the expression.

I like his son.   haben shelo motse khen be'einai
                           (lit: the-son of-his finds grace
                           in-my-eyes)

When the object is an infinitive, it follows it.

We like living   motse khen be'einenu lagur
   in a kibbutz.   bekibuts
                           (lit: it-finds grace in-our-eyes
                           to-live in-kibutz)

POSSESSION   שייכות

Possession is frequently expressed by the particle shel, meaning 'of'.
In the sentence hasefer shel harav (lit: the-book of the-rabbi),
notice that shel comes after the thing possessed and before the possessor. The object possessed is preceded by the definite article ha-.

Whose?   shel mi? (lit: of who?)
The student's.   shel hastudent
Whose book is this?   shel mi hasefer haze?
(This is) Justin's (book). (ze hasefer) shel justin

When the possessor is indicated by a pronoun, the pronoun suffixes are attached to the particle shel.

Possessive Pronouns		
	Masculine	Feminine
my	sheli	sheli
your	shelkha	shelakh
his/her	shelo	shela
our	shelanu	shelanu
your	shelakhem	shelakhen
their	shelahem	shelahen

GRAMMAR

my friends	hakhaverim sheli
his music	hamusika shelo
our futons	hafutonim shelanu
your (f) bananas	habananot shelakhen

Possessive Suffixes

All nouns can be conjugated with the possessive suffixes, but possessive suffixes are essentially used in spoken Hebrew with kin terms such as aba (father), ima (mother), akh (brother), akhot (sister), horim (parents) and so on. Possession can also be expressed by shel.

	Possessive Suffix	'shel'
my brother	akh-i	akh sheli
your (m, sg) brother	akh-ikha	akh shelkha
your (f, sg) brother	akh-ikh	akh shelakh
his brother	akh-iv	akh shelo
her brother	akh-iha	akh shela
our brother	akh-inu	akh shelanu
your (m, pl) brother	akh-ikhem	akh shelakhem
your (f, pl) brother	akh-ikhen	akh shelakhen
their (m) brother	akh-ihem	akh shelahem
their (f) brother	akh-ihen	akh shelahen

Feminine nouns add the -t ending before the possessive suffix, as in ishti (my wife), which is formed by adding -t to isha (wife) with the possessive form -i.

Plural nouns take on a slighly different form.

my brothers	akhai	akhim sheli
your (m, sg) brothers	akheikha	akhim shelkha
your (f, sg) brothers	akha'ikh	akhim shelakh
his brothers	ekhav	akhim shelo
her brothers	akheiha	ahim shela
our brothers	akheinu	akhim shelanu
your (m, pl) brothers	akheikhem	akhim shelakhem

GRAMMAR

your (f, pl) brothers	akheikhen	(akhim shelakhen)
their (m) brothers	akheihem	(akhim shelahem)
their (f) brothers	akheihen	(akhim shelahen)

QUESTIONS   שאלות

When forming a question to be answered with a simple 'yes' or
'no', the word order of the sentence remains the same as a
declarative sentence, and the question is indicated by rising
intonation on the last word of the sentence.

Is he Israeli?	hu israeli?
	(lit: he-is Israeli)
Yes, he's Israeli.	ken, hu israeli
	(lit: yes, he-is Israeli)
No, he's not Israeli.	lo, hu lo israeli
	(lit: no, he-is no Israeli)

Question Words

Simple questions such as 'what' (ma), 'who' (mi), 'how' (eikh),
'where' (eifo), 'when' (matay), 'where from' (me'ain), 'where to'
(le'an), 'how many' (kama) and 'why' (lama), place the question
word at the beginning of the sentence. Unlike in English, the
word order in the sentence isn't modified.

Who knows?	mi yode'a?
Yoram knows.	yoram yode'a
What's new?	ma khadash?
Nothing's new.	ein khadash
When did he come?	matai hu ba?
He came yesterday.	hu ba etmol
What did she say?	ma hi amra?
She said 'goodbye'.	hi amra lehitra'ot
Where do they come from?	me'ain hem?
They're from the kibbutz.	hem mehakibuts
Where's the toilet?	eifo hasherutim?

GRAMMAR

| The toilet is opposite the bank. | hasherutim mul habank (lit: the-toilet opposite the-bank) |

Questions can begin with the word ha'im, giving the sense of 'is it that ...?'.

| Will there be a lot of people there? | ha'im iheyu sham harbe anashim? (lit: is-it-that will-be there many people) |
| Is everybody here? | ha'im kulam po? (lit: is-it-that everybody here?) |

Another favourite way of asking a question is by adding the word nakhon, meaning 'isn't that right?', at the end of a sentence.

| All Israelis speak Hebrew, right? | kol haIsraelim medebrim ivrit, nakhon? (lit: all the-israelis speak Hebrew, isn't-that-right?) |

NEGATIVES   שלילה

The word lo is commonly used to negate a sentence. It's usually placed in front of the part of speech that's being negated. Lo can negate a noun, an adjective or a verb.

Saul is not a musician.	shaul lo musika'i (lit: Saul not musician)
The dress is not elegant.	hasimla lo elegantit (lit: the-dress not elegant)
They (m) are not working in the bank.	hem lo ovdim babank (lit: they-m not work in-the-bank)

GRAMMAR

The word ein (lit: there is/are not) is the opposite of yesh (there exists). Ein is part of some basic Israeli expressions.

No problems.	ein be'ayot
Nothing can be done.	ein ma la'asot
There's no time.	ein zman
Never mind.	ein davar

Several other words can be used to indicate the negative. When combined with lo, the word af, meaning 'not even, not also', followed by a singular noun, forms a double negative.

Not a single person came.	af ekhad lo ba
	(lit: not-even one not came)
Nobody speaks like Assaf.	af ekhad lo medaber kmo asaf
	(lit: not-even one not speak like Assaf)

The word af can be used in the expression af pa'am to mean 'not a single time' or 'never'.

They never drink water	hem af-pa'am lo shotim mayim
	(lit: they not-even-one-time not drink water)
We never dance polka.	anakhnu af-pa'am lo rokdim polka
	(lit: we not-even-one-time not dance polka)

The word 'never' meaning 'never before', or 'haven't had the experience at all', is me'olam and is followed in the sentence by lo.

I've never heard his name.	me'olam lo shama'ati alav
	(lit: never-before not I-heard about-him)

They've never studied Chinese.	hem me'olam lo lamdu sinit (lit: they never-before not studied Chinese)

The words shum and klum mean 'nothing'. While klum can stand on its own, shum must be followed by a noun (frequently the word davar, 'a thing') to give the meaning 'no thing'. The two can also come appear as a popular expression – shum klum, 'nothing of nothing'.

What happened? Nothing.	ma kara? shum davar (lit: what happened? no-thing)
What's the matter? Nothing.	ma yesh? klum (lit: what there-is? nothing)

THE IMPERSONAL   סתמי

In many languages, the subject of a verb, or the thing performing an action, needs to be explicitly stated.

david menagen leshaul
David (subject) plays (verb) for Saul (complement)

noa veofri lomdot birushala'im
Noa and Ofri (subject) study (verb) in Jerusalem (complement)

In Hebrew, it's possible to have complete sentences which don't have subjects. These are usually sentences where facts that are common knowledge are being stated, such as 'In Israel people speak Hebrew'. In English, the subject 'people' would be necessary, while in Hebrew, it can be omitted. The sentence would be beIsrael medabrim ivrit (lit: in-Israel speaking Hebrew). Likewise, 'In Italy people eat a lot of pasta'. This statement is equally true. When one longs for a delicious pasta dish, one should preferably travel to Italy and not to London. Again, English cannot do without the subject 'people', while Hebrew can dispense with it – beItalia okhlim harbe pasta (lit: in-Italy eating much pasta).

As well as the absence of a subject in the sentence, the mark of the impersonal form is the masculine plural form of the verb –in this case medabrim and okhlim.

The greatest convenience of the impersonal form, other than a light noncommitment while maintaining a certain aura of author-ity, is that it allows us, on occasion, to steer clear from the complica-tions of verb conjugations.

For example, the sentence:

How do you do this in   eikh osim zot etzlekhem?
    your country?'   (lit: how doing this at-your-
                                   place?)

would have forced us to write four possible sentences – two for the singular and two for the plural, depending on the number and gender of 'you'. By choosing to use the impersonal, this phrasebook is considerably simplified. The phrase 'how do you say ...?' will simply be expressed by eikh omrim ... (lit: how saying ...).

Another important variant of the impersonal is formed by replacing the verb 'can' with the expression efshar (it's possible). The verb 'can' always requires a subject. A polite phrase such as 'Can we use the phone?' has two possible translations, one for 'we' feminine and one for 'we' masculine. Instead, efshar letsaltsel? (lit: is-it-possible to-phone?) is much shorter, easier, and as polite, especially if you add bevakasha (please). The considerate question, 'Do you mind if I smoke?' has eight possible phrases if you insist upon manners! In comparison, efshar le'ashen? (lit: is-it-possible to-smoke?) makes you feel almost fluent!

Sentences like these abound in this phrasebook. Whenever possible, the impersonal efshar is used instead of yakhol. However, in sentences where there's no escape from using 'you' or 'I', both the masculine and feminine, as well as the plural, are given.

MEETING PEOPLE הכרויות חדשות

Israelis often refer to themselves as Sabra (cactus fruit), because as the story goes they are 'prickly on the outside but sweet and succulent on the inside'. The comparison is an apt one. Their body language reflects the society's inheritance as a nation of immigrants living in a harsh environment, surrounded by hostile peoples. Thus many Israelis appear to be brash, pushy, macho, argumentative and arrogant at first meeting. It's only after you get to know them that they relax and show their gracious and warm natures.

YOU SHOULD KNOW   כדאי לך לדעת

Yes.	ken	כן.
No.	lo	לא.
Excuse me.	slikha	סליחה.
Please.	bevakasha	בבקשה.
Thank you.	toda	תודה.
Many thanks.	toda raba	תודה רבה.

GREETINGS & GOODBYES   פגישה ופרידה

Shalom is an all-purpose greeting and way to say goodbye. Shalom means 'peace', as in 'come in peace', 'go in peace', 'leave in peace', and 'be at peace'. When asking someone about their health, the greeting is Ma shlomkha (shlomekh)? (lit: what's your peace?).

Hello.	shalom	שלום.
Hi.	hai	היי.
Goodbye.	lehitra'ot	להתראות.
Good morning.	boker tov	בוקר טוב.
Good evening.	erev tov	ערב טוב.
Good night	layla tov	לילה טוב.
Bye.	bai	ביי.

Civilities

You're welcome.
al lo davar

על לא דבר.

Sorry. (pol)
tislakh li; slikha

תסלח לי; סליחה.

May I?
efshar bevakasha?

אפשר בבקשה?

FIRST ENCOUNTERS

פגישות ראשונות

How are you?
ma shlom'kha (shlomekh)?

מה שלומך?

Fine, and you?
metsuyan, ve'ata (ve'at)?

מצוין, ואתה (ואת)?

What's your name?
ma shimkha (shmekh)?

מה שמך?

My name's ...
shmi ...

שמי ...

I'd like to introduce you to ...
takir bevakasha et ... (m, sg)
takiri bevakasha et ... (f, sg)

תכיר בבקשה את ...
תכירי בבקשה את ...

I'm pleased to meet you.
na'im me'od

נעים מאוד.

MEETING PEOPLE

BODY LANGUAGE

A common Israeli gesture to express 'I don't know' is to stick the bottom lip out, shrug the shoulders and hold the hands at chest height with the palms facing upward.

When asking someone to wait a moment, an Israeli might place the thumb, index and middle fingers together and squeeze, with the palm facing up.

MAKING CONVERSATION

שיחה

Do you live here?
  ata gar kan? (m)   אתה גר כאן?
  at gara kan? (f)   את גרה כאן?

Where are you going?
  le'an ata holekh? (m)   לאן אתה הולך?
  le'an at holekhet? (f)   לאן את הולכת?

What are you doing?
  ma ata ose? (m)   מה אתה עושה?
  ma at osa? (f)   מה את עושה?

What do you think about ...?
  ma da'atkh al ...? (m)   מה דעתך על ...?
  ma da'atekh al ...? (f)   מה דעתך על ...?

Can I take a photo (of you)?
  efshar letsalem otkha? (m)   אפשר לצלם אותך?
  efshar letsalem otakh? (f)   אפשר לצלם אותך?

What's this called?
  eikh kor'im leze?   איך קוראים לזה?

Beautiful, isn't it?
  yafe, nakhon?   יפה, נכון?

It's very nice here.
  me'od yafe po   מאוד יפה פה.

We love it here.
  me'od motse khen be'eineinu kan   מאוד מוצא חן בעינינו כאן.

What a cute baby!
  eize tinok khamud!   איזה תינוק חמוד!

Are you waiting too?
  gam ata mekhake? (m)   גם אתה מחכה?
  gam at mekhaka? (f)   גם את מחכה?

That's strange.   meshune   משונה.
That's funny (amusing).   mats'khik   מצחיק.

ARABIC

Arabic is Israel's second most widely spoken language, after Hebrew. The Arab population is concentrated mainly in the Gaza Strip and the West Bank.

Clearly you would need a separate phrasebook for Palestinian Arabic if you were planning to visit Arabic-speaking areas extensively. These two pages should allow you to initiate some communication and any attempts, however unsuccessful, to speak the language is likely to endear you to Arab people.

You Should Know

Please.	min fadlach
Thank you.	shoo-khran
You're welcome.	afwan
Yes.	ay-wah
No.	la
Pardon?	sa-mech-nee?
I don't understand.	mish faahim
Do you speak English?	tech-kee Ingleesi?

Greetings & Goodbyes

Hello.	a-halan/mahr-haba
Goodbye.	salaam aleicham; ma-ah-salameh
Good morning.	sabah-al-kheir
Good evening.	masa'al-kheir

Time & Days

Sunday	el-ahad	What's the time?	gaddesh saa'ah?
Monday	itnein	minute	da'iah
Tuesday	talaata	hour	saa'ah
Wednesday	el-arbi'a	day	yawm
Thursday	khamis	week	jum'a/usbuu'
Friday	jumu'a	month	shahr
Saturday	sabit	year	saneh

ARABIC

Getting Around

Which bus goes to ...?	ayya baas yaruh 'ala ...?
Is it far?	ba'id?
Stop here.	wa'if huna
Where?	feen?
right	yemine
left	she-mal
straight	doo-ree
airport	mataar
bus stop	mawif al-baas
railway station	mahattat train

Food & Accommodation

breakfast	futuur	restaurant	mat'am
coffee	kah-wah	tea	schai
dinner	'asha	water	may
food	akil	hotel	oteyl
lunch	ghada	room	odah
menu	menu	toilet	beyt al-may

Shopping

How much is this?	ah-desh hadah?
chemist (pharmacy)	farmashiyyeh
cheap	rakhis
expensive	ghaali
shop	dukkaan

Numbers

0	sifr	8	tamanyeh
1	wa-hid	9	taisah
2	tinen	10	ahsharah
3	talatay	100	miyyah
4	arbaha	500	khamsmiyyah
5	chamseh	1000	alf
6	sitteh	5000	khamasta alaf
7	sabah		

MEETING PEOPLE

Are you here on holiday?
ata (at) kan bekhufsha?   אתה (את) כאן בחופשה?

I'm here on/to ...   ani kan ...   ... אני כאן
  business   la'asakim   לעסקים
  holiday   bekhufsha   בחופשה
  study   lelimudim   ללימודים

How long are you here for?
lekama zman bata (bat)?   לכמה זמן באת (באת)?

I'm/We're here for ... weeks/days.
ani/anakhnu po ...   ... אני/אנחנו פה
shavu'ot/yamim   שבועות/ימים ...

Do you like it here?
motse khen be'eineikha (be'eina'ikh) kan?   מוצא חן בעיניך כאן?

I/We like it here very much.
me'od motse khen   מאוד מוצא חן
be'einai/be'einenu   בעיני/בעינינו.

Sure.	betakh	בטח.
Just a minute.	rak rega	רק רגע.
It's OK.	ze beseder	זה בסדר.
It's important.	ze khashuv	זה חשוב.
It's not important.	ze lo khashuv	זה לא חשוב.
It's possible.	efshar	אפשר.
It's not possible.	i-efshar	אי-אפשר.
Look!	tir'e! (tir'i!)	(תראי!) תראה!
Listen!	tishma! (tishme'i!)	(תשמעי!) תשמע!
Listen to this!	tishma (tishme'i) et ze!	את זה! (תשמעי) תשמע
Are you ready?	ata mukhan? (m)	אתה מוכן?
	at mukhana? (f)	את מוכנה?
I'm ready.	ani mukhan(a)	אני מוכן(ה).
Good luck!	behatslakha!	בהצלחה!
Just a second.	od shniya	עוד שניה.

MEETING PEOPLE

NATIONALITIES

לאומים

Unfortunately we can't list all countries here; however, you'll find that many country names in Hebrew are similar to English. Remember, though, that even if a word looks like the English equivalent, it will have a Hebrew pronunciation. For instance, Ireland is pronounced irland.

Where are you from?	me'ayin ata (at)?	?מאין אתה (אה)
I'm from ...	ani me ...	... אני מ
Australia	ostralia	אוסטרליה
Canada	canada	קנדה
England	anglia	אנגליה
Europe	eropa	אירופה
India	hodu	הודו
Ireland	irland	אירלנד
Japan	yapan	יפאן
Scotland	skotland	סקוטלנד
the US	artsot habrit	ארצות-הברית
I come from a/the ...	ani me ...	... אני מ
I live in a/the ...	ani gar(a) be ...	... אני גר(ה) ב
city	ba'ir	בעיר
countryside	mikhuts la'ir	מחוץ לעיר
mountains	be'harim	בהרים

MEETING PEOPLE

seaside	lekhof hayam	לחוף הים
suburbs of ...	beparvar shel ...	בפרבר של ...
village	kfar	כפר

FAMILY משפחה

Are you married?
ata nasui? (m) אתה נשוי?
at nesu'a? (f) את נשואה?

I'm single.
ani ravak(a) אני רווק(ה).

I'm married.
ani nasui (nesu'a) אני נשוי (נשואה).

How many children do you have?
kama yeladim yesh lekha (lakh)? כמה ילדים יש לך?

We don't have any children.
ein lanu yeladim אין לנו ילדים.

I have a son.	yesh li ben ekhad	יש לי בן אחד.
I have a daughter.	yesh li bat akhat	יש לי בת אחת.
I have (three) children.	yesh li (shlosha) yeladim	יש לי (שלושה) ילדים.

How many siblings do you have?
kama akhim ve'akhayot כמה אחים ואחיות
yesh lekha (lakh)? יש לך (יש לך)?

Is your husband/wife here?
ha'im ba'alekh (ishtekha) kan? האם בעלך (אשתך) כאן?

Do you have a girlfriend?
yesh lekha khavera? יש לך חברה?

Do you have a boyfriend?
yesh lakh khaver? יש לך חבר?

MEETING PEOPLE

brother	akh	אח
children	yeladim	ילדים
daughter	bat	בת
family	mishpakha	משפחה
father	aba	אבא
husband	ba'al	בעל
mother	ima	אמא
older brother	akh gadol	אח גדול
older sister	akhot gdola	אחות גדולה
sister	akhot	אחות
son	ben	בן
wife	isha	אישה

MEETING PEOPLE

DID YOU KNOW ...

The Israeli flag was created at the first Zionist Congress in 1897. Its simple design is a Star of David placed in the centre of a Jewish prayer shawl. The traditional blue colour formerly used in the tassel (tsitsit) of this type of shawl ceased to be used after the destruction of the Second Temple in 70AD. Some say the formula for the dye was lost, while others hold that the loss of the blue dye echoes the loss of the Temple.

The dye comes from a crustacean and, over the past 30 years, some Jewish sects have begun once again to dye one of the eight threads making up each tassel with this blue colour, to help remind worshippers of the ocean, the horizon, the sky and the sapphire throne of God.

CULTURAL DIFFERENCES

הבדלי תרבות

How do you do this in your country?

eikh osim zot etzlekhem?

איך עושים זאת אצלכם?

Is this a local or national custom?

ze minhag mekomi o le'umi?

זה מנהג מקומי או לאומי?

I don't want to offend you.

ani lo rotse lifgo'a bekha (m)

אני לא רוצה לפגוע בך.

ani lo rotsa lifgo'a bakh (f)

אני לא רוצה לפגוע בך.

I'm sorry, it's not the custom in my country.

ani mitsta'er(et),

אני מצטער(ת),

ze lo nahug etslenu

זה לא נהוג אצלנו

I'm not used to this.

ani lo ragil (regila) leze

אני לא רגיל (רגילה) לזה.

I don't mind watching, but I'd prefer not to participate.

lo ikhpat li litspot, aval ani

לא איכפת לי לצפות, אבל אני

ma'adif(a) lo lehishtatef

מעדיף(ה) לא להשתתף.

AGE

גיל

| How old are you? (m) | ben kama ata? | בן כמה אתה? |
| How old are you? (f) | bat kama at? | בת כמה את? |

How old is your ...		
daughter	bat kama bitkha?	בת כמה בתך?
son	ben kama binkha?	בן כמה בנך?

| I'm ... years old. | ani ben (bat) ... | אני בן (בת) ... |

See Numbers & Amounts on page 181 for your age.

OCCUPATIONS

מקצוע

What sort of work do you do?

bema ata oved? (m)

במה אתה עובד?

bema at ovedet? (f)

במה את עובדת?

MEETING PEOPLE

I'm a(n) ...	ani ...	... אני
artist	oman(it)	אמן(ית)
businessperson	ish (eshet) asakim	איש (אשת) עסקים
doctor	rofe (rof'a)	רופא (רופאה)
engineer	mehandes(et)	מהנדס(ת)
farmer	khakla'i(t)	חקלאי(ת)
journalist	itona'i(t)	עיתונאי(ת)
lawyer	orekh(et) din	עורך(ת) דין
mechanic	mekhona'i(t)	מכונאי(ת)
nurse	akh(ot)	אח(ות)
office worker	pakid (pkida)	פקיד (פקידה)
scientist	mad'an(it)	מדען(ית)
student	student(it)	סטודנט(ית)
teacher	more (mora)	מורה
waiter	meltsar(it)	מלצר(ית)
writer	sofer(et)	סופר(ת)

I'm studying ...	ani lomed(et) ...	... אני לומד(ת)
art	omanut	אמנות
arts/humanities	mada'ei haru'akh	מדעי הרוח
business	asakim	עסקים
teaching	hora'a	הוראה
engineering	handasa	הנדסה
languages	safot zarot	שפות זרות
law	mishpatim	משפטים
medicine	refu'a	רפואה

NATIONAL SERVICE

Most Israelis, even immigrants, must serve in Israel's armed forces – men for three years and women for two years. Men must also serve in the reserve forces for anywhere between a week to two months each year, usually until they're 55 years old. All this training enables the Israelis to mobilise, within a matter of hours, a huge force to defend the country.

MEETING PEOPLE

Hebrew	ivrit	עברית
Jewish studies	mada'ei hayahadut	מדעי היהדות
science	mada'im	מדעים
social science	mada'ei hakhevra	מדעי החברה

JUDAISM

The Hebrew Bible (tanakh) and the Christian Old Testament are not the same book. The various books of the Bible are rearranged in the Christian Old Testament to foretell the coming of Jesus of Nazareth, whereas the Hebrew Bible tells a story of freedom from slavery and redemption from oppression. The first five books – called khumash (from Hebrew khamesh, meaning 'five') or pentateuch (from Greek meaning 'five scrolls') – of the Hebrew Bible (tanakh) are collectively known as the torah. These five books in Hebrew are known as bereshit (Genesis), shmot (Exodus), vayikra (Leviticus), bamidbar (Numbers) and dvarim (Deuteronomy).

According to Judaism, Jews are bound by God to obey a total of 613 positive (do this) and negative (don't do this) command-ments, known as 'mitzvahs' (mitzvot). Non-Jewish civilisations are considered righteous if they follow the more general seven Laws of Noah, including the forbidding of incest and eating flesh cut from a live animal.

One sect of orthodox Judaism attempts to bring non-practicing Jews to Judaism through the use of 'mitzva tanks'. These auto-vans contain prayer books (sidurim), prayer shawls (talit) with tassels (tsitsit) and phylacteries (tfillin), and leather straps with leather boxes that Jews are commanded to wear on the left arm and on the fore-head during morning prayers each day except the Sabbath.

According to Jewish numerology, the tassels which many orthodox Jews wear on the four corners of their undershirts and show outside their clothing, are tied in a series of 613 knots. Thus, when looking at the tassels, a religious Jew is reminded of all 613 commandments. A similar number system applies to the two shin letters, שש, placed side-by-side on the forehead box of the tfillin, that also add up to 613 (see page 150).

MEETING PEOPLE

I'm unemployed.	ani muvtal (muvtelet)	אני מובטל(ת).
What are you studying?	ma ata lomed? (m)	מה אתה לומד?
	ma at lomedet? (f)	מה את לומדת?

FEELINGS רגשות

I'm ...	ani ...	... אני
Are you ...?	ata (at) ...?	?... (את) אתה
afraid	mefakhed(et)	מפחד(ת)
angry	ko'es(et)	כועס(ת)
cold	kar li	קר לי
grateful	asir(at) toda	אסיר(ת) תודה
happy	same'akh (smekha)	שמח (שמחה)
hot	kham li	חם לי
hungry	ani ra'ev (re'eva)	רעב (רעבה)
in a hurry	memaher(et)	ממהר(ת)
keen to ...	met(a) le ...	... ל "מת(ה)"
sad	atsuv(a)	עצוב(ה)
sleepy	menumnam	מנומנם
	(menumnemet)	מנומנמת
sorry (condolence)	tankhumay	תנחומי
sorry (regret)	mitsta'er(et)	מצטער(ת)

A NATION OF IMMIGRANTS

During this past century, Jews have come to the Holy Land as pioneers (khalutsim), as refugees of war and Nazi concentration camps, and as emigrants from the Jewish Diaspora. According to Israel's Law of Return, anyone whose mother is Jewish or who is a convert to Judaism is Jewish and therefore eligible for Israeli citizenship. Immigrants become Israelis through an absorption process in which they attend intensive Hebrew language schools (ulpanim) and receive economic assistance to help them settle in the country.

thirsty	tsame (tsme'a)	צמא (צמאה)
tired	ayef(a)	עייף(ה)
well	bari (bri'a)	בריא (בריאה)
worried	mud'ag (mud'eget)	מודאג (מודאגת)

LANGUAGE DIFFICULTIES קשיי שפה

Do you speak English?

ata medaber anglit? (m) אתה מדבר אנגלית?

at medaberet anglit? (f) את מדברת אנגלית?

Yes, I do.

ken, ani medaber(et) anglit כן, אני מדבר(ת) אנגלית.

No, I don't.

lo, ani lo medaber(et) anglit לא, אני לא מדבר(ת) אנגלית.

Does anyone here speak English?

mishehu po medaber anglit? מישהו פה מדבר אנגלית?

I speak a little English.

ani yode'a (yoda'at) ktsat anglit אני יודע (יודעת) קצת אנגלית.

THE JEWISH COMMUNITY

A distinguishing characteristic of the Orthodox Jewish community is that the men wear skull caps, called kipot or yarmulkas. Although there's no religious law that requires Jews to cover their heads, the skull cap is a custom that's developed over thousands of years. Observant Jews hold that certain customs have the power of law.

Various orthodox sects have adopted different styles of skull cap to identify their religious affiliation. Hassids wear black felt caps, while modern Young-Israel worshippers wear black-knit ones. Religious Sephardic Jews frequently wear non-black skull caps, which are worn off-centre of the head. Young Jews from the US or Canada often have their name or a design crocheted in their cap.

ETHNIC GROUPS

There are about 12 million Jewish people worldwide. Four million live in Israel, and six million in the US. Jewishness isn't a matter of blood inheritance, but one of soul inheritance – inherited from the mother. However, anyone can become a Jew by embracing the faith of Judaism.

Jews from European countries are called Ashkenazis, while those from the former Spanish and Ottoman Empires are Sephardis. Today, a third of all Israeli children are of both Ashkenazi and Sephardic descent.

Do you understand?		
ata mevin? (m)		אתה מבין?
at mevina? (f)		את מבינה?
I (don't) understand.		
ani (lo) mevin(a)		אני (לא) מבין(ה).
Could you speak more slowly?		
ata yakhol ledaber yoter le'at? (m)		אתה יכול לדבר יותר לאט?
at yekhola ledaber yoter le'at? (f)		את יכולה לדבר יותר לאט?
Could you repeat that?		
ata yakhol (at yekhola)		אתה יכול (את יכולה)
lomar zot shenit?		לאמר זאת שנית?
Please write it down.		
tirshom et ze bevakasha		תרשום את זה בבקשה.
How do you say ...?	eikh omrim ...?	?... איך אומרים
What does ... mean?	ma ze ...?	?... מה זה

MEETING PEOPLE

GETTING AROUND   מסתדרים

Israel's relatively small size is a major boon, one which allows for leisurely exploration. No location in Israel is more than eight hours' drive from anywhere else. The country's excellent road system makes travel by bus *the* way to get around.

FINDING YOUR WAY   איך להתמצא

Most Israeli towns of any size have at least one tourist information office, so look for these if you find yourself stuck or lost.

Where's the ...?	eifo ...?	?... איפה
aeroplane	aviron	אווירון
boat	oniya	אוניה
bus	otobus	אוטובוס
train	rakevet	רכבת

How do we get to ...?
eikh magi'im le ...?	?... איך מגיעים ל

Is it far from/near here?
ha'im ze rakhok	האם זה רחוק
mikan/karov lekan?	מכאן/קרוב לכאן?

Can we walk there?
efshar lalekhet lesham baregel?	אפשר ללכת לשם ברגל?

Can you show me on the map?
ata yakhol (at yekhola)	אתה יכול (את יכולה)
lehar'ot li al hamapa?	להראות לי על המפה?

Are there other means of getting there?
efshar lehagi'a lesham	אפשר להגיע לשם
bidrakhim akherot?	בדרכים אחרות?

GETTING AROUND

What ... is this?	eize ... ze (m)	איזה ... זה?
	eizo ... zot? (f)	איזו ... זאת?
street	rekhov	רחוב
city	ir	עיר
village	kfar	כפר

DIRECTIONS — כיוונים

Turn at the ...	pne (pni) ...	... פנה (פני)
next corner	bapina haba'a	בפינה הבאה
traffic lights	baramzor	ברמזור

Straight ahead.	yashar	ישר.
To the right.	yamina	ימינה.
To the left.	smola	שמאלה.

behind	me'akhorei	... מאחורי
in front of	lifnei	... לפני
opposite	batsad hasheni	בצד השני
near	karov	קרוב
far	rakhok	רחוק
here	kan/po	פה/כאן
there	sham	שם

north	tsafon	צפון
south	darom	דרום
east	mizrakh	מזרח
west	ma'arav	מערב

ADDRESSES — כתובות

Israel's small population often makes foreigners imagine that all Israelis know each other. However, sending a letter to 'Ohr Kedem, Givataim' is likely never to reach the Ohr you're writing to. Writing an address on a letter or postcard follows mostly the same practice as in the West. The top line of the address includes (at least) the last name of the addressee. The second line will be the street and number of the house, the apartment number or entrance number (if it's a large building), followed by the city and area code on the last line:

> Ohr Kedem
> Rehov Golomb 64
> Givataim 53464

Israelis mostly write addresses in Hebrew script, but postal workers are also able to read Roman script.

BUYING TICKETS
איך לקנות כרטיסים

Where can I buy a ticket?
eifo efshar liknot kartisim?   ?איפה אפשר לקנות כרטיסים

We want to go to ...
anakhnu rotsim linso'a le ...   ... אנחנו רוצים לנסוע ל

Do I need to book?
tsarikh lehazmin makom merosh?   ?צריך להזמין מקום מֵראש

I'd like to book a seat to ...
ani rotse lehazmin makom le ...   ... אני רוצה להזמין מקום ל

Can I get a stand-by ticket?
efshar liknot kartis stand-by?   ?אפשר לקנות כרטיס סטנד-ביי

I'd like (a) ...	ani rotse (rotsa) ...	... (אני רוצה (רוצה
one-way ticket	kartis bekivun ekhad	כרטיס בכיוון אחד
return ticket	kartis halokh vashov	כרטיס הלוך ושוב
two tickets	shnei kartisim	שני כרטיסים
child's fare	ta'arif leyeled	תעריף לילד
pensioner's fare	ta'arif kashish	תעריף קשיש
student's fare	ta'arif student	תעריף סטודנט
1st class	makhlaka rishona	מחלקה ראשונה
2nd class	makhlaka shniya	מחלקה שנייה

kol hamekomot nimkeru	It's full.	כל המקומות נמכרו.

AIR   שדה התעופה

Domestic air travel is limited to routes linking Eilat, Tel Aviv, Jerusalem, Haifa and Kiryat Shmona in the North Galilee region.

Is there a flight to Eilat?
   yesh tisa le'eilat?   יש טיסה לאילת?
When's the next flight to Kiryat Shmone?
   matay hatisa haba'a le'   מתי הטיסה הבאה
   kiryat shmone?   לקרית שמונה?
How long does the flight take?
   ma meshekh hatisa?   מה משך הטיסה?
What time do I have to check in at the airport?
   matay alai lavo lisde hate'ufa?   מתי עלי לבוא לשדה-התעופה?
What time does the plane leave/arrive?
   matay mamri/nokhet ha'aviron?   מתי ממריא/נוחת האווירון?
Where's the baggage claim?
   eifo masof hamizvadot?   איפה מסוף המזוודות?

WESTERN WALL

Israel's famous Western Wall lies in the Old City of Jerusalem. It formed part of the retaining wall built by Herod the Great in 20 BC to contain the landfill on which the Second Temple compound stood. Although the temple was destroyed in 70 AD, according to rabbinical texts, the shechina, or divine presence, remained with the wall and it came to be regarded as the most holy of all Jewish sites where Jews make pilgrimages to mourn their ancient loss – hence the term 'Wailing Wall'. The area in front of the wall acts as an open-air synagogue, with a small southern section for women and a larger northern section reserved for men. Giant Herodian stones with carved edges form the lower layers of the wall, while the stones forming the top layer were chiselled slightly differently and were laid at the time of the construction of the Al-Aqsa Mosque.

At Customs

Animals, plants, firearms and fresh meat may not be brought into the country.

I have nothing to declare.
ein li al ma lehats'hir   אין לי על מה להצהיר.

I've got something to declare.
yesh li al ma lehats'hir   יש לי על מה להצהיר.

Do I have to declare this?
tsarikh lehats'hir al ze?   צריך להצהיר על זה?

This is all my luggage.
elu kol hakhafatsim sheli   אלו כל החפצים שלי.

I didn't know I had to declare it.
lo yada'ati shetsarikh   לא ידעתי שצריך
lehats'hir al ze   להצהיר על זה.

BUS   אוטובוס

City buses are frequent, fairly inexpensive, and run from 5.30 am to midnight. Bus services don't run during the Sabbath, starting from one hour before sunset. Almost all drivers speak English, and will let you know where to get off. Intercity buses are dependable and inexpensive. Tel Aviv has the largest bus station in the world, with destinations throughout the country.

ISRAELI SOLDIERS

Israeli soldiers' main means of transport throughout the country is Egged, the national bus line. When travelling by bus in Israel, you'll encounter many olive-green uniformed men and women, all carrying one type of machine gun or another. If a rifle blocks your path, don't be afraid to say:

slikha, ata yakhol (at yekhola) lehaziz et harove, bevakasha?
Pardon me, could you move the gun?

GETTING AROUND

Where's the bus stop?
  eifo takhanat ha'otobus?   איפה תחנת האוטובוס?

Where's the bus station?
  eifo hatakhana hamerkazit?   איפה התחנה המרכזית?

Which bus goes to ...?
  eize otobus nose'a le ...?   איזה אוטובוס נוסע ל ...?

Does this bus go to ...?
  haotobus haze nose'a le ...?   האוטובוס הזה נוסע ל ...?

What time does the bus leave/arrive?
  matay yotse/magi'a ha'otobus?   מתי יוצא/מגיע האוטובוס?

How often do buses come?
  ma tkhifut ha'otobus?   מה תכיפות האוטובוס?

What time is	matay yotse	מתי יוצא
the ... bus?	haotobus ...?	?... האוטובוס
first	harishon	הראשון
last	ha'akharon	האחרון
next	haba	הבא

Could you let me know when we get to ...?
ata yakhol (at yekhola) lomar   אתה יכול (את יכולה) לאמר
li keshenagi'a le ...?   ?... לי כשנגיע ל

Where do I get the bus for ...?
eifo ha'otobus le ...?   ?... איפה האוטובוס ל

TRAIN   לרכבת

The Tel Aviv-Haifa-Nahariya line is modern and comfortable –
prices are on a par with bus travel, making train travel a viable
alternative. The train service extends south towards Rehovot, with
commuter services twice a day to and from Ashdod.

Where's the train station?
eifo takhanat ha'rakevet?   ?איפה תחנת הרכבת

What station is this?
eizo takhana zot?   ?איזו תחנה זאת

What is the next station?
mahi hatakhana haba'a?   ?מהי התחנה הבאה

Does this train stop at Netanya?
harakevet otseret benetanya?   ?הרכבת עוצרת בנתניה

What time does the train leave/arrive?
matay yotset/magi'a harakevet?   ?מתי יוצאת/מגיעה הרכבת

How long does the trip take?
ma meshekh hanesi'a?   ?מה משך הנסיעה

Is it a direct route?
ha'im zo derekh yeshira?   ?האם זו דרך ישירה

The train has been delayed/cancelled.
harakevet me'akheret/butla   .הרכבת מאחרת/בוטלה

How long will it be delayed?
bekama zman te'akher harakevet?   ?בכמה זמן תאחר הרכבת

Is that seat taken?
hamakom tafus?   ?המקום תפוס

I want to get off at ...
ani rotse (rotsa) laredet be ...   ... אני רוצה (רוצה) לרדת ב

TAXI   מוניות

Apart from regular taxis, you can catch shared taxis (moniyot sherut),
which depart from designated locations when filled with passengers
and follow a set route.

Is this taxi free?
hamonit pnuya?   ?המונית פנויה

Please take me to ...
bevakasha sa le ...   ... בבקשה סע ל

How much does it cost to go to ...?
kama ola hanesi'a le ...?   ?... כמה עולה הנסיעה ל

How much is the fare?
ma hamekhir?   ?מה המחיר

Do we pay extra for luggage?
yesh tashlum nosaf avur mit'an?   ?יש תשלום נוסף עבור מטען

Instructions

Continue.
hamshekh (hamshikhi)   .(המשך (המשיכי

The next street to the left/right.
barekhov haba pne (pni)   (ברחוב הבא פנה (פני
smola/yamina   .שמאלה/ימינה

Please slow down.	bevakasha ha'et	בבקשה האט.
Please wait here.	bevakasha khake kan	בבקשה חכה כאן.
Stop here.	atsor kan	עצור כאן.
Stop at the corner.	atsor bapina	עצור בפינה.

BOAT אוניה

Passenger boats tour the Bay of Haifa and the Sea of Galilee, although, as most Israelis catch a plane to where they want to be, pleasure cruises aren't as popular as they could be.

The only way into and out of Israel by scheduled sea services is via Haifa to Cyprus, then on to Greece. Two companies run services up to three times a week in summer and once a week in winter.

Where does the boat leave from?
  me'ayin yotset ha'oniya? מאין יוצאת האוניה?
What time does the boat leave/arrive?
  matay mafliga/magi'a ha'oniya? מתי מפליגה/מגיעה האוניה?

CAR מכונית

The Israeli road system is excellent, with bilingual Hebrew–English roadsigns. It's easy to travel from Jerusalem to Metulah, on the Lebanese border, and back to Tel Aviv on the same day. Licence plates from the Palestinian Territories are blue–grey, while Israeli cars have yellow plates.

Where can I rent a car?
  eifo efshar liskor mekhonit? איפה אפשר לשכור מכונית?
How much is it daily/weekly?
  ma hamekhir leyom/leshavu'a? מה המחיר ליום/לשבוע?
Does that include insurance/mileage?
  hamekhir kolel המחיר כולל
  bitu'akh/kilometrage? ביטוח/קילומטראז'?
Where's the next petrol station?
  eifo takhanat hadelek haba'a? איפה תחנת הדלק הבאה?

Please fill the tank.
   bevakasha lemale

בבקשה למלא.

I'd like ... litres.
   ani rotse (rotsa) ... litrim

אני רוצה (רוצה) ... ליטרים.

Please check	bevakasha livdok	בבקשה לבדוק
the ...	et ha ...	את ה ...
oil	shemen	שמן
tyre pressure	lakhats avir batsamig	לחץ אוויר בצמיג
water	mayim	מים

Can I park here?
   efshar lakhanot kan?

אפשר לחנות כאן?

How long can we park here?
   kama zman efshar lakhanot kan?

כמה זמן אפשר לחנות כאן?

Where's the road to ...?
   eifo haderekh le ...?

איפה הדרך ל ...?

Does this road lead to ...?
   zot haderekh le ...?

זאת הדרך ל ...?

air	avir	אוויר
battery	matsber	מצבר
brakes	balamim/breks	בלמים/ברקס
clutch	matsmed/clutch	מצמד/קלאץ'
driver's licence	rishyon nehiga	רישיון נהיגה
engine	mano'a	מנוע
garage	musakh	מוסך
indicator	panas itut	פנס איתות
leaded	mekhil oferet	מכיל עופרת
lights	orot	אורות
main road	derekh rashit	דרך ראשית
oil	shemen	שמן
puncture	pancher/teker	פנצ'ר/תקר
radiator	radiator	רדיאטור
regular	ragil	רגיל
roadmap	mapat drakhim	מפת דרכים

GETTING AROUND

seatbelt	khagorat btikhut	חגורת בטיחות
self-service	sherut atsmi	שירות עצמי
speed limit	hamehirut hamuteret	המהירות המותרת
tyres	tsmigim	צמיגים
unleaded	lelo oferet	ללא עופרת
windscreen	shimsha kidmit	שמשה קדמית

Car Problems

We need a mechanic.
anakhnu mekhapsim musakhnik — אנחנו מחפשים מוסכניק.

What make is it?
eizo mekhonit zot? — איזו מכונית זאת?

The car broke down at ...
hamekhonit hitkalkela be ... — המכונית התקלקלה ב ...

The battery is flat.
hamatsber rek — המצבר ריק.

The radiator is leaking.
yesh dlifa baradiator — יש דליפה ברדיאטור.

I have a flat tyre.
yesh li pancher — יש לי פנצ׳ר.

It's overheating.
hamekhonit mitkhamemet — המכונית מתחממת.

It's not working.
ze lo oved — זה לא עובד.

I've lost my car keys.
ibadti et maftekhot hamkhonit — איבדתי את מפתחות המכונית.

I've run out of petrol.
nigmar li hadelek — נגמר לי הדלק.

BICYCLE — אופניים

Is it within cycling distance?
ha'im ze bemerkhak — האם זה במרחק
rekhivat ofana'im? — רכיבת אופניים?

Where can I hire a bicycle?
eifo efshar liskor ofana'im? — איפה אפשר לשכור אופניים?

GETTING AROUND

Where can I find secondhand bikes for sale?

	eifo efshar limtso ofana'im	איפה אפשר למצוא אפניים
	yad shniya limkira?	יד שנייה למכירה?

I've got a flat tyre.	yesh li pancher	יש לי פנצ'ר.

How much is it for an/the ...?	ma hamekhir le ...?	מה המחיר ל ...?
afternoon	akhar-tsohora'im	אחר-צהריים
day	yom	יום
hour	sha'a	שעה
morning	boker	בוקר

bike	ofana'im	אופניים
brakes	ma'atsorim	מעצורים
to cycle	lirkav al ofana'im	לרכב על אופניים
gear stick	yadit hilukhim	ידית הילוכים
handlebars	kidon	כידון
helmet	kasdat magen	קסדת-מגן
inner tube	pnimit	פנימית
lights	orot	אורות
mountain bike	ofnei harim	אופני הרים
padlock	man'ul	מנעול
pump	mash'eva	משאבה
puncture	pancher	פנצ'ר
racing bike	ofnei meruts	אופני מרוץ
saddle	moshav	מושב
tandem	ofana'im lishna'im	אופניים לשניים
wheel	galgal	גלגל

ACCOMMODATION תאכסנות

Israel has a wide range of accommodation, with plenty of scope for both the big spender and the budget traveller. In comparison with the number of lower and mid-price beds available, Israel has a disproportionately high percentage of luxury accommodation with first-class service and facilities.

In the Dead Sea region and Mitzpe Ramon, hostels are the sole accommodation choice. In the mid-price range are kibbutz guest-houses, which have access to good facilities such as swimming pools and beaches, renowned restaurants and organised activities, and Christian hospices. In many popular tourist areas you'll find accommodation in private homes – inquire at the local tourist information office or look for signs posted in the street.

FINDING ACCOMMODATION מחפשים חדר

I'm looking for a ...	ani mekhapes(et) ...	... (אני מחפש(ת
camping ground	atar camping	אתר קמפינג
guesthouse	beit ha'arakha	בית-הארחה
hotel	malon	מלון
motel	motel	מוטל
youth hostel	akhsaniyat no'ar	אכסניית נוער

Where can I find a ... hotel?	eifo yesh malon ...?	?... איפה יש מלון
clean	naki	נקי
good	tov	טוב
nearby	karov	קרוב

Where's the ... hotel?	eifo hamalon ... beyoter?	איפה המלון ... ביותר?
best	hatov	הטוב
cheapest	hazol	הזול

ACCOMMODATION

| What's the address? | ma haktovet? | ?מה הכתובת |

Could you write down the address, please?
ata yakhol (at yekhola) lirshom
li et haktovet bevakasha?

אתה יכול (את יכולה) לרשום לי
את הכתובת בבקשה?

BOOKING AHEAD
זמנה מראש

I'd like to book a room please.
ani rotse (rotsa) lehazmin
kheder bevakasha

אני רוצה (רוצה) להזמין
חדר בבקשה.

Do you have any rooms available?
yesh khadarim pnuyim?

?יש חדרים פנויים

For three nights.
lishlosha leylot

לשלושה לילות.

We'll be arriving at ... nagi'a be ... ... נגיע ב
My name's ... shmi ... ... שמי

CHECKING IN
רישום בדלפק הקבלה

Do you have any rooms available?
yesh lakhem khadarim pnuyim?

?יש לכם חדרים פנויים

Sorry, we're full.
ani mitsta'er(et), hakol tafus

אני מצטער(ת), הכל תפוס.

Do you have a room with two beds?
yesh kheder im shtei mitot?

?יש חדר עם שתי מיטות

Do you have a room with a double bed?
yesh kheder im mita kfula?

?יש חדר עם מיטה כפולה

I'd like ...	hayiti rotse (rotsa) ...	... הייתי רוצה (רוצה)
to share a dorm	lehitkhalek bekheder bame'onot	להתחלק בחדר במעונות
a single room	kheder leyakhid	חדר ליחיד

ACCOMMODATION

We want a room with a ...	anakhnu rotsim kheder im ...	אנחנו רוצים חדר עם ...
bathroom	ambatya	אמבטיה
shower	miklakhat	מקלחת
TV	televisia	טלוויזיה
window	khalon	חלון

Can I see it?	efshar lir'ot?	אפשר לראות?
Are there any others?	yesh od akherim?	יש עוד אחרים?
Where's the bathroom?	eifo hasherutim?	איפה השרותים?

Is there hot water all day?

yesh mayim khamim kol hayom?   יש מים חמים כל היום?

How much for ...?	ma hamekhir le ...?	מה המחיר ל...?
one night	layla ekhad	לילה אחד
a week	shavu'a	שבוע
two people	shnei anashim	שני אנשים

Is there a discount for children/students?

yesh hanakha liladim/listudentim?   יש הנחה לילדים/לסטודנטים?

It's fine. I'll take it.

| ze beseder, ani loke'akh (lokakhat) et ze | זה בסדר, אני לוקח (לוקחת) את זה. |

KIBBUTZIM & MOSHAVIM

Kibbutzim (collective farms) and moshavim (cooperative farms) sprang up at the end of the 19th century as idealistic communities which had to face inhospitable geographical and climatic conditions. Today, only about three percent of the population now actually live on a kibbutz. Every year, thousands of young foreigners arrive in Israel to work on a kibbutz or moshav. Kibbutz volunteers work six days a week, usually for a minimum of two months. Those working on a moshav usually work with an individual farmer for a minimum of five weeks.

REQUESTS & COMPLAINTS

קשות ותלונות

I need a ...
    ani tsarikh (tsrikha) ...

אני צריך (צריכה) ...

Do you have a safe where I can leave my valuables?
    yesh po kasefet she'ani
    yakhol (yekhola) lehafkid
    ba et divrei ha'erekh sheli?

יש פה כספת שאני
יכול (יכולה) להפקיד
בה את דברי הערך שלי?

Could I have a receipt for them?
    efshar lekabel kabala?

אפשר לקבל קבלה?

Is there somewhere to wash clothes?
    eifo efshar lirkhots bgadim?

איפה אפשר לרחוץ בגדים?

Can we use the telephone?
    efshar lehishtamesh batelefon?

אפשר להשתמש בטלפון?

My room is too dark.
    hakheder khashukh midai

החדר חשוך מידי.

It's too cold/hot.
    ze kar/kham midai

זה קר/חם מידי.

It's too noisy.
    mar'ish midai

מרעיש מידי.

I can't open/close the window.
    ani lo yakhol (yekhola)
    lifto'akh/lisgor et hakhalon

אני לא יכול (יכולה)
לפתוח/לסגור את החלון.

This ... isn't clean.	ha ... lo naki (nekia)	ה ... לא נקי (נקיה)
blanket	smikha	שמיכה
pillow	karit	כרית
pillow case	tsipit	ציפית
sheet	sadin	סדין

Please change them/it.
    bevakasha lehakhlif otam/oto

בבקשה להחליף אותם/אותו.

CHECKING OUT

עזיבה

Can I pay with a travellers cheque?

efshar leshalem betraveler cheque?   אפשר לשלם בטרוולר צ'ק?

Could I have the bill please?

efshar lekabel et   אפשר לקבל את
hakheshbon bevakasha?   החשבון בבקשה?

There's a mistake in the bill.

slikha, yesh ta'ut bakheshbon   סליחה, יש טעות בחשבון.

Useful Words

air-conditioning	mizug-avir	מיזוג-אוויר
clean	naki	נקי
key	mafte'akh	מפתח
face cloth	magevet lapanim	מגבת לפנים
bottle of water	bakbuk mayim	בקבוק מים
lamp	menora	מנורה
lock	man'ul	מנעול
mosquito coil	takhshir dokhe yatushim	תכשיר דוחה יתושים
soap	sabon	סבון
toilet	sherutim	שירותים
toilet paper	neyar twalet	נייר טואלט
towel	magevet	מגבת
water (hot/cold)	mayim (khamim/karim)	מים (חמים/קרים)

PAPERWORK

ניירת

address	ktovet	כתובת
age	gil	גיל
baptismal certificate	te'udat tvila	תעודת טבילה
customs	mekhes	מכס
date of birth	ta'arikh leida	תאריך לידה
driver's licence	rishyon nehiga	רישיון נהיגה
ID	te'udat zehut	תעודת זהות
(last) name	shem mishpakha	שם משפחה

ACCOMMODATION

ACCOMMODATION

(first) name	shem prati	שם פרטי
nationality	le'om	לאום
passport number	mispar darkon	מספר דרכון
place of birth	mekom leida	מקום לידה
profession	miktsoa	מקצוע
purpose of visit	matrat habikur	מטרת הביקור
business	asakim	עסקים
holiday	khufsha	חופשה
immigration	bikoret darkonim	ביקורת דרכונים
visiting the homeland	bikur moledet	ביקור מולדת
visiting relatives	bikur krovim	ביקור קרובים
marital status	matsav mishpakhti	מצב משפחתי
divorced	garush (grusha)	גרוש (גרושה)
married	nasui (nesu'a)	נשוי (נשואה)
single	ravak(a)	רווק(ה)
widow/widower	alman(a)	אלמן(ה)
reason for travel	matrat hanesi'a	מטרת הנסיעה
religion	dat	דת
sex	min	מין
visa	visa	ויזה

AROUND TOWN

בעיר

LOOKING FOR ...

מחפשים ...

Where's a ...?	eifo ha ... ?	<div dir="rtl">?... איפה ה</div>
bank	bank	<div dir="rtl">בנק</div>
consulate	konsulya	<div dir="rtl">קונסוליה</div>
embassy	shagrirut	<div dir="rtl">שגרירות</div>
post office	do'ar	<div dir="rtl">דואר</div>
public telephone	telefon tsiburi	<div dir="rtl">טלפון ציבורי</div>
public toilet	sherutim tsiburi'im	<div dir="rtl">שירותים ציבוריים</div>
town square	kikar ha'ir	<div dir="rtl">כיכר העיר</div>

AT THE BANK

בבנק

Most Israelis talk in terms of US dollars, not shekels (the Israeli currency), a habit acquired in the days when the national currency was constantly being devalued. Upmarket hotels still quote their prices in dollars, as do many hostels, car hire companies and airlines. At such places, payment in dollars is accepted and, for the customer, it's preferable because payments made in foreign currency are free of Value Added Tax (VAT).

Many bank foyers are equipped with cash-dispensing ATMs accepting all major international cards. Travellers cheques are also widely accepted, though commission charges can be quite high.

Although banking hours vary, generally they are Sunday to Tuesday and Thursday from 8.30 am to 12.30 pm and 4 to 5.30 pm. On Wednesday, Friday and the eves of holy days, they're usually open from 8.30 am until noon. In Nazareth, banks are open Friday and Saturday mornings, but are closed on Sundays.

Can I use my credit card to withdraw money?

efshar limshokh kesef
be'emtsa'ut kartis ashra'i? אפשר למשוך כסף
באמצעות כרטיס אשראי?

Can I exchange money here?

efshar lehakhlif kan kesef? אפשר להחליף כאן כסף?

Please write it down.

ata yakhol lirshom
et ze, bevakasha? (m) אתה יכול לרשום
את זה בבקשה?

at yekhola lirshom
et ze, bevakasha? (f) את יכולה לרשום
את זה בבקשה?

Can I have smaller notes?

efshar lekabel shtarot
ktanim yoter? אפשר לקבל שטרות
קטנים יותר?

The automatic teller swallowed my card.

hakaspomat bala li et
kartis ha'ashra'i כספומט בלע לי את
כרטיס האשראי.

<table>
<tr><td>I want to change (a) ...</td><td>ani rotse (rotsa)
lehakhlif ...</td><td>אני רוצה (רוצה)
להחליף ...</td></tr>
<tr><td>cash/money</td><td>mezumanim/kesef</td><td>מזומנים/כסף</td></tr>
<tr><td>cheque</td><td>chek</td><td>צ'ק</td></tr>
<tr><td>travellers cheque</td><td>hamkha'at nos'im</td><td>המחאת נוסעים</td></tr>
</table>

What time does the bank open?

matay potkhim et habank? מתי פותחים את הבנק?

Where can I cash a travellers cheque?

eifo ani yakhol (yekhola)
lifdot hamkha'at nos'im? איפה אני יכול (יכולה)
לפדות המחאת נוסעים?

What's the exchange rate?

mahu sha'ar hakhalifin? מהו שער החליפין?

Can I transfer money here from my bank?

efshar leha'avir lekan
kesef mehabank sheli? אפשר להעביר לכאן
כסף מהבנק שלי?

How long will it take to arrive?

betokh kama zman ze yagi'a? בתוך כמה זמן זה יגיע?

AT THE POST OFFICE   בדואר

Letters posted in Israel take seven to 10 days to reach North America and Australia, and reach Europe a little sooner. Incoming mail takes about three or four days to arrive from Europe and around a week from places further afield.

I want to buy ...	ani rotse (rotsa) liknot ...	... אני רוצה לקנות
postcards	gluyot	גלויות
stamps	bulim	בולים

I want to send a(n) ...	ani rotse (rotsa) lishlo'akh ...	... אני רוצה (רוצה) לשלוח
aerogram	igeret-avir	איגרת-אוויר
letter	mikhtav	מכתב
parcel	khavila	חבילה
telegram	mivrak	מברק

Please send it by ...
bevakasha lishlo'akh be ...   ... בבקשה לשלוח ב
How much does it cost to send this to ...?
kama ole lishlo'akh et ze le ...?   ?... כמה עולה לשלוח את זה ל

air mail	do'ar avir	דואר אוויר
envelope	ma'atafa	מעטפה
express mail	do'ar express	דואר אקספרס
mail box	teivat do'ar	תיבת דואר
parcel	khavila	חבילה
pen	et	עט
postcode	mikud	מיקוד
registered mail	do'ar rashum	דואר רשום
surface mail	do'ar yam	דואר ים

AROUND TOWN

TELECOMMUNICATIONS   קשורת אלקטרונית

Israel has a state-of-the-art, card-operated public telephone system. International calls can be made from any public telephone. Faxes can be sent at post offices.

Israel is a remarkably well-connected Internet society, with many businesses on the Web. However, Internet cafés do come and go – Jerusalem currently leads the pack with cafés to access your email and surf the Net.

Could I please use the telephone?
slikha, efshar lehishtamesh
batelefon?

סליחה, אפשר להשתמש
בטלפון?

I want to call ...
ani rotse (rotsa) letalpen le ...

אני רוצה (רוצה) לטלפן ל ...

The number is ...
hamispar ...

המספר ...

How much does a three-minute call cost?
kama ola sikha bat
shalosh dakot?

כמה עולה שיחה בת
שלוש דקות?

I want to make a long-distance call to Australia.
ani rotse (rotsa) la'asot
sikhat khuts leOstralia

אני רוצה (רוצה) לעשות
שיחת חוץ לאוסטרליה.

I want to make a reverse charges call.
ani rotse (rotsa) la'asot
sikhat collect

אני רוצה (רוצה) לעשות
שיחת קולקט.

What's the area code for ...?
mahu ezor hakhiyug shel ...?

מהו אזור החיוג של ...?

It's engaged.   tafus   תפוס
I've been cut off.   nutakti   נותקתי

Is there a local Internet café?
yesh po kafe Internet?

יש פה קפה אינטרנט?

I want to get Internet access.

ani tsarikh (tsrikha)   אני צריך (צריכה)

gisha laInternet   גישה לאינטרנט.

I want to check my email.

ani tsarikh (tsrikha) livdok et   אני צריך (צריכה) לבדוק את

hado'ar ha'elektroni sheli   הדואר האלקטרוני שלי.

operator	merkazan(it)	מרכזן(ית)
phone book	madrikh telefon	מדריך טלפון
phone box	ta telefon	תא טלפון
phonecard	kartis telefon	כרטיס טלפון
telephone	telefon	טלפון
urgent	dakhuf	דחוף

Making a Call

Hello, is ... there?	Halo, ha'im ... sham?	הלו, האם ... שם?
Hello.	halo	הלו.
May I speak to ...?	efshar ledaber im ...?	אפשר לדבר עם ...?
Who's calling?	mi mevakesh?	מי מבקש?
It's ...	ze ...	זה ...
Yes, he (she) is here.	ken, hu (hi) po	כן, הוא (היא) פה.

One moment.

rak rega bevakasha   רק רגע, בבקשה.

I'm sorry, he's not here.

ani mitsta'er(et), hu lo po   אני מצטער(ת), הוא לא פה.

What time will she be back?

matay hi takhzor?   מתי היא תחזור?

Can I leave a message?

efshar lehash'ir hoda'a?   אפשר להשאיר הודעה?

Please tell her I called.

bevakasha tagid la shetsiltsalti   בבקשה תגיד לה שצלצלתי.

I'll call back later.

etkasher shuv me'ukhar yoter   אתקשר שוב מאוחר יותר.

AROUND TOWN

SIGHTSEEING

טיול ותיור

Where's the tourist office?
eifo hamodi'in letayarim?

איפה המודיעין לתיירים?

Do you have a local map?
yesh lekha (lakh) mapa shel ha'ezor?

יש לך מפה של האזור?

I'd like to see ...
ani rotse (rotsa) levaker be ...

... אני רוצה (רוצה) לבקר ב

What time does it open/close?
matay potkhim/sogrim?

מתי פותחים/סוגרים?

What's that building?
mahu habinyan hahu?

מהו הבנין ההוא?

What's this monument?
mahu ha'atar haze?

מהו האתר הזה?

May we take photographs?
efshar letsalem?

אפשר לצלם?

I'll send you the photograph.
eshlakh lekha (lakh) et hatmuna

אשלח לך (לך) את התמונה.

Could you take a photograph of me?
ata yakhol letsalem oti? (m)

אתה יכול לצלם אותי?

at yekhola letsalem oti? (f)

את יכולה לצלם אותי?

castle	tira	טירה
cathedral	katedrala	קתדרלה
church	knesiya	כנסייה
cinema	bet-kolno'a	בית-קולנוע
concert	concert	קונצרט
crowded	tsafuf	צפוף
museum	moze'on	מוזיאון
park	gan tsiburi	גן ציבורי
statue	pesel	פסל
university	universita	אוניברסיטה

AROUND TOWN

SIGNS

חם/קר	**HOT/COLD**
כניסה	**ENTRANCE**
יציאה	**EXIT**
אין כניסה	**NO ENTRY**
אסור לעשן	**NO SMOKING**
פתוח/סגור	**OPEN/CLOSED**
אסור	**PROHIBITED**
שירותים	**TOILETS**

AROUND TOWN

PLACENAMES

Jerusalem	yerushala'im	ירושלים
East Jerusalem	yerushala'im hamizrakhit	ירושלים המזרחית
Giv'at Ram	giv'at ram	גבעת רם
Kidron Valley	emek kidron	עמק קידרון
Mamilla	mamila	ממילה
Mount of Olives	har hazeitim	הר הזיתים
Mount Scopus	har hatsofim	הר הצופים
Mt Zion	har tsion	הר ציון
Museum Row	shderat hamuze'onim	שדרת המוזיאונים
Rehavia	rekhavia	רחביה
Talbiyeh	talbiye	טלביה
Talpiot	talpiot	תלפיות
Tel Aviv	tel aviv	תל-אביב
Ashdod	ashdod	אשדוד
Ashkelon	ashkelon	אשקלון
Bat Yam	bat yam	בת-ים
B'nei Brak	b'nei brak	בני-ברק
Herzlia	herzlia	הרצליה
Jaffa	yaffo	יפו
Lod	lod	לוד
Netanya	netanya	נתניה
Ramla	ramla	רמלה
Rehovot	rekhovot	רחובות
Rishon Lezion	rishon letsion	ראשון לציון
Haifa	khaifa	חיפה
Akko	ako	עכו
Atlit	atlit	עתלית
Beit She'arim	beit she'arim	בית שערים
Caesarea	keisariya	קיסריה
Daliyat al-Karmel	daliyat al-karmel	דלית אל-כרמל
Dor	dor	דור
Ein Hod	ein hod	עין הוד
Meggido	megido	מגידו
Nahariya	nahariya	נהריה

PLACENAMES

Peqi'in	peqi'in	פקיעין
Rosh HaNikra	rosh hanikra	ראש הניקרה
Usfiya	usafiye	עוספיה
Zichron Ya'akov	zikhron ya'akov	זכרון יעקב

The Galilee	hagalil	**הגליל**
Beit She'an	beit she'an	בית שאן
Belvior	kokhav hayarden	כוכב הירדן
Nazareth	natsrat	נצרת
Safed	tsfat	צפת
Tiberias	tveriya	טבריה
Sea of Galilee	kineret	כנרת

Upper Galilee	hagalil ha'elyon	**הגליל העליון**
& The Golan	hagolan	**הגולן**
Banias	banias	בניאס
Gamla	gamla	גמלה
Hazor	khatsor	חצור
Hula Valley &	emek hakhula	עמק החולה
Nature Reserve	veshmurat hateva	ושמורת הטבע
Hurshat Tal National	khurshat tal	חורשת טל
Park		
Katzrin	katzrin	קצרין
Kibbutz Kfar Gil'adi	kibutz kfar gil'adi	כפר גלעדי
Kiryat Shmona	kiryat shmona	קרית שמונה
Majdal Shams	majdal shams	מג'דל שאמס
Mas'ada	mas'ada	מסעדה
Metula	metula	מטולה
Nahal Yehudiya	shmurat hateva shel	שמורת הטבע
Nature Reserve	nakhal yehudiya	של נחל יהודיה
Nimrod Castle	kala'at nimrod	קלעת נמרוד
Quneitra Viewpoint	taspit al-kuneitra	תצפית אל-קונייטרה
Rosh Pina	rosh pina	ראש פינה
Tel Dan	tel dan	תל דן
Tel Hai	tel hai	תל חי

PLACENAMES

The Dead Sea	yam hamelakh	ים המלח
Attrakzia	atrakzia	אטרקציה
Ein Bokek	ein bokek	עין בוקק
Ein Feshkha	ein feshkha	עין פשחה
Ein Gedi	ein gedi	עין גדי
Hamme Zohar	khamei zohar	חמי זוהר
Masada	metsada	מצדה
Neve Zohar	neve zohar	נווה זוהר
Qumran	qumran	קומרן
Sodom	sdom	סדום
The Negev	hanegev	הנגב
Arad	arad	ערד
Avdat	avdat	עבדת
Be'er Sheva	be'er sheva	באר שבע
Dimona	dimona	דימונה
Eilat	eilat	אילת
Mitzpe Ramon	mitzpe ramon	מצפה רמון
Sde Boker	sde boker	שדה בוקר
Tel Arad	tel arad	תל ערד
Gaza Strip	retsu'at aza	רצועת עזה
The West Bank	hagada hama'aravit; yosh	הגדה המערבית; יו״ש
Bethlehem	bet lekhem	בית לחם
Hebron	khevron	חברון
Jericho	yerikho	ייריחו
Nablus	shkhem	שכם

INTERESTS

תחביבים

A youthful nation still imbued with a pioneering spirit, Israelis are very much outdoor types which isn't surprising, considering Israel is a geologically diverse, yet compact, country. A two hour drive from Tel Aviv can have you skiing on the slopes of Mt Hermon or rafting on the Jordan River. Alternatively, head off in another direction and you're into the desert, riding dune buggies or camel trekking. Most of these activities have been developed for the benefit of the locals, but they're also a great way for visitors to experience the natural beauty of the country.

COMMON INTERESTS

תחביבים שכיחים

What do you do in your spare time?

ma ata ose bizmankha hapanui? (m)	מה את/ה עושה בזמנך הפנוי?
ma at osa bizmanekh hapanui? (f)	מה את/ה עושה בזמנך הפנוי?

I like ...	ani ohev(et) ...	... אני אוהב(ת)
I don't like ...	ani lo ohev(et) ...	... אני לא אוהב(ת)
Do you like ...?	ata ohev ...? (m)	?... אתה אוהב
	at ohevet ...? (f)	?... את אוהבת

art	omanut	אמנות
dancing	rikudim	ריקודים
cooking	bishul	בישול
film	seret	סרט
music	musika	מוסיקה
going out	latset levalot	לצאת לבלות
playing games	lesakhék miskhakim	לשחק משחקים
playing soccer	lesakhek kaduregel	לשחק כדורגל
playing sport	la'asot sport	לעשות ספורט
reading books	likro sfarim	לקרוא ספרים
shopping	la'asot shopping	לעשות שופינג
travelling	letayel	לטייל

watching TV	lir'ot televisia	לראות טלוויזיה
photography	tsilum	צילום
the theatre	teatron	תיאטרון
writing	ktiva	כתיבה

SPORT

ספורט

Do you like sport?

   ata ohev la'asot sport?   אתה אוהב לעשות ספורט?

   at ohevet la'asot sport?   את אוהבת לעשות ספורט?

I like playing sport.

   ani ohev(et) la'asot sport   אני אוהב(ת) לעשות ספורט.

I prefer to watch rather than play sport.

   ani ma'adif lehistakel   אני מעדיף להסתכל

   me'asher lesakhek   מאשר לשחק.

INTERESTS

Do you play ...?
ata mesakhek ...? (m)		אתה משחק ...?
at mesakheket ...? (f)		את משחקת ...?

Would you like to play ...?
ata rotse lesakhek ...? (m)		אתה רוצה לשחק ...?
at rotsa lesakhek ...? (f)		את רוצה לשחק ...?

baseball	baseball	בייסבול
basketball	kadur-sal	כדור-סל
boxing	he'avkut	האבקות
cricket	cricket	קריקט
diving	tslila	צלילה
football	kaduregel amerikani	כדורגל אמריקני
hockey	hockey	הוקי
gymnastics	hit'amlut	התעמלות
keeping fit	lishmor al kosher	לשמור על כושר .
martial arts	omanuyot lekhima	אמנויות לחימה
rugby	rugby	רגבי
soccer	kaduregel	כדורגל

THE GATES TO JERUSALEM

The walls of the Old City of Jerusalem were built
by Suleyman the Great between 1537 and 1542.
It had seven gates, while an eighth was added in
the 19th century. Each of the gates – Damascus
Gate, Herod's Gate, St Stephen's Gate, Golden
Gate, Dung Gate, Zion Gate, Jaffa Gate and New
Gate – has at least three names, one used by
Arabs, one used by Jews, as well as the anglicised
names given here.

INTERESTS

surfing	glisha	גלישה
swimming	skhiya	שחייה
tennis	tennis	טניס
skiing	la'asot ski	לעשות סקי

WRITING LETTERS כותבים מכתב

Once you get back home, you may want to drop a line to people you met. Here are a few suggestions to help you.

Dear ...	... היקר/ה,
I'm sorry it's taken me so long to write.	סליחה שלא כתבתי קודם.
It was great to meet you.	היה נפלא להכיר אותך.
Thank you so much for your hospitality.	המון תודות על הכנסת האורחים הנפלאה.

| I miss you (sg). | אני מתגעגע אליך. |
| I miss you (pl). | אני מתגעגע אליכם. |

I had a fantastic time in (Arad).	ביליתי נהדר (בערד).
My favourite place was ...	המקום שנמצא חן בעיני ביותר היה ...
I hope to visit ... again.	אני מקווה לבקר ב ... שוב.

Say hello to ... and ... for me.	ד"ש ל ... ול ... ממני.
I'd love to see you again.	אשמח לראותך שוב.
Write soon.	תכתוב/תכתבי בקרוב.
Yours ...	... שלך

INTERESTS

SHOPPING

עושים קניות

The most important thing to know is that on Shabbat, the Jewish Sabbath, all Israeli shops, offices and places of entertainment are closed down. You'll also do well to be prepared for any Jewish religious holidays (see page 169) that are celebrated during your visit. The Jewish holidays are effectively like long bouts of Shabbat, and if you're caught off-guard you can be rendered immobile for a couple of days at a time, maybe without food, maybe without money.

Not all your shopping needs to be done in markets. Some of Israel's best buys are luxury items from regular shops and galleries. It's worth remembering that that some shops give a special discount if you pay in foreign currency.

LOOKING FOR ...

מחפשים ...

Where can I buy ...?
eifo efshar liknot ...?   ?.... איפה אפשר לקנות
Where's the nearest ...?
eifo ha ... hakarov (hakrova)?   ?(איפה ה ... הקרוב (הקרובה

barber	sapar	ספר
bookshop	khanut sfarim	חנות ספרים
camera shop	khanut tsilum	חנות צילום
chemist (pharmacy)	bet mirkakhat	בית-מרקחת
clothing store	khanut bgadim	חנות בגדים
general store	kol bo	כל-בו
laundry	makhbesa	מכבסה
market	shuk	שוק
souvenir shop	khanut mazkarot	חנות מזכרות

SHOPPING

MAKING A PURCHASE

קנייה

I'd like to buy ...
ani rotse (rotsa) liknot ...

אני רוצה (רוצה) לקנות ...

Do you have others?
yesh akherim?

יש אחרים?

I don't like it.
ani lo ohev(et) et ze.

אני לא אוהב(ת) את זה.

Can I look at it?
ani yakhol (yekhola)
lehistakel mikarov?

אני יכול (יכולה)
להסתכל מקרוב?

I'm just looking.
ani rak mistakel(et).

אני רק מסתכל(ת).

How much is this?
kama ze ole?

כמה זה עולה?

Can you write down the price?
ata yakhol lirshom et
hamekhir al daf?

אתה יכול לרשום את
המחיר על דף?

Do you accept credit cards?
efshar leshalem bekartis ashra'i?

אפשר לשלם בכרטיס אשראי?

Please wrap it.
bevakasha la'atof

בבקשה לעטוף.

BARGAINING

התמקחות

The golden rules are: don't start bargaining with a shopkeeper
unless you're really interested in buying; have a good idea of the
item's value both locally and back home; and don't be intimi-
dated. Easier said than done. Don't use large notes or travellers
cheques, as getting change can be a problem.

I think it's too expensive.
ani khoshev(et) sheze
yoter miday yakar

אני חושב(ת) שזה
מידי יקר.

It's too much for us.
ze yoter miday yakar bishvilenu

זה יותר מידי יקר בשבילנו.

Can you lower the price?
efshar lekabel hanakha?

אפשר לקבל הנחה?

SHOPPING

SHOPPING HOURS

Standard Israeli shopping hours are Monday to Thursday from 8 am to 1 pm and 4 to 7 pm or later, and Friday from 8 am to 2 pm, with some places opening after sundown on Saturday.

SHOPPING

ESSENTIAL GROCERIES

		מצרכי יסוד
Where can I find?	eifo efshar limtso ...?	איפה אפשר למצוא ...?
I'd like ...	ani rotse (rotsa) ...	אני רוצה (רוצה) ...

batteries	solelot	סוללות
bread	lekhem	לחם
butter	khem'a	חמאה
cheese	gvina	גבינה
chocolate	shokolad	שוקולד
eggs	beitsim	ביצים
flour	kemakh	קמח
gas cyclinder	balon gas	בלון גז
ham	hem	הם
honey	dvash	דבש
margarine	margarina	מרגרינה
matches	gafrurim	גפרורים
milk	khalav	חלב
pepper	pilpel	פלפל
salt	melakh	מלח
shampoo	shampoo	שמפו
soap	sabon	סבון
sugar	sukar	סוכר
toilet paper	neyar twalet	נייר טואלט
toothpaste	mishkhat shina'im	משחת שיניים
washing powder	avkat kvisa	אבקת כביסה
yoghurt	yoghurt	יוגורט

FOOD

baklava – toasted, shredded wheat stuffed with pistachios
or hazelnuts and smothered in honey
kunafeh – made with cheese, wheat, sugar and honey

SHOPPING

SOUVENIRS

מזכרות

Israel is full of shops stocked with souvenirs. To find bargains and quality items you'll need the time to shop around and the patience to haggle.

Popular items available for purchase include antiquities, modern and traditional ceramics, copper and brassware, olive-wood carvings (crucifixes, camels, worry beads and carvings of biblical scenes and characters), glassware, canework and basketware, and handmade jewellery. Products made out of mud and minerals from the Dead Sea are popular.

baskets	salim	סלים
brassware	avodot nekhoshet	עבודות נחושת
cane ware; furniture	klei netsarim; rahitim	כלי נצרים; רהיטים
handicraft	avodot yad	עבודות יד
woodcarved figure	dmut megulefet	דמות מגולפת
souvenirs made of shell	mazkarot mitsdafim	מזכרות מצדפים

CLOTHING

ביגוד

jacket	jacket	ז'קט
jumper (sweater)	sveder	סוודר
pants	mikhnasa'im	מכנסיים
raincoat	me'il geshem	מעיל גשם
shirt	khultsa	חולצה
shoes	na'ala'im	נעליים
socks	garba'im	גרביים
swimsuit	beged yam	בגד-ים
T-shirt	khultsat ti	חולצת-טי
underwear	levanim	לבנים

SHOPPING

COLOURS   צבעים

black	shakhor	שחור
blue	kakhol	כחול
brown	khum	חום
green	yarok	ירוק
grey	afor	אפור
orange	katom	כתום
pink	varod	ורוד
purple	sagol	סגול
red	adom	אדום
white	lavan	לבן
yellow	tsahov	צהוב
dark	kehe	כהה
light	bahir	בהיר

Place the adjectives 'dark' and 'light' after the colour.

| dark blue | kakhol kehe |
| light brown | khum bahir |

TOILETRIES   צרכי רחצה

condoms	condomim	קונדומים
deodorant	deodorant	דאודורנט
moisturiser	krem lakhut	קרם לחות
razor	sakin gilu'akh	סכין גילוח
sanitary napkins	takhboshot higyeniyot	תחבושות היגייניות
shampoo	shampoo	שמפו
shaving cream	mishkhat gilu'akh	משחת גילוח
soap	sabon	סבון
sunblock	krem shizuf	קרם שיזוף
tampons	tamponim	טמפונים
toilet paper	neyar twalet	נייר טואלט

SHOPPING

FOR THE BABY   לתינוק

tinned baby food	mazon tinokot meshumar	מזון תינוקות משומר
baby powder	avkat tinokot	אבקת תינוקות
bib	sinor shel tinok	סינור של תינוק
disposable nappies	khitulim khad pe'ami'im	חיתולים חד-פעמיים
dummy (pacifier)	motsets	מוצץ
feeding bottle	bakbuk	בקבוק
nappy	khitulim	חיתולים
nappy rash cream	mishkha neged geruyei or	משחה נגד גרויי עור
powdered milk	avkat khalav	אבקת חלב

STATIONERY & PUBLICATIONS   צרכי כתיבה ועיתונות

The *Jerusalem Post* is the country's only English-language daily (except for Saturday) – on Fridays it includes an extensive 'what's on' supplement. Western newspapers are readily available and they're usually only a day old.

Do you sell ...?	atem mokhrim ...?	?... אתם מוכרים
dictionaries	milonim	מילונים
envelopes	ma'atafot	מעטפות
magazines	shvu'onim	שבועונים
newspapers	itonim	עיתונים
postcards	gluyot	גלויות
English-language newspapers	itonim be'anglit	עיתונים באנגלית
paper	neyar	נייר
pens (ballpoint)	etim (kaduri'im)	עטים (כדוריים)
stamps	bulim	בולים
... maps	mapot ...	... מפות
city	ir	עיר
regional	azori	אזורי
road	derekh	דרך

SHOPPING

Is there an English-language bookshop here?
yesh kan khanut sfarim be'anglit? יש כאן חנות ספרים באנגלית?

Is there an English-language section?
yesh mador sifrei anglit? יש מדור סיפרי אנגלית?

Is there a local entertainment guide?
yesh madrikh biluyim? יש מדריך בילויים?

MUSIC מוסיקה

I'm looking for a ... CD.
ani mekhapes(et) CD shel ... ... אני מחפש(ת) סי-די של

Do you have any ...?
yesh lakhem ...? ...? יש לכם

What is his (her) best recording?
mahu habitsu'a hatov מהו הביצוע הטוב
beyoter shelo (shela)? ביותר שלו (שלה)?

I heard a band/singer called ...
shama'ati lahaka/zamar beshem ... ... שמעתי להקה/זמר בשם

Can I listen to this CD here?
ani yakhol (yekhola) lehakshiv אני יכול (יכולה) להקשיב
la-CD haze kan? לסי-די הזה כאן?

I need a blank tape.
ani tsarikh (tsrikha) kaletet reika אני צריך (צריכה) קלטת ריקה.

PHOTOGRAPHY צילום

Whatever you run out of or whatever needs replacing on your
camera, you'll be able to find it in Israel, but there's a good chance
that it would've been way cheaper back home.

What will it cost to process this film?
kama ya'ale pitu'akh hafilm haze? כמה יעלה פיתוח הפילם הזה?

When will it be ready?
matay ze iheye mukhan? מתי זה יהיה מוכן?

I'd like a film for this camera.
ani rotse (rotsa) film bishvil אני רוצה (רוצה) פילם
hamatslema hazot בשביל המצלמה הזאת.

SHOPPING

battery	solela	סוללה
B&W film	film shakhor-lavan	פילם שחור-לבן
camera	matslema	מצלמה
colour film	film tsiv'oni	פילם צבעוני
film	film	פילם
flash (bulb)	(nurit) flesh	נורית (פלש)
lens	adasha	עדשה
light metre	mad or	מד-אור
slides	shikufiyot	שיקופיות
videotape	videotape	וידאו-טייפ

SMOKING

עישון

A packet of cigarettes, please.

kufsat sigaryot, bevakasha

קופסת סיגריות, בבקשה.

Are these cigarettes strong or mild?

hasigaryot ha'ele khazakot
o khalashot?

הסיגריות האלה חזקות
או חלשות?

Do you have a light?

yesh lekha (lakh) esh?

יש לך (לך) אש?

Please don't smoke.

bevakasha al te'ashen

בבקשה אל תעשן.

Do you mind if I smoke?

efshar le'ashen?

אפשר לעשן?

JERUSALEM

The Old City of Jerusalem is divided into four vaguely defined
quarters. The Christian and Armenian quarters have developed
in homage to the Church of the Holy Sepulchre, where it has
traditionally been thought that Jesus was crucified. The Muslim
Quarter gravitates toward the Haram ash-Sharif (Temple Mount,
site of the Dome of the Rock), while the Jewish Quarter is ori-
ented toward the Western Wall.

SHOPPING

I'm trying to give up.

| | ani menase (menasa) | אני מנסה (מנסה) |
| | lehafsik le'ashen | להפסיק לעשן. |

cigarettes	sigaryot	סיגריות
cigarette papers	neyar sigaryot	נייר סיגריות
filtered	sigaryot filter	סיגריות פילטר
lighter	matsit	מצית
matches	gafrurim	גפרורים
menthol	menthol	מנתול
pipe	mikteret	מקטרת
tobacco	tabak	טבק

SIZES & COMPARISONS   דלים והשוואות

big	gadol (gdola)	גדול (גדולה)
small	katan (ktana)	קטן (קטנה)
heavy	kaved (kveda)	כבד (כבדה)
light	kal(a)	קל(ה)
more	od	עוד
little (amount)	me'at	מעט
too much/many	yoter/harbe miday	יותר/הרבה מידי
many	harbe	הרבה
enough	maspik dai	מספיק, די
also	gam	גם
a little bit	ktsat	קצת

FOOD

According to Judaism, every meal is a religious rite and so has to be kosher, which roughly translated means 'ritually acceptable'. All fruits and vegetables are permitted, but there are rules about which animals may be consumed, how they must be slaughtered and which parts may be eaten. There is also a rule forbidding the mixing of meat and dairy products.

That said, there is a wide variety of cuisines available in Israel, from kosher, vegetarian and Oriental Jewish to Eastern European Jewish and Palestinian. Israel has a delicious selection of breads, including pita, hallah (baked for Shabbat), matza (unleavened bread), bagels and sweet breads.

Although tea and coffee are the most popular beverages in Israel, beer, wine and spirits are available in most supermarkets and grocery shops.

breakfast	arukhat boker	ארוחת בוקר
lunch	arukhat tsohora'im	ארוחת צהריים
dinner	arukhat erev	ארוחת ערב

VEGETARIAN & SPECIAL MEALS

מאכלים צמחוניים ומיוחדים

Israel is a dream for vegetarians, with numerous dairy-only restaurants.

I'm a vegetarian.
  ani tsimkhoni(t)   אני צמחוני(ת).
I don't eat meat.
  ani lo okhel(et) basar   אני לא אוכל(ת) בשר.
I don't eat chicken, fish or ham.
  ani lo okhel(et) of, dag o ham   אני לא אוכל(ת) עוף, דג או הם.
I can't eat dairy products.
  ani lo okhel(et) mutsarei khalav   אני לא אוכל(ת) מוצרי חלב.

Do you have any vegetarian dishes?
    yesh lakhem ma'akhalim
    tsimkhoni'im?

יש לכם מאכלים
צמחוניים?

Does this dish have meat?
    yesh basar bama'akhal haze?

יש בשר במאכל הזה?

Can I get this without meat?
    efshar lekabel et hamana
    hazot bli basar?

אפשר לקבל את המנה
הזאת בלי בשר?

Does it contain eggs?
    yesh baze beitsim?

יש בזה ביצים?

I'm allergic to (peanuts).
    ani alergi(t) le ... (botnim)

אני אלרגי(ת) ל ... (בוטנים)

Is there a kosher restaurant here?
    yesh mis'ada kshera basviva?

יש מסעדה כשרה בסביבה?

Is this kosher?	ha'im ze kasher?	האם זה כשר?
Is this organic?	ha'im ze organi?	האם זה אורגני?

BREAKFAST & DINNER   ארוחת בוקר וארוחת ערב

Some Israelis don't mix milk and meat at a single meal because of kosher laws. Since religious law requires that there be an interval of about six hours between meals, the pace of meals for many Israelis means a milk meal for breakfast (7 to 9 am), followed by a main and heavy meat meal for lunch (supper), followed by a breakfast-like milk dinner.

Breakfast and dinner include lots of fresh milk dishes such as leben (a light yogurt), shamenet khamutsa (sour cream), gvinat katshkeval (goats' cheese) and kotaj (cottage cheese), along with fresh farm vegetables like cucumbers and green peppers. For cheese to be kosher, it can't be made with the rennet typically used to make blue cheese and swiss cheese. Israeli vegetables and milk products are so flavoursome that visitors can't eat the vegetables in their home countries without apologising to their tastebuds.

There are also hard boiled eggs, blintzes, picked herring, tuna fish, scrambled and poached eggs, and of course bagels. The bagel is given profound respect in Israel. A poster for tourism to Israel with an enormous bagel on it asked, 'Is this the only thing left of 4000 years of Jewish culture?' Israel itself is the emphatic reply to this question, although bagels do reign supreme in Jewish culinary heritage.

LUNCH   ארוחת צהריים

Chicken is king in Israel – potatoes are the staple for European Israelis, as rice is for Middle Eastern Israelis. Israelis eat lots of chicken schnitzel dishes, kreplakh (meat filled dumpling), kebabs, pot roast (basar tsaluy), sausages (naknik), leg of lamb (keves) and shish-kebab (shishlik). As for seafood, kosher laws dictate that Jews only eat sea life with both scales and fins. That means no shellfish, sharks, catfish or eels, although they can be found on the menus of many Israeli restaurants. But there's plenty of carp (karpiyon), herring (dag maluakh), and 'St Peter's Fish' (amnun) from the Sea of Galilee. If you're blessed, you might find a shekel (coin) in its mouth.

Many Israelis also love to eat Middle Eastern-style salads with their meat dishes. These include humous (puréed chick peas), tahina (ground sesame paste), baba gnoush (puréed eggplant) and tabouli (cracked wheat, parsley, mint, tomatoes, cucumbers). Such salads are served in pita bread with shawarma (doner kebabs), chicken kebabs, and falafel (fried chick pea balls) at fast-food sandwich shops for lunch, dinner and snacks.

Religious Jews are forbidden from cooking on the Sabbath. For Shabbat lunch, it's become traditional for Israelis to eat a slow-cooked stew, called khamin in Hebrew, and 'cholent' in Yiddish, that begins cooking before the Sabbath begins. Khamin is often made of beef and beans. Timing seems to be a real art with this dish, since dried-out khamin can be frequently encountered. Kugel, a baked potato pudding, is also popular, as are fried potato pancakes (latkes).

Although pork is not kosher, and pigs aren't allowed to set foot on Israeli soil, ingenious farmers raise pigs in pens with raised wooden boards covering the ground, so ham and pork products are widely available in Israel. Pork products are especially popular with recent Russian immigrants, who tend to be non-practicing. Again, Chinese restaurants are the great repository of non-kosher 'forbidden fruits' such as pork and shellfish.

KOSHER FOOD

Kashrut (kosher law) is a system of food classification based on biblical laws. Land animals that are within the kosher classification are those that both chew their cud and have cloven hooves. Kosher animals are killed in a way that drains all the blood from their flesh. Kosher seafood must have both scales and fins.

According to kosher rules, meat ('fleishic' or basar) can't be eaten or cooked with milk ('milchic' or halavi). Food that's considered neither milk nor meat, such as eggs and fish, are called parve, 'neutral', and can be consumed with either milk or meat. Wine is deemed kosher if only Jews are involved in its production. Kosher wine is so sacred that if a non-Jew looks upon an open bottle, it's no longer considered to be kosher. To allow non-Jews to consume wine at religious events, the wine is first boiled.

Although Israel is known as the 'land of milk and honey' (see the Bible, Numbers 14:8), bees, and therefore honey, weren't always considered kosher. Many biblical scholars believe the term 'honey' actually refers to date jam. Over the years, honey was deemed to be kosher, which was a good thing as the phrase 'the land of milk and date jam' doesn't have the same ring.

FOOD

EATING OUT   אוכלים בחוץ

Table for (five), please.

shulkhan le(khamisha), bevakasha   שולחן ל(חמישה), בבקשה.

May we see the menu?

efshar lir'ot et hatafrit?   אפשר לראות את התפריט?

Please bring some ...

bevakasha tavi kama ...   בבקשה תביא כמה ...

Do I get it myself or do they bring it to us?

ha'im ze sherut atsmi   האם זה שרות עצמי
o yesh meltsar?   או יש מלצר?

Please bring a/the/an ...	tavi bevakasha ...	... תביא בבקשה
ashtray	ma'afera	מאפרה
bill	et hakheshbon	את החשבון
fork	mazleg	מזלג
glass of water	kos mayim	כוס מים
with/without ice	im/bli kerakh	עם/בלי קרח
knife	sakin	סכין
plate	tsalakhat	צלחת

No ice in my beer, please.

bli kerakh babira sheli, bevakasha   בלי קרח בבירה שלי, בבקשה.

Is service included in the bill?

ha'im hasherut kalul bamekhir?   האם השירות כלול במחיר?

Useful Words

cup	sefel	ספל
fresh	tari	טרי
spicy	kharif	חריף
stale/spoiled	tafel/mekulkal	תפל/מקולקל
sweet	matok	מתוק
toothpick	keisam shinayin	קיסם שיניים

FOOD

TYPICAL DISHES

מאכלים אופייניים

International cuisine is very well represented in Israel, particularly in the big cities. Although there's no 'national dish' or typical Israeli cuisine per se, there are many popular dishes and foods, many which are Mediterranean, that taste especially good in Israel.

Breakfast

Breakfast in Israel is a meal based on dairy products. A common breakfast dish is eggs, prepared your favourite way.

eggs with cheese	beitsa im gvina	ביצה עם גבינה
eggs with mushrooms	beitsa im pitriyot	ביצה עם פיטריות
garden salad	salat yerakot tari	סלט ירקות טרי
omelette	khavita	חביתה
sunny side up	beitsa im a'in	ביצה עם עין
scrambled egg	beitsa mekushkeshet	ביצה מקושקשת
soft boiled egg	beitsa raka	ביצה רכה
hard boiled egg	beitsa kasha	ביצה קשה

Bread is an important component of breakfast, and there's a variety to choose from.

bread roll	lakhmaniya	לחמניה
khala	khala	חלה
pita	pita	פיתה
pumpernikel	pumpernikel	פומפרניקל
rye bread	lekhem shakhor	לחם שחור
white bread	lekhem lavan	לחם לבן
whole wheat	lekhem mekhita	לחם מחיטה
	mele'a	מלאה

FOOD

Khala is the special bread eaten on the Sabbath, and is easily recognised by its braided appearance. You can find it all week round, but it's freshest and tastiest on Friday mornings. There are several varieties of khala:

regular	khala regila	חלה רגילה
round	khala agula	חלה עגולה
sweet	khala metuka	חלה מתוקה
with poppy seed	khala im pereg	חלה עם פרג

Yoghurt is another popular breakfast food. There are many different products, but the basics include:

yoghurt	yogurt	יוגורט
bio-yoghurt	yogurt-bio	יוגורט ביו

Cheeses

Israel is a champion in making cream cheeses. Not even in Paris, where cheese is a matter of national pride, will you find such a large, varied, and above all delicious array of cream cheese. The various kinds are grouped under the generic name gvina levana (white cheese). They differ in taste and in percentage of fat, from half a percent to around 12 per cent. All are simply delicious.

cottage cheese	cotaj	קוטג'
goat's milk cheese (hard)	gvinat kna'an	גבינת כנען
goat's milk cheese (soft)	gvina tsfatit	גבינה צפתית
hard cheese	gvina tsehuba	גבינה צהובה
salty cheese	gvina melukha	גבינה מלוחה
sour cheese	labane	לבנה
white cream cheese	gvina levana	גבינה לבנה

FOOD

Drinks

Tea and coffee are Israel's most popular beverages. A wide selection of beer, wine and spirits is available in most supermarkets and grocery stores.

... coffee	kafe ...	... קפה
black	shakhor	שחור
white	hafukh	הפוך
Turkish coffee	kafe turki	קפה תורכי
with cardamom	im hel	עם הל
without cardamom	bli hel	בלי הל
espresso	kafe espreso	קפה אספרסו
capuccino	kaputshino	קפוצ'ינו
tea ...	te ...	תה ...
with milk	bekhalav	תה בחלב
with mint	im na'ana	תה עם נענע
herbal tea	te tsmakhim	תה צמחים
lemon tea	te limon	תה לימון
sugar	sukar	סוכר
artificial sweetener	sukrazit	סוכרזית
with/without sugar	im/bli sukar	עם/בלי סוכר
fruit juice	mits	מיץ
freshly squeezed juice	mits tiv'i	מיץ טבעי
grapefruit juice	mits eshkoliyot	מיץ אשכוליות
orange juice	mits tapuzim	מיץ תפוזים
hot chocolate	kaka'o	קקאו
(boiled) water	mayim (retukhim)	מים (רתוחים)

FOOD

| mineral water | mayim mineralim | מים מינרליים |
| lemonade | limonada | לימונדה |

Falafel, Shawarma & Sabikh

Between meals, many places offer falafel, shawarma or sabikh, all of them served inside a pita bread.

felafel	falafel	פלפל
shawarma	shawarma	שווארמה
pita with eggplant	sabikh	סביח

They're all served with a sliced salad rich in cilantro, and tehina sauce. The deep-fried falafel balls are made of chickpea purée and flavoured with tasty exotic spices. Important additions are the varied pickles arranged in bowls around the counter.

cabbage (pickled)	kruv kavush	כרוב כבוש
capsicum (grilled)	pilpel bagril	פלפל בגריל
cauliflower	kruvit khamutsa	כרובית חמוצה
chilli (hot, pickled whole)	pilpel kharif	פלפל חריף
eggplant slices (fried)	prusot khatsilim	פרוסות חצילים
	metuganot	מטוגנות
eggplant (pickled)	khatsilim kvushim	חצילים כבושים
olives	zeitim	זיתים
pickles	khamutsim	חמוצים
turnips	lefet	לפת

Usually there's a fixed price for a pita, and as long as you stay next to the counter, you can stuff your pita to your heart's content. A number of bowls filled with colourful sauces are also usually provided. Tehina has a pale ivory colour. The deep red and fruity green spicy sauces, kharif, are made from red and green hot chilli. Often they're pretty diluted, alas, so don't worry too much. Amba, a rich, creamy mustardy yellow sauce, has a refreshing sour taste. Although not commonly used in falafel, it's an essential ingredient of sabikh.

Of Iraqi origin, sabikh originated in Ramat Gan almost 30 years ago. Sabikh pita is spread lavishly with hummous, with slices of fried eggplant, and a beitsa khuma, a 'brown egg' (an egg that's been cooked for a long time). This is topped with a layer of salad, minced onion and tehina, kharif and amba. Delicious!

A shawarma is a pita bread stuffed with lamb, thinly sliced from a vertically rotating and roasting huge chunk of meat. Salad and tehina are added, and sometimes French fries, tchipsim.

Salads

garden salad	salat yerakot	סלט ירקות
Turkish salad (tomatoes, peppers, onions and parsley in spicy tomato sauce)	salat turki	סלט טורקי
Madbukha (a Moroccan salad based on tomatoes, tomato sauce and peppers)	madbukha	מדבוחה
eggplant salad ... with mayonnaise with tehini sauce	salat khatsilim ... bemayonez bitkhina	סלט חצילים ... במיונז בטחינה
fried eggplants	khatsilim metuganim	חצילים מטוגנים
potato salad	salat tapukhei adama	סלט תפוחי אדמה

FOOD

| tuna salad | salat tuna | סלט טונה |
| broad beans | fool | פול |

(served with tehini sauce and a hard boiled egg)

artichoke hearts	levavot artichoke	לבבות ארטישוק
chickpea puree	khumus	חומוס
tehini	tkhina	טחינה
pickled vegetables	khamutsim	חמוצים
skewers	shipudim	שיפודים

Meats

FOOD

Israeli shipudim, also known as 'shishkebab', can be made with different meats.

chicken	of	עוף
heart	levavot	לבבות
lamb	keves	כבש
chicken liver	kaved of	כבד עוף
goose liver	kaved avaz	כבד אווז
turkey	hodu	הודו

Another kind of skewer is me'orav yerushalmi, 'Jeruselmite Mélange' (מעורב ירושלמי). Although as popular as 'regular' skewers, and preparation in similar ways, me'orav and shipdim shouldn't be confused. While shipudim is made of chunks of meat grilled on burning coal, me'orav contains offal which is grilled on an electric plate.

| pork steak | steik lavan | סטייק לבן |

(for kashrut reasons,
pork is also known as
para nemukha 'low cow')

meat balls	ktsitsot	קציצות
schnitzel	schnitsel	שניצל
tongue	lashon	לשון
moussaka (layers of fried eggplant and fried minced meat, served in tomato sauce)	musaka	מוסקה

SELF-CATERING

הכנה עצמית

bread	lekhem	לחם
bread roll	lakhmaniya	לחמנייה
butter	khem'a	חמאה
cheese (hard)	gvina tsehuba	גבינה צהובה
chocolate	shokolad	שוקולד
cream cheese	gvina levana	גבינה לבנה
dried fruits	peirot yeveshim	פירות יבשים
eggs	beitsim	ביצים
flour	kemakh	קמח
ham	hem	הם
honey	dvash	דבש
margarine	margarina	מרגרינה
milk	khalav	חלב
olive oil	shemen zayit	שמן זית
olives	zeitim	זיתים
pepper	pilpel	פלפל
pickles	khamutsim	חמוצים
salt	melakh	מלח
spices	tavlinim	תבלינים
sugar	sukar	סוכר
sunflower seeds	gar'inim	גרעינים
yoghurt	yogurt	יוגורט

FOOD

AT THE MARKET

בשוק

FOOD

Meat

beef	bakar	בקר
chicken	of	עוף
goat	ez	עז
gyros	shawarma	שווארמה
hot dog	naknikiya	נקניקיה
lamb	keves	כבש
liver	kaved	כבד
(fatty/lean) meat	basar (shamen/raze)	בשר (שמן/רזה)
pork	khazir	חזיר
ribs	tsla'ot	צלעות
sausage	naknik	נקניק
skewers	shipudim	שיפודים
steak	steik	סטייק
turkey	hodu	הודו
baked	batanur	בתנור
grilled	al ha'esh	על האש

Seafood

clams	tsdafot	צדפות
lobster	sartan	סרטן
mussels	tsdafot	צדפות
oysters	oysters	אויסטרס
shrimps	khasilonim	חסילונים

Vegetables

artichoke	kharshaf	חרשף
bean sprouts	nevatim	נבטים
beetroot	selek	סלק
cabbage	kruv	כרוב
carrot	gezer	גזר
cauliflower	kruvit	כרובית

chickpeas	humus	חומוס
cucumber	melafefon	מלפפון
eggplant (aubergine)	khatsil	חציל
garlic	shum	שום
green beans	she'u'it yeruka	שעועית ירוקה
lettuce	khasa	חסה
lima beans	she'u'it levana	שעועית לבנה
mushrooms	pitriyot	פיטריות
onion	batsal	בצל
pepper	pilpel	פלפל
potato	tapu'akh adama	תפוח אדמה
spinach	tered	תרד
spring onion	batsal yarok	בצל ירוק
tomato	agvaniya	עגבניה
vegetables	yerakot	ירקות
zucchini	kishu	קישוא

FOOD

Fruit

apple	tapu'akh	תפוח
apricot	mishmish	משמש
avocado	avocado	אבוקדו
banana	banana	בננה
clementine	klementina	קלמנטינה

MO-RE RED WINE?

At first, you'll probably be inclined to pronounce more (teacher) as in 'more red wine' and nose (topic) as in 'my nose is bleeding'. But these words each have two syllables and should be said as mo-re and no-se respectively. Also, when two vowels follow each other but are part of different syllables, they're separated by the symbol ' ". Thus, me'il (overcoat) is pronounced me-il and not 'meil', and me'al (above) should be read as me-al and not as 'meal'.

FOOD

dates	tmarim	תמרים
figs	te'enim	תאנים
grapefruit	eshkolit	אשכולית
grapes	anavim	ענבים
loquat	shesek	שסק
melon	melon	מלון
orange	tapuz	תפוז
peach	afarsek	אפרסק
pear	agas	אגס
pineapple	ananas	אננס
plum	shezif	שזיף
pomelo	pomela	פומלה
raisins	tsimukim	צימוקים
strawberries	tut sade	תות שדה
watermelon	avati'akh	אבטיח

Spices & Condiments

garlic	shum	שום
ginger	ginger	ג'ינג'ר
red/black pepper	pilpel adom/shakhor	פלפל אדום/שחור
salt	melakh	מלח
sesame seed	sumsum	שומשום
tehine	tehina	טחינה

IN THE COUNTRY מחוץ לעיר

CAMPING
קמפינג

While there are numerous camping areas around the country, usually equipped with all necessary amenities, they aren't always the expected cheap alternative. Still, there are plenty of opportunities to pitch your tent for free. Camping seems to be tolerated on most public beaches, though notable exceptions include the shore of the Dead Sea, the Mediterranean coast north of Nahariya and in the Gaza Strip.

Do you have any sites available?
    yesh mekomot pnuyim ba'atar?   יש מקומות פנויים באתר?

How much is it per person/per tent?
    ma hamekhir le'adam/le'ohel?   מה המחיר לאדם/לאוהל?

Where can I hire a tent?
    eifo efshar liskor ohel?   איפה אפשר לשכור אוהל?

Can we camp here?
    efshar lehakim po ohel?   אפשר להקים פה אוהל?

Are there shower facilities?
    yesh kan miklakhot?   יש כאן מקלחות?

backpack	tarmil gav	תרמיל גב
campfire	medura	מדורה
camping	camping	קמפינג
campsite	atar camping	אתר קמפינג
can opener	potkhan kufsa'ot	פותחן קופסאות
compass	matspen	מצפן
firewood	zradim	זרדים
gas cartridge	mekhal gas	מיכל גז
hammer	patish	פטיש
hammock	arsal	ערסל
mat	makhtselet	מחצלת
mattress	mizron	מזרון

rope	khevel	חבל
sleeping bag	sak shena	שק שינה
tent	ohel	אוהל
tent pegs	yetedot	יתדות
torch (flashlight)	panas	פנס
water bottle	meimiya	מימיה

HIKING

מסעות

With its changing landscapes, Israel offers a wealth of superb hiking opportunities, both leisurely and more strenuous. Both Makhtesh Ramon, the world's largest crater, and Ein Avdat, which involves some canyon climbing to reach an ice-cold spring, are popular.

Are there any tourist attractions near here?
yesh atarei tayarut basviva?　　　　　　יש אתרי תיירות בסביבה?

Where's the nearest village?
eifo hayishuv hakarov beyoter?　　　　איפה הישוב הקרוב ביותר?

Is it safe to climb this mountain?
ha'im batu'akh letapes　　　　　　　　האם בטוח לטפס
al ha'har haze?　　　　　　　　　　　　על ההר הזה?

Is there a hut up there?
yesh bikta lema'ala?　　　　　　　　　יש ביקתה למעלה?

Do we need a guide?
yesh tsorekh bemadrikh?　　　　　　　　יש צורך במדריך?

Where can I find out about hiking trails in the region?
eifo efshar levarer al　　　　　　　　איפה אפשר לברר על
maslulei halikha basviva?　　　　　　מסלולי הליכה בסביבה?

Are there guided treks?
yesh maslulim mudrakhim?　　　　　　　יש מסלולים מודרכים?

I'd like to talk to someone who knows this area.
ha'iti rotse (rotsa) ledaber im　　　　הייתי רוצה (רוצה) לדבר עם
mishehu shemitmatse ba'ezor　　　　　מישהו שמתמצא באזור.

How long is the trail?
ma orekh hamaslul?　　　　　　　　　　מה אורך המסלול?

Is the track well marked?
    ha'im hamaslul mesuman heitev?   ?האם המסלול מסומן היטב
How high is the climb?
    le'eize gova metapsim?   ?לאיזה גובה מטפסים
Which is the shortest route?
    mahi haderekh haktsara beyoter?   ?מהי הדרך הקצרה ביותר
Which is the easiest route?
    mahi haderekh hakala beyoter?   ?מהי הדרך הקלה ביותר
Is the path open?
    ha'im hashvil avir?   ?האם השביל עביר
When does it get dark?
    matay makhshikh?   ?מתי מחשיך
Is it very scenic?
    hanof me'od yafe?   ?הנוף מאוד יפה
Where can I hire mountain gear?
    eifo nitan liskor tsiyud   איפה ניתן לשכור ציוד
    tipus harim?   ?טיפוס הרים
Where can we buy supplies?
    eifo efshar liknot tseida?   ?איפה אפשר לקנות צידה

On the Path

Where have you come from?
    me'ain atem magi'im? (m)   ?מאין אתם מגיעים
    me'ain aten magi'ot? (f)   ?מאין אתן מגיעות
How long did it take you?
    kama zman lakakh lekha (lakh)?   ?כמה זמן לקח לך (לך)
Does this path go to ...?
    ha'im hashvil movil le ...?   ?... האם השביל מוביל ל
I'm lost.
    ta'iti baderekh   .תעיתי בדרך
Where can we spend the night?
    eifo efshar lishon halayla?   ?איפה אפשר לישון הלילה
Can I leave some things here for a while?
    efshar lehash'ir kan mispar   אפשר להשאיר כאן מספר
    khafatsim lizman ma?   ?חפצים לזמן מה

IN THE COUNTRY

altitude	gova	גובה
backpack	tarmil gav	תרמיל גב
binoculars	mishkefet	משקפת
candles	nerot	נרות
to climb	letapes	לטפס
compass	matspen	מצפן
downhill	yerida	ירידה
first-aid kit	tarmil ezra rishona	תרמיל עזרה ראשונה
gloves	kfafot	כפפות
guide	madrikh	מדריך
guided trek	maslul munkhe	מסלול מונחה
hiking	tiyul ragli	טיול רגלי
hiking boots	na'alei halikha	נעלי הליכה

hunting	tsa'yid	צייד
ledge	tsuk	צוק
lookout	mitspe	מצפה
map	mapa	מפה
mountain climbing	tipus harim	טיפוס הרים
pick	makosh	מכוש
provisions	tseida	צידה
rock climbing	tipus tsukim	טיפוס צוקים
rope	khevel	חבל
signpost	tamrur	תמרור
steep	talul	תלול
trek	maslul	מסלול
uphill	ma'ale hahar	מעלה ההר
to walk	lalekhet baregel	ללכת ברגל

AT THE BEACH
על חוף הים

With the Red and Mediterranean seas and the Sea of Galilee, there are plenty of opportunities to enjoy the pleasures of swimming, windsurfing and sailing.

Can we swim here?
mutar liskhot po?
מותר לשחות פה?
Is it safe to swim here?
batu'akh liskhot po?
בטוח לשחות פה?
What time is high/low tide?
be'eizo sha'a hage'ut/hashefel?
באיזו שעה הגאות/השפל?

coast	khof	חוף
fishing	da'ig	דיג
reef	shunit	שונית
rock	sela	סלע
sand	khol	חול
sea	yam	ים
snorkelling	tslila im snorkel	צלילה עם שנורקל
sunblock	mishkhat shizuf	משחת שיזוף
sunglasses	mishkefei shemesh	משקפי שמש
surf	glisha	גלישה
surfing	galshanut	גלשנות
surfboard	keresh glisha	קרש גלישה
swimming	skhiya	שחייה
towel	magevet	מגבת
waterskiing	ski mayim	סקי-מים
waves	galim	גלים
windsurfing	glishat ru'akh	גלישת רוח

Diving
Although Eilat is the watersports capital of Israel and a major diving centre, the diving sites along the Sinai coast are considered by many to be the best. Other diving options include Caesarea, where you can explore the underwater ruins of Herod's city.

scuba diving   scuba   סקובה

IN THE COUNTRY

Are there good diving sites here?

    yesh kan atarei tslila tovim?   ?יש כאן אתרי צלילה טובים

Can we hire a diving boat/guide?

    efshar liskor sirat/   /אפשר לשכור סירת

    madrikh tslila?   ?מדריך צלילה

We'd like to hire diving equipment.

    anakhnu rotsim liskor   אנחנו רוצים לשכור

    tsiyud tslila   .ציוד צלילה

I'm interested in exploring wrecks.

    ani me'unyan litslol   אני מעוניין לצלול

    le'oniyot trufot   .לאוניות טרופות

WEATHER   מזג האוויר

The regional climatic variations are part of what makes Israel so fascinating. For example, in Jerusalem during the winter months it's generally cold and wet and you may even experience snow, but hop on a bus down to the Dead Sea (little more than an hour's ride away) and you can change into your shorts and T-shirt and bask in 23⁰ C sunshine.

In general, Israel's climate is temperate, with two seasons – winter (cold and rainy) and summer (hot and dry). Rainfall is concentrated between November and March. The hottest areas are those below sea level – the Jordan Valley, the shores of the Sea of Galilee and the Dead Sea, and the Arava Valley.

IN THE COUNTRY

SEASONS

summer	ka'its	קיץ
autumn	stav	סתיו
winter	khoref	חורף
spring	aviv	אביב
dry season	ona yevesha	עונה יבשה
rainy season	onat hagshamim	עונת הגשמים

What's the weather like?	eikh mezeg ha'avir?	?איך מזג האוויר
Today it's ...	hayom ...	... היום
cloudy	me'unan	מעונן
cold	kar	קר
hot	kham	חם
warm	khamim	חמים
windy	yesh ru'akh	יש רוח
It's raining heavily.	yored mabul	.יורד מבול
It's raining lightly.	yored geshem kal	.יורד גשם קל
It's flooding.	yesh hatsafot	.יש הצפות
dry season	ona yevesha	עונה יבשה
monsoon season	onat hamonsunim	עונת המונסונים
rainy season	onat hagshamim	עונת הגשמים
storm	se'ara	סערה
sun	shemesh	שמש
typhoon	typhoon	טייפון

IN THE COUNTRY

GEOGRAPHICAL TERMS   מונחים גיאוגרפיים

beach	khof	חוף
bridge	gesher	גשר
cave	me'ara	מערה
cliff	tsuk	צוק
earthquake	re'idat adama	רעידת אדמה
farm	khava	חווה
footpath	shvil leholkhei regel	שביל להולכי רגל
forest	ya'ar	יער
harbour	namal	נמל
hill	giv'a	גבעה
hot springs	ma'ayanot khamim	מעיינות חמים
island	yi	אי
lake	agam	אגם

mountain	har	הר
mountain path	shvil harim	שביל הרים
narrow pass	shvil tsar	שביל צר
pass	ma'avar	מעבר
peak	pisga	פיסגה
river	nahar	נהר
sea	yam	ים
valley	emek	עמק
waterfall	mapal mayim	מפל מים

FAUNA

חיות בר

bird	tsipor	ציפור
butterfly	parpar	פרפר
cat	khatul	חתול
chicken	tarnegolet	תרנגולת
cockroach	tikan	תיקן
cow	para	פרה
dog	kelev	כלב
donkey	khamor	חמור
duck	barvaz	ברווז
fish	dag	דג
fly	zvuv	זבוב
hen	tarnegolet	תרנגולת
horse	sus	סוס
mosquito	yatush	יתוש
pig	khazir	חזיר
sheep	kivsa	כבשה
snake	nakhash	נחש
spider	akavish	עכביש
tiger	namer	נמר
mountain goat	ya'el	יעל

IN THE COUNTRY

FLORA & AGRICULTURE

		צמחיה וחקלאות
agriculture	khakla'ut	חקלאות
corn	tiras	תירס
crops	yevulim	יבולים
flower	perakh	פרח
to harvest	liktsor	לקצור
irrigation	hashkaya	השקייה
leaf	ale	עלה
planting	lata'at	לטעת
sowing	lizro'a	לזרוע
tobacco	tabak	טבק
tree	ets	עץ

HEALTH

בריאות

Israel presents no major health hazards for the visitor. If you do need to see a doctor or visit a hospital, bear in mind that doctors and hospitals in Israel generally expect immediate cash payment for health services.

AT THE DOCTOR

אצל הרופא

Where's the ...?	eifo ha ...?	?... איפה ה
chemist	roke'akh	רוקח
dentist	rofe shinayim	רופא שיניים
doctor	rofe (rof a)	רופא (רופאה)
hospital	bet kholim	בית חולים

I'm sick.
   ani khole (khola) — אני חולה (חולה).

My friend is sick.
   hakhaver sheli khole — החבר שלי חולה.

I need a doctor who speaks English.
   ani tsarikh rofe — אני צריך רופא
   dover anglit — דובר אנגלית.

It hurts there.
   ko'ev li sham — כואב לי שם.

I feel nauseous.
   yesh li bkhila — יש לי בחילה.

I've been vomiting.
   heketi — הקאתי.

I feel better/worse.
   ani margish(a) yoter tov/ra — אני מרגיש(ה) יותר טוב/רע.

THE DOCTOR MAY SAY

ma habe'aya? What's the matter?	מה הבעייה?
ata margish ke'ev? Do you (m) feel any pain?	אתה מרגיש כאב?
at margisha ke'ev? Do you (f) feel any pain?	את מרגישה כאב?
eifo ko'ev lekha (lakh)? Where does it hurt?	איפה כואב לך?
yesh lakh veset? Are you menstruating?	יש לך וסת?
yesh lekha (lakh) khom? Do you have a temperature?	יש לך חום?
kama zman ze kvar nimshakh? How long have you been like this?	כמה זמן זה כבר נמשך?
ze kvar kara lekha (lakh) be'avar? Have you had this before?	זה כבר קרה לך בעבר?
ata mekabel trufot? Are you (m) on medication?	אתה מקבל תרופות?
at mekabelet trufot? Are you (f) on medication?	את מקבלת תרופות?
ata me'ashen? Do you (m) smoke?	אתה מעשן?
at me'ashenet? Do you (f) smoke?	את מעשנת?
ata shote? Do you (m) drink?	אתה שותה?
at shota? Do you (f) drink?	את שותה?

THE DOCTOR MAY SAY

ata loke'akh samim? (m)	?אתה לוקח סמים
at lokakhat samim? (f)	?את לוקחת סמים
Do you take drugs?	
ata alergi lemashehu? (m)	?אתה אלרגי למשהו
at alergit lemashehu? (f)	?את אלרגית למשהו
Are you allergic to anything?	
at beherayon?	?את בהריון
Are you pregnant?	

AILMENTS   מחלות

I'm ill.

ani khole (khola)   .(אני חולה (חולה

I've been vomiting.

heketi   .הקאתי

I feel under the weather.

ani margish(a) lo kmo atsmi   .אני מרגיש(ה) לא כמו עצמי

I feel nauseous.

yesh li bkhila   .יש לי בחילה

I can't sleep.

yesh li nedudei shena   .יש לי נדודי שינה

I feel ...	ani margish(a) ...	... (אני מרגיש(ה
dizzy	skharkhoret	סחרחורת
shivery	tsmarmorot	צמרמורות
weak	khulsha	חולשה

I have (a/an) ...	yesh li ...	... יש לי
allergy	alergia	אלרגיה
anaemia	anemia	אנמיה
burn	kvi'ya	כוויה
cancer	sartan	סרטן
cold	tsinun	צינון

HEALTH

constipation	atsirut	עצירות
cystitis	daleket shalpukhit	דלקת שלפוחית
	hasheten	השתן
cough	shi'ul	שיעול
diarrhoea	shilshul	שלשול
fever	khom	חום
gastroenteritis	daleket hakeyva	דלקת הקיבה
	ve'hame'ayim	והמעיים
headache	ke'ev rosh	כאב ראש
heart condition	be'ayot lev	בעיות לב
indigestion	kilkul keiva	קלקול קיבה
infection	zihum	זיהום
lice	kinim	כינים
migraine	migrena	מיגרנה
pain	ke'ev	כאב
sore throat	ke'ev garon	כאב גרון
sprain	neka	נקע
stomachache	ke'ev beten	כאב בטן
sunburn	makat shemesh	מכת שמש
thrush	pitriya	פיטריה
toothache	ke'ev shina'im	כאב שיניים
travel sickness	bkhila binsi'ot	בחילה בנסיעות
urinary infection	zihum bedarkei	זיהום בדרכי
	hasheten	השתן
venereal disease	makhalat min	מחלת מין
worms	tola'im	תולעים

This is my usual medicine.

zo hatrufa she'ani loke'akh
(lokakhat)

זו התרופה שאני לוקח
(לוקחת).

I've been vaccinated.

kibalti khisun

קיבלתי חיסון.

HEALTH

I don't want a blood transfusion.

ani lo rotse (rotsa) iru'i dam   .אני לא רוצה (רוצה) עירוי דם

Can I have a receipt for my insurance?

efshar lekabel kabala avur   אפשר לקבל קבלה עבור

khevrat habitu'akh?   ?חברת הביטוח

WOMEN'S HEALTH   בריאות האישה

Could I see a female doctor?

ani yekhola lir'ot rof'a?   ?אני יכולה לראות רופאה

I'm pregnant.

ani beherayon   .אני בהריון

I think I'm pregnant.

ani khoshevet she'ani beherayon   .אני חושבת שאני בהריון

I'm on the pill.

ani lokakhat glulot   .אני לוקחת גלולות

I haven't had my period for ... weeks.

haveset sheli me'akheret kvar   הווסת שלי מאחרת כבר

... shavu'ot   .שבועות ...

I'd like to get the morning-after pill.

ani rotsa lekabel et glulat   אני רוצה לקבל את גלולת

haboker she'akharei   .הבוקר שאחרי

I'd like to use contraception.

ani rotsa lehishtamesh   אני רוצה להשתמש

be'emtsa'ei meni'a   .באמצעי מניעה

abortion	hapala	הפלה
cystic fibrosis	cystic fibrosis	סיסטיק פיברוזיס
cystitis	daleket shalpukhit	דלקת שלפוחית
	hasheten	השתן
diaphragm	di'aphragma	דיאפרגמה
IUD	hetken tokh rakhmi	התקן תוך רחמי
mammogram	memograma	ממוגרמה
menstruation	veset	וסת

miscarriage	hapala tiv'it	הפלה טבעית
pap smear	pap smear	פאפ סמיר
period pain	ke'evei makhzor	כאבי מחזור
the Pill	glula	גלולה
premenstrual tension	metakh shelifnei	מתח שלפני
	haveset	הווסת
thrush	pitria	פטריה
ultrasound	ultrasound	אולטרה-סאונד

SPECIAL HEALTH NEEDS צרכי בריאות מיוחדים

I'm ...	yesh li ...	... יש לי
anaemic	anemia	אנמיה
asthmatic	asthma	אסטמה
diabetic	sakeret	סכרת

I'm allergic to ...	ani alergi(t) le ...	... אני אלרגי(ת) ל
antibiotics	antibiotika	אנטיביוטיקה
aspirin	aspirin	אספירין
bees	dvorim	דבורים
codeine	codein	קודאין
dairy products	mutsarei khalav	מוצרי חלב
penicillin	penicillin	פניצילין
pollen	avkat prakhim	אבקת פרחים

I have a skin allergy.
yesh li tguva alergit ba'or   יש לי תגובה אלרגית בעור.

I've had my vaccinations.
kibalti et kol hakhisunim   קיבלתי את כל החיסונים.

I have my own syringe.
yesh li mazrek misheli   יש לי מזרק משלי.

I'm on medication for ...
ani mekabel(et) trufot neged ...   ... אני מקבל(ת) תרופות נגד

I need a new pair of glasses.
ani tsarikh (tsrikha)   (אני צריך (צריכה
mishkafa'im khadashim   משקפיים חדשים.

HEALTH

addiction	hitmakrut	התמכרות
bee sting	akitsat dvora	עקיצת דבורה
blood test	bdikat dam	בדיקת דם
contraceptive	emtsa'ei meni'a	אמצעי מניעה
dog bite	neshikhat kelev	נשיכת כלב
injection	zrika	זריקה
injury	ptsi'a	פציעה
snake bite	hakashat nakhash	הכשת נחש
vitamins	vitaminim	ויטמינים
wound	petsa	פצע

ALTERNATIVE TREATMENTS   רפואה אלטרנטיבית

acupuncture	akupunktura	אקופונקטורה
aromatherapy	aromatherapia	ארומתראפיה
faith healer	merape	מרפא
herbalist	metapel be'isbey marpe	מטפל בעשבי מרפא
homeopathy	homeopatia	הומאופתיה
massage	isui	עיסוי
meditation	meditatsia	מדיטציה
naturopath	rofe tiv'oni	רופא טבעוני
reflexology	reflexologia	רפלקסולוגיה
yoga	yoga	יוגה

PARTS OF THE BODY   אברי הגוף

ankle	karsul	קרסול
appendix	apenditsit	אנפנדיציט
arm	zro'a	זרוע
back	gav	גב
bladder	shalpukhit hasheten	שלפוחית השתן

OUCH!		
Ouch!	aiii!	אי!

HEALTH

blood	dam	דם
bone	etsem	עצם
chest	khaze	חזה
ears	ozna'im	אוזניים
eye	a'in	עין
finger	etsba	אצבע
foot	regel	רגל
hand	yad	יד
head	rosh	ראש
heart	lev	לב
kidney	kilya	כליה
knee	berekh	ברך
legs	ragla'im	רגליים
liver	kaved	כבד
lungs	re'ot	ריאות
mouth	pe	פה
muscle	shrir	שריר
ribs	tsla'ot	צלעות
shoulder	katef	כתף
skin	or	עור
stomach	keiva	קיבה
teeth	shina'im	שיניים
throat	garon	גרון
vein	vrid	וריד

HEALTH

AT THE CHEMIST   בבית-המרקחת

Many Israeli chemists speak English or French. Israeli chemists, bet mirkakhat, take turns in staying open 24 hours a day. Chemists post the name of the nearest 24-hour store, or you can get a list at hotels.

I need something for ...
  ani tsarikh (tsrikha) mashehu le ...   ... אני צריך (צריכה) משהו ל
Do I need a prescription for ...?
  tsarikh mirsham bishvil ... ?   ? ...צריך מרשם בשביל
How many times a day?
  kama pe'amim beyom?   ?כמה פעמים ביום

antibiotics	antibiotika	אנטיביוטיקה
antiseptic	khomer mekhate	חומר מחטא
aspirin	aspirin	אספירין
bandage	takhboshet	תחבושת
Band-aids	plaster	פלסטר
condoms	condomim	קונדומים
contraceptives	emtsa'ei meni'a	אמצעי מניעה
cotton balls	kadurei tsemer gefen	כדורי צמר גפן
cough medicine	trufa neged shi'ul	תרופה נגד שיעול
gauze	gaza	גזה
laxatives	khomer meshalshel	חומר משלשל
painkillers	kadurim neged ke'evim	כדורים נגד כאבים
rubbing alcohol	alkohol me'a akhuz	אלכוהול 100%
sleeping pills	kadurei shena	כדורי שינה

AT THE DENTIST   אצל רופא השיניים

I have a toothache.
  yesh li ke'ev shina'im   .יש לי כאב שיניים
I have a cavity.
  yesh li khor bashen   .יש לי חור בשן
I've lost a filling.
  nafla li stima   .נפלה לי סתימה
I've broken my tooth.
  nishbera li shen   .נשברה לי שן
My gums hurt.
  ko'avot li hakhanikha'im   .כואבות לי החניכיים

HEALTH

I don't want it extracted.

   ani lo rotse (rotsa) la'akor
   et hashen

אני לא רוצה (רוצה) לעקור
את השן.

Please give me an anaesthetic.

   ani mevakesh(et) hardama

אני מבקש(ת) הרדמה.

GEMATRIA (NUMEROLOGY)

In gematria, or Hebrew numerology, each letter of the alphabet has a numerical value. Of the 22 letters, the first 10, from alef to yod, are given the values from one to 10. The next eight, from kaf to tsadi, correspond to every tenth number from 20 to 90, and the last four letters, from kof to tav, are given the values 100, 200, 300 and 400.

The origins of gematria in Jewish tradition go back as early as the 2nd century BC. It became a powerful system of knowledge in the Middle Ages. The Kabbalists used numerology as a method of gaining mystic insights into the holy scripts. It's believed the numerical equivalence of two words or phrases in a text reveals an interrelationship between the two, and a hidden meaning, even if there's no etymological connection.

There are many ways to compute the numerical value of a word, the simplest being to add the numerical value of the corresponding letters.

For example, ahava (love) is: alef (1) + he (5) + bet (2) + he (5) = 13, and the word ekhad (one) is: alef (1) + khet (8) + dalet (4) = 13.

SPECIFIC NEEDS צרכים מסויימים

DISABLED TRAVELLERS   הנוסע הנכה

Many hotels and most public institutions in Israel provide ramps, specially equipped toilets and other conveniences for people with disabilities. Several hostels also have rooms specially adapted for wheelchair access.

I'm disabled (handicapped).
    ani nekhe (nekha)   אני נכה (נכה).

I need assistance.
    ani tsarikh (tsrikha) ezra   אני צריך (צריכה) עזרה.

What services do you have for disabled people?
    elu sherutim lenekhim   אילו שירותים לנכים
    yesh lakhem?   יש לכם?

Is there wheelchair access?
    yesh knisa lekise galgalim?   יש כניסה לכסא גלגלים?

I'm deaf. Speak more loudly, please.
    ani kheresh(et) na   אני חרש(ת). נא
    ledaber bekol ram   לדבר בקול רם.

I can lipread.
    ani kore(t) tnu'ot sfata'im   אני קורא(ת) תנועות שפתיים.

I have a hearing aid.
    yesh li makhshir shmi'a   יש לי מכשיר שמיעה.

Does anyone here know sign language?
    mishehu po makir   מישהו פה מכיר
    et sfat hasimanim?   את שפת הסימנים?

Are guide dogs permitted?
    mutar lehikanes im kelev mankhe?   מותר להכנס עם כלב מנחה?

braille library	sifriyat braille	ספריית בראייל
disabled person	nekhe (nekha)	נכה (נכה)
guide dog	kelev mankhe	כלב מנחה
wheelchair	kise galgalim	כסא גלגלים

SPECIFIC NEEDS

GAY & LESBIAN TRAVELLERS   "הנוסע ה"עליז

Homosexuality isn't illegal in Israel, but it's an anathema to the country's large religious population. As a result, the gay and lesbian community are obliged to keep a low profile. The Society for the Protection of Personal Rights (SPPR) represents gay and lesbian people.

The biggest scene, and the annual gay-pride parade, is in largely secular, free-wheeling Tel Aviv.

Where are the gay hangouts?
    mahem mekomot habilui   מהם מקומות הבילוי
    shel hahomosexualim?   של ההומוסקסואלים?
Is there a gay district?
    yesh po rova homosexualim?   יש פה רובע הומוסקסואלים?
Are we/Am I likely to be harassed ?
    kayemet po hatrada minit?   קיימת פה הטרדה מינית?
Is there a gay bookshop around here?
    yesh kan khanut sfarim   יש כאן חנות ספרים
    lehomosexualim?   להומוסקסואלים?
Is there a local gay guide?
    yesh madrikh homosexualim   יש מדריך הומוסקסואלים
    mekomi?   מקומי?
Where can I buy some gay/lesbian magazines?
    eifo efshar liknot kitvei   איפה אפשר לקנות כתבי
    et lehomosexualim/lesbiyot?   עת להומוסקסואלים/לסביות?
Is there a gay telephone hotline?
    yesh kav patu'akh lehomosexualim?   יש קו פתוח להומוסקסואלים?

TRAVELLING WITH A FAMILY   לטייל עם משפחה

Are there facilities for babies?
    yesh mitkanim letinokot?   יש מתקנים לתינוקות?
Do you have a child-minding service?
    yesh lakhem sherutei beibi-siting?   יש לכם שירותי בייבי-סיטינג?

Where can I find a English-speaking baby-sitter?
eifo efshar limtso beibi-siter
dover(et) anglit?

איפה אפשר למצוא בייבי-סיטר
דובר(ת) אנגלית?

Can you put an extra bed/cot in the room?
efshar lehosif mitat
tinok lakheder?

אפשר להוסיף
מיטת תינוק לחדר?

I need a car with a child seat.
ani tsarikh (tsrikha) mekhonit
im moshav leyeled

אני צריך (צריכה) מכונית
עם מושב לילד.

Is it suitable for children?
ha'im ze mat'im liladim?

האם זה מתאים לילדים?

Are there any activities for children?
yesh po pe'iluyot liladim?

יש פה פעילויות לילדים?

Is there a family discount?
yesh hanakha lemishpakha?

יש הנחה למשפחה?

Are children allowed?
haknisa liladim muteret?

הכניסה לילדים מותרת?

Do you have a children's menu?
yesh tafrit yeladim?

יש תפריט ילדים?

LOOKING FOR A JOB   מחפשים עבודה

Many people automatically associate a visit to Israel with a stint
as a kibbutz or moshav volunteer, and every year thousands of
young people descend on the Holy Land for the experience. Other
volunteer projects include Palestinian work camps, medical and
social work, including teaching, nursing and counselling, and
Volunteers for Israel. Most archeological digs require that you
pay to work and have full personal insurance.

Where can I find local job advertisements?
eifo efshar limtso
moda'ot drushim ba'ezor?

איפה אפשר למצוא
מודעות דרושים באזור?

Do I need a work permit?
tsarikh rishyon avoda?

צריך רשיון עבודה?

SPECIFIC NEEDS

I've had experience.
yesh li nisayon
יש לי נסיון.

I've come about the position advertised.
ani ba(a) bekesher lamoda'a
אני בא(ה) בקשר למודעה.

I'm ringing about the position advertised.
ani metsaltsel(et) bekesher lamoda'a
אני מצלצל(ת) בקשר למודעה.

What is the wage?
ma hamaskoret?
מה המשכורת?

Do I have to pay tax?
ani khayav (khayevet) bemas?
אני חייב (חייבת) במס?

I can start ...	ani yakhol (yekhola) lehatkhil ...	אני יכול (יכולה) להתחיל ...
today	hayom	היום
tomorrow	makhar	מחר
next week	bashavu'a haba	בשבוע הבא

casual	lo formali	לא פורמאלי
employee	sakhir	שכיר
employer	ma'asik	מעסיק
full-time	misra mele'a	משרה מלאה
job	avoda	עבודה
occupation/trade	miktso'a	מקצוע
part-time	misra khelkit	משרה חלקית
résumé/cv	toldot khayim	תולדות חיים
traineeship	hitmakhut	התמחות
work experience	nisayon ba'avoda	נסיון בעבודה

DASH!

'Dash' is the abbreviation for drishat shalom, meaning something like 'say hello to' (lit: x asks for peace for y).

SPECIFIC NEEDS

ON BUSINESS
בעסקים

We're attending a ...	anakhnu mishtatfim be ...	... אנחנו משתתפים ב
conference	yeshiva	ישיבה
meeting	pgisha	פגישה
trade fair	ta'arukhat miskhar	תערוכת מסחר

I'm on a course.
ani lomed(et) bekurs — אני לומד(ת) בקורס.

I have an appointment with ...
yesh li pgisha im ... — ... יש לי פגישה עם

Here's my business card.
hine kartis habikur sheli — הנה כרטיס הביקור שלי.

I need an interpreter.
ani tsarikh (tsrikha) meturgeman — אני צריך (צריכה) מתורגמן.

I want to use a computer.
ani tsarikh (tsrikha) makhshev — אני צריך (צריכה) מחשב.

I want to send a(n) fax/email.
ani tsarikh (tsrikha) liskhlo'akh — אני צריך (צריכה) לשלוח
fax/do'ar elektroni — פקס/דואר אלקטרוני.

client	lako'akh	לקוח
colleague	colega	קולגה
distributor	mefits	מפיץ
email	do'ar elektroni	דואר אלקטרוני
exhibition	ta'arukha	תערוכה
manager	menahel	מנהל
mobile phone	telephon nayad	טלפון נייד
profit	revakh	רווח
proposal	hatsa'a	הצעה

JERUSALEM – RELIGIOUS EPICENTRE

If the Holy Land is the spiritual core of some of the world's major religions, then Jerusalem is its epicentre. Jews from all over the world come to pray at the Western Wall, or kotel, the site of the ancient Temple. Muslim pilgrims worship on the Temple Mount in the El Aqsa Mosque and visit the Dome of the Rock, both among Islam's holiest sites. Muhammad is believed to have ascended to heaven from this spot. It's also the site where Abraham, the patriarch of the Jewish, Christian, Muslim and Baha'i faiths, attempted to sacrifice his son. Christian pilgrims walk the Via Dolorosa, the path Jesus is thought to have followed on the way to his crucifixion. Nearby, pilgrims visit Bethlehem, the site of Jesus' birth and the Sea of Galilee, where he walked on water. Jews make pilgrimages to Tsfat (Sefad), an ancient centre of Kabbalistic mystical teachings. And at one of the most remarkable pilgrimage sites, the tomb of Abraham in the volatile West Bank city of Hebron, Muslims and Jews alternate prayer times under the gaze of Israeli soldiers.

Nearby in Haifa is the spiritual centre and pilgrimage site of the planet's most recent world religion, the Baha'i faith. Pilgrims visit the World Center and the shrines of their prophet Baha'u'llah and his Herald, the Bab, with their spectacular gardens. While most Israelis frequent the site, they know nothing of the content of the Baha'i faith that teaches the oneness of God, all religions, and the peoples of the world. Apart from individual Baha'is that work at the Center, there are no Baha'i communities in Israel, they don't teach about their faith here, and so those Israelis who become Baha'i are required to leave the country. The Baha'i faith forbids its nearly six million followers to travel to or work in Israel without the permission of its governing body. Those Baha'i pilgrims who are allowed to visit Haifa (for a maximum of 10 days), are given the rare opportunity to see a photo of their prophet, which is only available at the World Center.

SPECIFIC NEEDS

ON TOUR

בטיול המאורגן

We're part of a group.

anakhnu shayakhim likvutsa

אנחנו שייכים לקבוצה.

We're on tour.

anakhnu betiyul me'urgan

אנחנו בטיול מאורגן.

I'm with the ...	ani im ha ...	... אני עם ה
band	khavura	חבורה
crew	tsevet	צוות
group	kvutsa	קבוצה
team	tsevet	צוות

Please speak with our manager.

bevakasha daber (dabri)
im hamenahel

בבקשה דבר (דברי)
עם המנהל.

We've lost our equipment.

ibadnu et hatsiyud shelanu

איבדנו את הציוד שלנו.

We sent equipment on this ...	shalakhnu et hatsiyud ba ... haze (hazot)	שלחנו את הציוד ב ... הזה (הזאת).
bus	otobus	אוטובוס
flight	tisa	טיסה
train	rakevet	רכבת

We're taking a break for ... days.

anakhnu yots'im lekhufsha
bat ... yamim

אנחנו יוצאים לחופשה
בת ... ימים.

We're playing on ...

anakhnu mesakhakim be ...

אנחנו משחקים ב ...

SPECIFIC NEEDS

FILM & TV CREWS

קולנוע וצוותי טלוויזיה

We're on location.
anakhnu ba'atar hatsilumim

אנחנו באתר הצילומים.

We're filming!
metsalmim!

מצלמים!

May we film here?
efshar letsalem po?

אפשר לצלם פה?

We're making a ...   anakhnu osim ...   ... אנחנו עושים
   documentary   seret ti'udi   סרט תיעודי
   film   seret   סרט
   TV series   sidrat televisia   סדרת טלוויזיה

LUNAR CONSCIOUSNESS

In order to calibrate the lunar calendar with the solar year, Jewish sages added a 29-day month, seven times every 19 years.

While this sounds somewhat convoluted, it ingeniously allows the Jewish ritual cycle to follow a lunar 'consciousness' while at the same time keeping the holiday schedule within the agricultural seasons they celebrate.

The Jewish leap year systematically takes place in the 3rd, 6th, 8th, 11th, 14th, 17th and 19th years. The leap month, added after the month of Adar, is called Adar II and immediately precedes the month of Nisan (the first month of the Jewish agricultural calendar).

It's this leap year system that causes Jewish holidays to take place at a different time each year on the Western calendar.

The names of the months of the Jewish calendar were borrowed from the Babylonians, after their conquest of Jerusalem in 587 BC.

HEBREW PRAYERS

Shma (unifying prayer)

שמע ישראל ה' אלוהינו ה' אחד.

shma israel adonai eloheinu adonai ekhad

Hear O Israel, the Lord our God, the Lord is one.

Over wine

ברוך אתה ה' אלוהינו מלך העולם בורא פרי הגפן.

barukh ata adonai eloheinu melekh ha'olam bore pri hagafen

Blessed are you, Lord our God, King of the Universe, who creates the fruit of the vine.

Over bread

ברוך אתה ה' אלוהינו מלך העולם המוציא לחם מן הארץ.

barukh ata adonai eloheinu melekh ha'olam hamotsi lekhem min ha-arets

Blessed are you, Lord our God, King of the Universe, who brings forth bread from the earth.

Over fruits from trees

ברוך אתה ה' אלוהינו מלך העולם בורא פרי העץ.

barukh ata adonai eloheinu melekh ha'olam bore pri ha-ets

Blessed are you, Lord our God, King of the Universe, who creates the fruit of the tree.

On seeing the beauties of nature

ברוך אתה ה' אלוהינו מלך העולם שככה לו בעולמו.

barukh ata adonai eloheinu melekh ha'olam shekakha lo be'olamo

Blessed are you, Lord our God, King of the Universe, who has such as these in your world.

HEBREW PRAYERS

On seeing a rainbow

ברוך אתה ה' אלוהינו מלך העולם זוכר הברית ונאמן בבריתו וקיים במאמרו.

barukh ata adonai eloheinu melekh ha'olam zokher habrit vene-eman bivrito vekyam bema-amaro

Blessed are you, Lord our God, King of the Universe, who remembers the covenant and keeps your promise faithfully.

On seeing the ocean

ברוך אתה ה' אלוהינו מלך העולם שעשה את הים הגדול.

barukh ata adonai eloheinu melekh ha'olam she'asa et hayam hagadol

Blessed are you, Lord our God, King of the Universe, who has made the great sea.

On seeing a person of abnormal appearance

ברוך אתה ה' אלוהינו מלך העולם משנה הבריות.

barukh ata adonai eloheinu melekh ha'olam meshane habriyot

Blessed are you, Lord our God, King of the Universe, who varies the aspect of your creatures.

Priestly Blessing

יברכך ה' וישמרך, יאר ה' פניו אליך ויחונך, ישא ה' פניו אליך וישם לך שלום.

yevarekhekha adonai veyishmrekha; yaer adonai panav eleikha viyekhunekha; yisa adonai panav eleikha veyasem lekha shalom

May the Lord bless you and protect you, may the Lord countenance you and be gracious to you; may the Lord favour you and grant you peace.

SPECIFIC NEEDS

PILGRIMAGE & RELIGION

עליה לרגל וענייני דת

What's your religion?
ma hadat shelkha (shelakh)?

מה הדת שלך (שלך)?

I'm ...	ani ...	אני ...
Buddhist	budhisti(t)	בודהיסטי(ת)
Catholic	katholikatoli(t)	קתולי(ת)
Christian	notsri(t)	נוצרי(ת)
Hindu	hindi(t)	הינדי(ת)
Jewish	yehudi(a)	יהודי(ה)
Muslim	muslemi(t)	מוסלמי(ת)

I'm not religious.
ani lo dati(a)

אני לא דתי(ה).

I'm Christian, but not devout.
ani notsri(t) aval lo dati(a)

אני נוצרי(ת) אבל לא דתי(ה).

I think I believe in God.
ani khoshev(et) she'ani
ma'amin(a) be'elohim

אני חושב(ת) שאני
מאמין(ה) באלוהים.

I believe in destiny.
ani ma'amin(a) bagoral

אני מאמין(ה) בגורל.

I'm interested in astrology/philosophy.
ani mit'anyen(et)
be'astrologia/filosofia

אני מתעניין(ת)
באסטרולוגיה/פילוסופיה.

I'm an atheist.
ani ate'isti(t)

אני אתאיסט(ית).

I'm agnostic.
ani agnosti(t)

אני אגנוסטי(ת).

Can I attend this service/mass?
efshar lehishtatef batfila?

אפשר להשתתף בתפילה?

Can I pray here?
efshar lehitpalel kan?

אפשר להתפלל כאן?

Where can I pray/worship?

| eifo efshar lehitpalel? | ?איפה אפשר להתפלל |

Where can I make confession (in English)?

| eifo efshar lehitvadot (be'anglit)? | איפה אפשר להתוודות (באנגלית)? |

baptism/christening	tvila	טבילה
church	knesiya	כנסייה
communion	akhilat lekhem hakodesh	אכילת לחם הקודש
confession	vidu'i	וידוי
funeral	levaya	לוויה
God	elohim	אלוהים
monk	nazir	נזיר
prayer	tfila	תפילה
priest	komer	כומר
relic	sarid	שריד
religious procession	tahalukha datit	תהלוכה דתית
sabbath	shabbat	שבת
saint	kadosh	קדוש
shrine	mikdash	מקדש
temple	mikdash	מקדש

TRACING ROOTS & HISTORY   חיפוש שורשים והיסטוריה

I think my ancestors came from this area.

| ani khoshev(et) sheavotai ba'u meha'ezor haze | אני חושב(ת) שאבותי באו מהאזור הזה. |

I'm looking for my relatives.

| ani mekhapes(et) krovei mishpakha | אני מחפש(ת) קרובי משפחה. |

I have/had a relative who lives around here.

| yesh/haya li karov shegar kan basviva | יש/היה לי קרוב שגר כאן בסביבה. |

Is there anyone here by the name of ...?

| yesh po mishehu beshem ...? | יש פה מישהו בשם ...? |

I'd like to go to the cemetary/burial ground.
  ha'iti rotse (rotsa) lalekhet
  lebeit hakvarot

הייתי רוצה (רוצה) ללכת
לבית הקברות.

I think he fought/died near here.
  ani khoshev(et) shehu
  nilkham/neherag po

אני חושב(ת) שהוא
נלחם/נהרג פה.

TIME, DATES & FESTIVALS

Israelis work five or five-and-a-half days a week, with the day of rest, called Shabbat, beginning at sundown on Friday night and ending Saturday when three stars are visible in the night sky. In Israel, all days begin at sundown, but time is still calculated as it is in Western countries. The work day resumes on Sunday, which is called Yom Rishon, 'the first day'.

TELLING THE TIME

לקרוא את השעון

What time is it?

mahasha'a?   מה השעה?

(It's) one o'clock.

(hasha'a) akhat   (השעה) אחת.

(It's) ten o'clock.

(hasha'a) eser   (השעה) עשר.

(It's) half past one.

(hasha'a) akhat vakhetsi   (השעה) אחת וחצי.

(It's) half past three.

(hasha'a) shalosh vakhetsi   (השעה) שלוש וחצי.

DAYS

ימים

In Israel the week starts on Sunday and ends on Saturday. The week days, Sunday through to Friday, are designated by ordinal numbers – the first day, the second day, the third day and so on. This follows the biblical designation of days as God progressed through the creation of the universe. The name of Shabbat, the only day of the week to be given its own name, means 'to cease' or 'to rest'. According to the Torah, on that day God stopped his work and rested. Thus, Jews are expected to refrain from work on that day, and simply enjoy.

Sunday	yom rishon	יום ראשון
Monday	yom sheni	יום שני
Tuesday	yom shlishi	יום שלישי
Wednesday	yom revi'i	יום רביעי
Thursday	yom khamishi	יום חמישי
Friday	yom shishi	יום שישי
Saturday	shabbat	שבת

MONTHS   חודשים

Two calendars are used in Israel – the Gregorian and the Jewish lunar. There are two words in Hebrew to say 'month', and both express a close relationship to the moon. The less common word, yerakh, derives from yare'akh (moon), while khodesh derives from the word khadash (new), referring to a new moon. The religious calendar has traditionally associated the beginning of the month with the observation of the crescent of the new moon.

However, the Jewish calendar is not based on the cyclical movement of the moon only, but is lunisolar – regulated by the movements of both the moon and the sun. The lunar months are of 29 or 30 days each, as compared with the 30 or 31 days of the solar months. The lunar year is adjusted to the solar year by a periodic introduction of leap years, to ensure that major festivals fall in their proper season. The added month is a second month of Adar, and thus in leap years there are Adar 1 and Adar 2. The names of the months of the Jewish calendar were borrowed from the Babylonians, after their conquest of Jerusalem in BC 587.

January	yanu'ar	ינואר
February	febru'ar	פברואר
March	mertz	מרץ
April	april	אפריל
May	ma'i	מאי
June	yuni	יוני

TIME, DATES & FESTIVALS

July	yuli	יולי
August	august	אוגוסט
September	september	ספטמבר
October	oktober	אוקטובר
November	november	נובמבר
December	detsember	דצמבר

Jewish Lunar Calendar

first month	tishrei	תשרי
second month	kheshvan	חשוון
third month	kislev	כסלו
fourth month	tevet	טבת
fifth month	shvat	שבט
sixth month	adar	אדר
seventh month	nisan	ניסן
eighth month	iyar	אייר
ninth month	sivan	סיוון
tenth month	tamuz	תמוז
eleventh month	av	אב
twelfth month	elul	אלול

DATES

תאריכים

For religious reasons, the term 'Anno Domini' (AD), the year of our Lord, and 'Before Christ' (BC) aren't used in Israel. Instead, the notation CE (Common Era) and BCE (Before the Common Era) are used for the same periods. The Muslim calendar uses 'AH' (After *hajira*, 622 AD) and the Baha'is use 'BE' (Baha'i Era 1844).

What date it is today?
   ma hata'arikh hayom?   מה התאריך היום?
It's 18 October.
   (hayom) hashmona   (היום) השמונה
   asar be'october   עשר באוקטובר.

TIME, DATES & FESTIVALS

Present

today	hayom	היום
this morning	haboker	הבוקר
tonight	halayla	הלילה
this week	hashavu'a	השבוע
this year	hashana	השנה
now	akhshav	עכשיו

Past

yesterday	etmol	אתמול
day before yesterday	shilshom	שלשום
yesterday morning	etmol baboker	אתמול בבוקר
last night	etmol balayla	אתמול בלילה
last week	hashavu'a she'avar	השבוע שעבר
last year	hashana she'avra	השנה שעברה

Future

tomorrow	makhar	מחר
day after tomorrow	mokhrota'im	מחרתיים
tomorrow morning	makhar baboker	מחר בבוקר
tomorrow afternoon	makhar akhar hatsohora'im	מחר אחר הצהריים
tomorrow evening	makhar ba'erev	מחר בערב
next week	hashavu'a haba	השבוע הבא
next year	hashana haba'a	השנה הבאה

During the Day

afternoon	akhar hatsohora'im	אחר הצהריים
dawn	shakhar	שחר
day	yom	יום
early	mukdam	מוקדם
midnight	khatsot	חצות
morning	boker	בוקר
night	layla	לילה

noon	tsohora'im	צהריים
sunrise	zrikhat hashemesh	זריחת השמש
sunset	shki'at hashemesh	שקיעת השמש

HOLIDAYS & FESTIVALS   חגים ומועדים
Rosh Hashana & Yom Kippur

The Jewish holiday cycle begins with Rosh Hashana, literally the 'head of the year'. It begins in September–October, around the start of autumn, and is celebrated on both the first and second days of the Hebrew month of Tishrei. The observance of Rosh Hashana, which is commanded in the Bible, is regarded as a celebration of the beginning of the universe, the day God 'let there be light' through the Big Bang. During the previous month of Elul, called 'the days of conciliation and forgiveness' prior to the New Year, a ram's horn (shofar) is blown during certain prayers in the synagogue. The ram's horn is also blown during Rosh Hashana and the subsequent Day of Atonement, Yom Kippur. The shofar can be made from the horns of any animal except a cow, which is a reminder of the sin of the golden calf at Mount Sinai. The shofar is used to mark the beginning of 'the ten days of penitence' and to commemorate the destruction of the Temple (see Tish'a BeAv, page 177).

The New Year initiates an autumn holiday period that is fast and furious. Rosh Hashana is a time when families come together for a festive meal held on the first and second nights of Rosh Hashana. During the meal, a piece of bread and apple are dipped in honey to symbolise the hope that the upcoming year will be a sweet one. On the first afternoon of Rosh Hashana, some Jews participate in a Tashlikh ceremony, in which they go to a place where there's running water, like a river or the ocean, and throw bread upon it to symbolise the sins they've committed over the past year. This tradition stems from the prophet Micah, who stated that on Rosh Hashana Jews should 'cast their sins into the depths of the sea'.

Rosh Hashana begins a time of reflection called the '10 days of penitence' (aseret yeme tshuva). These are the 10 days in which God judges the world and decides who will live and who will die during the coming year. During this time, Jews ask forgiveness from God, and reflect on the wrongs they've committed during the past year. Jews believe that God only forgives sins committed against God, and only the individuals you've wronged can pardon your sins toward them. During these 10 days, people visit or call one another to ask for forgiveness.

HAPPY BIRTHDAY

When's your birthday?	
matay yom hahuledet	מתי יום ההולדת
shelkha (shelakh)?	שלך (שלך)?
My birthday is on ...	
yom huladeti ba ...	יום הולדתי ב ...
Congratulations!	
mazal tov!	מזל טוב!
Happy Birthday!	
yom huledet same'akh!	יום הולדת שמח!
Many happy returns!	
ad me'a ve'esrim!	עד מאה ועשרים!
birthday cake	
ugat yom huledet	עוגת יום הולדת
candles	
nerot	נרות
to blow out the candles	
linshof al hanerot	לנשוף על הנרות
presents	
matanot	מתנו

The tenth day, Yom Kippur (the Day of Atonement), is the most solemn, when God seals the decree for each person's future life on earth. The evening of Yom Kippur begins a 24-hour fast. According to tradition, Jews perform kaparot, in which they wave money or a live chicken over their heads to beg forgiveness. The chicken is slaughtered to atone for the repentant person's sins, taking their place in death so they can gain another year on earth. During this time of 'atonement', Jews spend most of their time praying in a synagogue, where the day is punctuated by solemn hymns. The local community often goes to a lake or river and throws bread into the water to symbolically carry their sins away. Yom Kippur ends with a long blast of the shofar, to open the Gate of Mercy. When leaving the synagogue, people wish each other gmar khatima tova, a good entry in the Book of the Living.

Sukkot

Five days after Yom Kippur, the thanksgiving harvest festival of Sukkot, meaning 'huts', is celebrated over seven or eight days. To celebrate this festival, people build 'huts', or sukkot, in their back yards – these are replicas of the simple huts the Israelites lived in as they wandered the Sinai desert. For Jews living in Israel, the holidays of Sukkot and Pesakh (Passover) are observed for seven days. Outside Israel, such holidays are observed for eight days to ensure that the new moon that begins the holiday is reckoned properly.

Sukkot, with its emphasis on the environment and on Mother Nature, is growing in popularity. The huts, built with ceilings which give a view of the sky, are decorated with fruit and vegetables. Some people spend the night in a sukka to sleep under the stars. As part of religious worship, people select etrogs (citron), a yellow citrus fruit, and palm branches (lulavs) with willow and myrtle attached. During the synagogue ritual, with the etrog in the left hand and lulav in the right, blessings are said while shaking the etrog and lulav in the four cardinal directions, as well as upward and downward. This symbolises God's presence in all directions. During this time, mitsva tanks with orthodox volunteers invite passersby to 'shake, shake, shake'.

Khanuka

While many in the West see the candle-lighting holiday of Khanuka as the Jewish alternative to Christmas, this eight-day holiday in which Jews exchange gifts actually began as Judaism's most revolutionary holiday. Khanuka begins on the 25th day of the Hebrew month of Kislev (November–December), and is observed to commemorate the rededication of the Temple after it was desecrated in 165BC. When the Greek–Syrian king Antiochus ordered all people living in his empire to worship Hellenistic gods, he ordered the seven-branched candelabrum (menora) and all consecrated oil removed from the Temple and replaced with pagan statues.

In response to this sacrilege, Judah Maccabee, a member of the Hasmonean family which ruled Jerusalem at the time, organised a successful rebellion and then rededicated the Temple to Jewish worship on the 25th day of Kislev. After removing the pagan statues and installing a new menora, Maccabees needed consecrated oil to keep the menora lit. However, only one vat of holy oil – about a day's worth – was found. Miraculously, it lasted for eight days, until new consecrated oil could be produced.

In order to commemorate this miracle of oil, Jews light a special lamp for the eight days of Khanuka. This lamp is called a khanukiya, which is a type of menora containing eight candleholders, as well as one used to light the other candles. One candle is lit on the first day, two on the second, and so on.

Originally, Jews were expected to follow the Maccabee lead and expel all foreign ideas and thoughts from their inner being on Khanuka, as a kind of spiritual cleansing.

Interestingly, many sports teams in Israel are named after the Maccabees. In opposition to the priestly Maccabees, whose government leadership was considered to be violating Jewish law, a group of Jews known as the Essenes, the groups to which Jesus of Nazareth is believed to have belonged, took refuge in the Dead Sea region.

Over time, certain traditions emerged surrounding this holiday. Many Khanuka traditions focus on children. During the holiday, children play a game for chocolate money, called 'gelt' in Yiddish, by spinning a top (dreidel) on which the letters NGHP (in Israel) and NGHSh (outside Israel) are written. The letters

TIME, DATES & FESTIVALS

HATIKVA

Israel's national anthem, Hatikva, was written in the late 19th century and put to a Moldavian folk melody.

For as long as within his heart		
kol od balevav pnima	כל עוד בלבב פנימה	
the soul of the Jew longs.		
nefesh yehudi homiya	נפש יהודי הומיה	
As he turns eastward		
ulfaatei mizrakh kadima	ולפאתי מזרח קדימה	
his eye looks toward Zion		
a'in letsiyon tsofiya	עין לציון צופיה	
Our hope has not yet lost		
od lo avda tikvatenu	עוד לא אבדה תקוותנו	
the hope of thousands of years		
hatikva shnot alpayim	התקווה שנות אלפים	
to be a free people in our land		
lihiyot am khofshi be-artsenu	להיות עם חופשי בארצנו	
the land of Zion and Jerusalem.		
erets tsiyon yerushala'im	ארץ ציון ירושלים	

stand for Nes Gadol Haya Po (a great miracle happened here) and Nes Gadol Haya Sham (a great miracle happened there). Bets are placed on which letter the dreidel will stop at after each spin.

Among Ashkenazi Jews (Jews of Northern and Eastern European descent), it's become customary to eat food cooked in oil, such as latkes (potato pancakes), on this holiday.

Purim

Purim is a carnivalesque holiday celebrated on the 14th day of Adar (February–March), to commemorate the foiling of a plot by a Persian minister named Haman to kill the Jews of Persia – a story recounted in the Book of Esther (Megilat Esther) of the Bible.

Haman's murderous plot developed after Mordecai, a Jew, refused to bow to him. The Persian king Ahaseurus approved Haman's plot, but Mordecai and his niece Esther, who just happened to be Ahaseurus' favourite wife, exposed the plan, along with her previously unknown Jewish identity. On the 14th day of Adar, Esther succeeded in foiling the plot and King Ahaseurus had Haman executed on the gallows. The holiday is called Purim, meaning 'lots', because Haman drew lots to determine the day on which the Jews would be slaughtered.

To celebrate this holiday, Jews dress in a variety of costumes and listen to a reading of the Megilat Esther. Under Italian influence, Purim carnivals have become common in many countries, with performances retelling the story of Purim. As part of the holiday, Jews are commanded to obliterate Haman's name throughout the generations. During services, while the Megilat Esther is being read, it's customary for children to rattle their ra'ashanim, or noisemakers, in an attempt to blot out the name of Haman. The irony of the command is that in order to remember to obliterate the name of Haman, it must ultimately be remembered.

Purim celebrations are marked by feasting and merriment. In the late afternoon, a festive meal is eaten. Foods typically enjoyed include boiled eggs, beans and three-cornered pies known as oznei haman (Haman's ears). In Yiddish they're called 'hamantashen' (Haman's pockets). They were originally called 'mohntashen' (poppy-seed pockets), which was so similar to 'hamantashen' that they became associated with the villain.

During Purim, Jewish revellers are allowed to indulge in excesses such as smoking and even drinking to intoxication. In fact, according to tradition, men are supposed to drink until they can't distinguish between a good person and an evil person.

Pesakh (Passover)

Pesakh is a seven-to-eight day holiday beginning on the 15th day of Nissan (March–April). It celebrates the Jewish liberation from slavery and subsequent exodus from Egypt in the 13th century BC. The name originates from when the Angel of Death, who slaughtered the Egyptians, passed over the homes of Jews. The Israelites fled so quickly they didn't have time to let their bread rise.

Jews eat matsa, or unleavened bread, to commemorate this haste. During the entire festival, Jews aren't permitted to eat anything containing leavening. In fact, the day before Pesakh, Jews must cleanse their homes of khamets (leavening), and remove all bread from their homes.

The history and traditions of Pesakh are a reminder of Jewish unity, and it's customary to reunite with the family to celebrate this holiday. Anyone who might be alone on Pesakh is also invited to take part in their Pesakh evening meal, called seder.

On this holiday, people are required to retell Biblical events during seder, on the first night of Pesakh. The seder follows the

STRESS

In Hebrew, stress is usually placed on the last syllable (as in Israel), or on the second last (as in Yerushalaim).

In words borrowed from other languages, stress is usually placed on the first syllable (as in telephone).

Pesakh haggadah, or telling, along with the seder plate containing symbolic food, which is placed on the table and eaten during the recounting of Israelites' bondage in Egypt, the 10 plagues, liberation and freedom. A full cup of wine is placed on the table for Elijah, the herald of the coming messiah.

On the seder plate, a roasted egg symbolises oppression, and bitter herbs dipped in salt water represent the tears and bitterness of slavery. A mixture of chopped apples, almonds and wine, called kharoset, represents the mortar used in slave labour. Wine represents the plagues and those who perished, and a roasted bone represents the sacrificial sheep whose blood marked the doors of Israelites homes as a Pesakh signal to the Angel of Death. Prior to the destruction of the Second Temple in 70 AD, Jews were required to sacrifice a lamb on the Pesakh holiday, and many thousands of Jews would go to Jerusalem to perform this sacrifice.

Shavuot

Shavuot, meaning 'weeks', also known as Pentecost (the 50th day), is held at the end of the seven-week period between Pesakh (passover) and the holiday of Shavuot. Shavuot is a one to two-day holiday observed in Israel on the 6th day of Sivan (May–June).

Traditionally, Shavuot celebrated the beginning of the wheat harvest. But like Sukkot, which is observed as an agricultural festival and in commemoration of Israelites wandering the desert and living in huts, Shavuot was transformed from an agricultural festival into an anniversary of the giving of the Torah at Mount Sinai. God's bestowal of the Torah upon the Israelites at Mount Sinai is believed to be the wedding between God and the Jewish people. A popular interpretation holds that, when God offered the commandments to the Israelites, God held Mount Sinai over the Israelites' heads as a coersion to go through with the 'nuptuals'.

During Shavuot, religious Jews often stay up the entire night in group study, preparing their souls for prayers that begin with the first ray from the sun as it rises. In Jerusalem, Jews gather at the Kotel (Western Wall) on Shavuot morning, waiting for the first rays of sun to come over the Wall before all bow their heads and begin prayers in unison.

Yom Ha'atsma'ut

Yom Ha'atsmaut (Independence Day), was first held on 14 May 1948 (the 5th day of Iyar), after the UN voted to establish the State of Israel. The holiday is celebrated according to the Jewish calendar in April–May.

Tu BiShvat

Tu BiShvat (the 15th day of Shvat, usually January-February) is known as the 'New Year for trees'. This is an ecological holiday marking the point when, according to rabbis, the fruits of trees begin to form, having been nourished by winter rains.

Israeli school children plant trees on Tu BiShvat, as part of a 100-year-old effort to reforest the country, an effort urged particularly by the Jewish National Fund. The effort has grown in importance after arsonists set a huge area of national forest ablaze in Jerusalem.

Tu BiShvat also signals the upcoming harvest and the arrival of spring. In the time of the ancient Jewish Temple, Tu BiShvat was important for agricultural bookkeeping, marking the start of the fiscal year, when farmers were taxed on their harvests.

Tish'a BeAv

Tish'a BeAv (the 9th day of the month of Av, which falls in July) is a 24-hour fast allowing neither food nor drink to mourn the destruction of the First and Second Temples (585 BC and 70 AD respectively). These temples stood atop the Temple Mount, which has the Western Wall (Kotel) on one side, and which now contains the Muslim holy sites of the Dome of the Rock and Al-Aqsa Mosque.

Although Reform Jews in the West refer to their synagogues as temples, according to Orthodox Jews only the First and Second

Temples can be referred to as such. By using the term 'temple', Reform Jews reject the possibility that a Messiah will come to lead Jews in the 'world to come', or ha-olam ha-ba.

The expulsion of 100,000 Jews from Spain took place on the 9th day of Av, the very day in 1492 that Columbus set sail on his way to the Americas. Consequently, Tish'a BeAv now commemorates both these painful events. In fact, today, Tish'a BeAv commemorates all Jewish tragedies except the Holocaust, which has its own memorial day called Yom Hasho'a.

As on Yom Kippur, Jews are required to fast on Tish'a BeAv, but many worshippers go further to be uncomfortable on this day. While not going as far as some Shi'ites, who beat their bodies with chains to mourn the Caliph Hussain, some Jews place rocks in their shoes or sleep on the floor. During the synagogue service, the Book of Lamentations is read in a haunting melody and, to express their sorrow, worshippers usually sit on the floor.

Yom Hazikaron (Memorial Day)

This day, which falls during April-May, one week after Yom Hasho'a, commemorates the fallen martyrs of Israel and civilian victims of terrorism.

Yom Hasho'a

Yom Hasho'a (Holocaust Memorial Day) commemorates the six million Jewish martyrs (kdoshim) who perished in the Nazi Holocaust (hasho'a). It takes place on the 27th day of the Jewish month of Nissan (in late April), the day that began the Warsaw Ghetto uprising against the Nazis.

Shabat (Sabbath)

Shabat or Shabbos (the Sabbath) is known as the 'bride', and for this day Jews dress in their 'wedding' best. The Jewish week is divided between the 'holy' (kodesh) Shabat and the 'profane' (khol) working week.

Beginning on Friday at sundown, Shabat follows the Biblical command to rest on the seventh day. 'Resting' means a cessation of 'creating', so those who observe Shabat don't drive, carry anything outside the home, cook, write, read anything non-spiritual, bathe or bleed (so teeth aren't brushed in case the gums bleed). Since tearing paper is forbidden, toilet paper must be torn in preparation for Shabat. In order to allow worshippers to carry books or push prams during Shabat, an eruv is formed by stringing a high wire around the perimeter of the community, which forms a 'gate' within which people may act as though in their own home. Observant Jews only break the Sabbath to rescue a person whose life is in danger, such as through accident or illness.

The Shabat evening meal begins when the female head of the household lights the two Shabbat candles and makes a blessing. Next, the male head of the household makes a blessing (kiddush) over wine (see page 160) that's been poured into a special goblet, called a 'Kiddush Cup'. Finally, a bread blessing (motzi) is made over the braided khala bread (see page 160). During the meal, family and friends enjoy a leisurely dinner.

After a day of peaceful meditation in the synagogue and at home, Shabat ends with a farewell service, called Havdala (the division between the holy Sabbath and the profane working week). A glass of wine, a braided havdala candle and a spice box filled with sweet smelling spices are three key symbols of the Havdala service. The spice box, with its sweet smell, wakes people from the dreamlike state of Shabat. The flame of the havdala candle is reflected in worshippers' fingernails, representing the glow of the Shabat light. Worshippers reluctantly part with the beauty of Shabat by extinguishing the candle into the wine cup and by singing a song praying for the coming week.

The rest of Shabat is a time for complete relaxation, and is well worth the experience. However, only about 20 per cent of the Israeli population refrain from 'creating' on Shabat. Many orthodox communities block off their streets to cars on Shabat.

The division between Shabat-observant and partially or non-observant Jews has led to heated confrontations, and might over the long-run split the nation in two, as in ancient times. The non-religious believe that their rights are being restricted by the religious in their country, which by law is a secular one. Israel has debated the role of Judaism in daily life ever since Israel's founding. This unresolved issue has prevented Israel from adopting a Constitution.

NUMBERS & AMOUNTS

CARDINAL NUMBERS מספרים יסודיים

Hebrew has a set of cardinal numbers for counting feminine objects, and one for counting masculine objects. Feminine numbers are used in straightforward counting.

	Feminine		Masculine	
0	efes	אפס	efes	אפס
1	akhat	אחת	ekhad	אחד
2	shta'im	שתיים	shna'im	שניים
3	shalosh	שלוש	shlosha	שלושה
4	arba	ארבע	arba'a	ארבעה
5	khamesh	חמש	khamisha	חמישה
6	shesh	שש	shisha	שישה
7	sheva	שבע	shiv'a	שבעה
8	shmone	שמונה	shmona	שמונה
9	tesha	תשע	tish'a	תשעה
10	eser	עשר	asara	עשרה
11	akhat-esre	אחת-עשרה	akhad-asar	אחד-עשר
12	shteim-esre	שתים-עשרה	shneim-asar	שניים-עשר
13	shlosh-esre	שלוש-עשרה	shlosha-asar	שלושה-עשר
14	arba esre	ארבע-עשרה	arba'a-asar	ארבעה-עשר
15	khamesh-esre	חמש-עשרה	khamisha-asar	חמישה-עשר
16	shesh-esre	שש-עשרה	shisha-asar	שישה-עשר
17	shva-esre	שבע-עשרה	shiv'a-asar	שבעה-עשר
18	shmone-esre	שמונה-עשרה	shmona-asar	שמונה-עשר
19	tsha-esre	תשע-עשרה	tish'a-asar	תשעה-עשר
20	esrim	עשרים	esrim	עשרים
21	esrim ve'akhat	עשרים ואחת	esrim ve'ekhad	עשרים ואחד
22	esrim ushta'im	עשרים ושתיים	esrim ushna'im	עשרים ושניים
30			shloshim	שלושים

40	arba'im	ארבעים
50	khamishim	חמישים
60	shishim	שישים
70	shiv'im	שבעים
80	shmonim	שמונים
90	tish'im	תשעים
100	me'a	מאה
1000	elef	אלף
one million	million	מליון

When used to modify a noun, cardinal numbers (except the number 'one') precede the noun they qualify.

| kamisha muze'onim | five museums |
| kamesh kafeteryot | five cafeterias |

The number 'one' follows the noun it qualifies.

| student ekhad (m) | one student |
| studentit akhat (f) | one student |

When the number is 'two', it precedes the noun, but it's form is modified from shna'im (m) to shnei and shta'im (f) to shtei.

| shnei khaverim (m) | two friends |
| shtei khaverot (f) | two friends |

NUMBERS & AMOUNTS

THE HOLY LAND

In Hebrew, Jerusalem is called Yerushala'im, the 'City of Peace'. Israel's capital has three distinct areas – East Jerusalem, the Old City and the New City.

The Old City contains many important Jewish, Muslim and Christian sites. Har HaBayit, the 'Temple Mount', is where the sacred First and Second Temples were built. The Hakotel Hama'aravi, or 'the Western Wall', the only remaining part of the Second Temple, is the most holy of all Jewish sites.

THE HOLY LAND

The Temple Mount, or 'Haram ash-Sharif' (Noble Sanctuary) in Arabic, is also home to the Dome of the Rock, which enshrines the sacred rock on which Abraham prepared to sacrifice his son. According to Islamic tradition, this is where the Prophet Mohammed rose to heaven to take his place alongside Allah.

The Old City also hosts the christian Church of the Holy Sepulchre, believed to be the site of Jesus' cruxifixion, burial and resurrection.

Jerusalem's first known settlement, mentioned in texts dating from the 20th century BC, was conquered in 997 BC by the Israelites. Their leader, King David, made the city his capital and began construction of the First Temple. Several centuries later, Jerusalem fell to Babylon, and both city and Temple were destroyed. After a time of exile in Babylon, which marked the beginning of the Diaspora, Jews returned to the city and built the Second Temple around 520 BC.

The Romans conquered Jerusalem in around 63 BC. The city was administered by Herod the Great, followed by a series of procurators – among them Pontius Pilate, best known for ordering Jesus' crucifixion in around 30 AD.

Thirty-six years later, an unsuccessful revolt led to the destruction of the Second Temple and the enslavement or exile of many Jews. In 132 AD, after a second revolt sparked by the complete destruction of Jerusalem, Jews were forbidden entry to Aelia Capitolina, the city built on the ruins of Jerusalem, which served as the foundation for today's Old City.

A period of almost 1300 years of Muslim supremacy began around 639, after an Arab army led under the banner of Islam swept through Palestine. After the Turkish sultan issued the Edict of Toleration for all religions in 1856, Jews and Christians again settled in the city, and Jewish immigrant settlements outside the city walls developed into what is now the New City.

In the 1948 War, the Jordanians took control of the Old City and East Jerusalem, while the Jews held the New City. Jerusalem remained divided for 19 years, until its reunification after the 1967 Six Day War, since which they city has undergone a period of restoration.

NUMBERS & AMOUNTS

ORDINAL NUMBERS

מספרים סידוריים

Like cardinal numbers, ordinal numbers have both masculine
and feminine forms. They're formed by changing the suffix of
the masculine cardinal number to -i, and changing the vowel of
the second-last syllable to i. To get the feminine form, the suffix
-t is added.

10 (m)	asara	עשרה
10th	asiri(t)	עשירי(ת)

The numbers '1st', '2nd' and '4th' are formed differently from
other ordinals. The masculine form of the number 'one', ekhad,
becomes rishon, and the feminine form, akhat, becomes rishona.
These words derive from the word rosh, meaning 'head' (the first
in line is the 'head' of the line).

The number 'two', shna'im (m), becomes sheni, and shta'im (f)
becomes shniya. The number four, arba'a, loses its first syllable to
become revi'i (m) and revi'it (f).

1st	rishon(a)	ראשון(ה)
2nd	sheni (shniya)	שני (שניה)
3rd	shlishi(t)	שלישי(ת)
4th	revi'i(t)	רביעי(ת)

For numbers from 11 and up, the ordinal number is created by
adding the article ha- in front of the cardinal number.

13th	ha-shlosha asar (m)
	ha-shlosh esre (f)

EMERGENCIES

Help!	hatsilu!	הצילו!
Stop!	atsor!	עצור!
Go away!	lekh mipo!	לך מפה!
Thief!	ganav!	גנב!
Fire!	sreifa!	שריפה!
Watch out!	zehirut!	זהירות!
It's an emergency!	ze mikre kherum!	זה מקרה חרום!
Call a doctor!	likro lerofe!	לקרוא לרופא!
Call an ambulance!	likro le'ambulance!	לקרוא לאמבולנס!
I'm ill.	ani khole (khola)	אני חולה (חולה).

My friend is ill.
hakhaver(a) sheli khole (khola)
החבר(ה) שלי חולה (חולה).

I have medical insurance.
yesh li bitu'akh refu'i
יש לי ביטוח רפואי.

Could you help us please?
ata yakhol la'azor lanu?
אתה יכול לעזור לנו?

Could I please use the telephone?
slikha, efshar lehishtamesh
batelefon?
סליחה, אפשר להשתמש בטלפון?

I'm lost.
ta'iti baderekh
תעיתי בדרך.

Where are the toilets?
eifo hasherutim?
איפה השירותים?

Call the police!
likro lamistara!
לקרוא למשטרה!

Where's the police station?
eifo takhanat hamishtara?
איפה תחנת המשטרה?

I've been raped.
ne'enasti
נאנסתי.

I've been assaulted.	
hutkafti	הותקפתי.

I've been robbed.	
shadedu oti	שדדו אותי.

My possessions are insured.	
hakhafatsim sheli mevutakhim	החפצים שלי מבוטחים.

My ... was/were stolen.	ganvu li et ha ...	... גנבו לי את ה ...
backpack	tarmil gav	תרמיל גב
bags	tikim	תיקים
handbag	tik yad	תיק יד
money	kesef	כסף
papers	te'udot	תעודות
passport	darkon	דרכון
travellers cheques	travelers cheks	טרוולרס צ'קס
wallet	arnak	ארנק

DEALING WITH THE POLICE   בתחנת המשטרה

We want to report an offence.	
anakhnu rotsim ledave'akh al avera	אנחנו רוצים לדווח על עבירה.

I'm sorry/I apologise.	
ani mitsta'er(et)	אני מצטער(ת).

I didn't realise I was doing anything wrong.	
lo te'arti le'atsmi she'asiti	לא תארתי לעצמי שעשיתי
mashehu lo nakhon	משהו לא נכון.

I didn't do it.	
lo asiti et ze	לא עשיתי את זה.

We're innocent.	
anakhnu khapim mipesha	אנחנו חפים מפשע.

We're foreigners.	
anakhnu zarim	אנחנו זרים.

I want to contact my embassy/consulate.	
ani rotse (rotsa) lehitkasher im	אני רוצה (רוצה) להתקשר עם
hashagrirut/hakonsulia sheli	השגרירות/הקונסוליה שלי.

Can I call someone?

| ani yakhol (yekhola) | אני יכול (יכולה) |
| letsaltsel lemishehu? | לצלצל למישהו? |

Can I have a lawyer who speaks English?

| ani yakhol (yekhola) lekabel | אני יכול (יכולה) לקבל |
| orekh-din dover anglit? | עורך-דין דובר אנגלית? |

Is there a fine we can pay to clear this?

| efshar leshalem knas | אפשר לשלם קנס |
| ulehasdir zot? | ולהסדיר זאת? |

Can we pay an on-the-spot fine?

| efshar leshalem et haknas miyad? | אפשר לשלם את הקנס מיד? |

I understand.

| ani mevin(a) | אני מבין(ה). |

I don't understand.

| ani lo mevin(a) | אני לא מבין(ה). |

I know my rights.

| ani makir(a) et zkhuyotai | אני מכיר(ה) את זכויותי. |

What am I accused of?

| bema ani mu'asham | במה אני מואשם |
| (mu'ashemet)? | (מואשמת)? |

arrested	asur	אסור
cell	ta	תא
consulate	konsulia	קונסוליה
embassy	shagrirut	שגרירות
fine (payment)	knas	קנס
guilty	ashem	אשם
lawyer	orekh din	עורך דין
not guilty	zaka'i	זכאי
police (officer)	(ktsin) mishtara	(קצין) משטרה
police station	takhanat mishtara	תחנת משטרה
prison	bet sohar	בית סוהר
trial	mishpat	משפט

THE POLICE MAY SAY

tu'asham (tu'ashmi) be ...
  You'll be charged with ...   תואשם (תואשמי) ב ...

hi tu'asham be ...
  She'll be charged with ...   היא תואשם ב ...

hu yu'asham be...	He'll be charged with ...	הוא יואשם ב ...
pe'ilut anti-memshaltit	anti-government activity	פעילות אנטי-ממשלתית
tkifa	assault	תקיפה
hafarat seder	disturbing the peace	הפרת סדר
hakhzakat samim	possession (of illegal substances)	החזקת סמים
knisa bilti khukit	illegal entry	כניסה בלתי חוקית
retsakh	murder	רצח
lelo visa	not possessing a visa	ללא ויזה
pki'at tokef ha'ashra	overstaying your visa	פקיעת תוקף האשרה
ones	rape	אונס
shod	robbery	שוד
skhiva mekhanut	traffic violation	"סחיבה" מחנות
averat tnu'a	shoplifting	עבירת תנועה
gneiva	theft	גניבה
avoda lelo rishayon	working without a permit	עבודה ללא רישיון

The consonants in the transliteration of the Hebrew words have the same sound value as they do in English. You may find, however, that some words are a trifle difficult to pronounce, since a consonant is not always followed by a vowel. Words like atsma'i, zkhuyot and shkhakh take some practice. See pages 17-19 or page 223 for the pronunciation of vowels and consonants.

You'll probably be inclined to pronounce more (teacher) as in 'have *more* wine' and nose (question) as in 'my *nose* is bleeding', but these words in Hebrew have two syllables and should be pronounced as mo-re and no-se respectively, with the 'e' pronounced as in 'karate'. Also, when two vowels follow each other but are pronounced as two different syllables, they are separated by the "'"symbol. Me'il (overcoat) is pronounced 'me-il' and not 'meil', and me'al (above) is pronounced 'me-al' and not 'meal'. Good luck!

A

able (to be); can	liheyot yakhol yakhol	להיות יכול

Can (may) I take your photo?
efshar letsalem otkha?

אפשר לצלם אותך?

Can you show me on the map?
ata yakhol lehar'ot li al hamapa?

אתה יכול להראות לי על המפה?

aboard	be	ב
abortion	hapala	הפלה
above	me'al	מעל
abroad	khuts la'arets	חוץ לארץ
to accept	lehaskim	להסכים
accident	te'una	תאונה
accommodation	diyur	דיור
across	me'ever	מעבר
activist	pa'il	פעיל
addiction	hitmakrut	התמכרות
address	ktovet	כתובת
to admire	leha'arits	להעריץ

admission (to a museum)	dmei knisa	דמי כניסה
to admit	lehodot be ...	להודות ב ...
adult	boger	בוגר
advantage	yitaron	יתרון
advice	etsa	עצה
aeroplane	matos	מטוס
to be afraid of	lefakhed me ...	לפחד מ ...
after	akhrei	אחרי
afternoon	akhar hatsohora'im	אחר הצהריים
this afternoon	hayom akhar hatsohora'im	היום אחר הצהריים
again	shuv	שוב
against	neged	נגד
age	gil	גיל
aggressive	tokpani	תוקפני
(a while) ago	lifnei (zman ma)	לפני (זמן מה)
(half an hour) ago	lifnei (khatsi sha'a)	לפני (חצי שעה)
(three days) ago	lifnei (shlosha yamim)	לפני (שלושה ימים)

to agree	lehaskim	להסכים
I don't agree.		
ani lo maskim(a).		.(אני לא מסכים(ה
Agreed!		
muskam!		!מוסכם
agriculture	khakla'ut	חקלאות
ahead	kadima	קדימה
aid (help)	ezra	עזרה
AIDS	aids	איידס
air	avir	אוויר
air-conditioned	mizug avir	מיזוג אוויר
air mail	do'ar avir	דואר אוויר
airport	sde te'ufa	שדה תעופה
airport tax	mas namal	מס נמל
alarm clock	sha'on me'orer	שעון מעורר
all	hakol	הכל
an allergy	alergya	אלרגיה
to allow	leharshot	להרשות
it's allowed	efshar	אפשר
it's not allowed	yi efshar	אי אפשר
almost	kim'at	כמעט
alone	levad	לבד
already	kvar	כבר
also	gam	גם
altitude	gova	גובה
always	tamid	תמיד
amateur	khovev	חובב
ambassador	shagrir	שגריר
among	bein	בין
anarchist	anarkhist	אנרכיסט
ancient	atik	עתיק
and	ve ...	ו ...
angry	ko'es	כועס
animals	khayot	חיות
annual	shnati	שנתי
answer	tshuva	תשובה

to answer	la'anot	לענות
ant	nemala	נמלה
antibiotics	antibiotika	אנטיביוטיקה
antinuclear	anti-gar'ini	אנטי-גרעיני
antiques	atikot	עתיקות
antiseptic	mekhate	מחטא
any	kolshehu	כלשהו
appointment	pgisha	פגישה
archaeological	arkhe'ologi	ארכיאולוגי
architect	arkhitekt	ארכיטקט
architecture	arkhitektura	ארכיטקטורה
to argue	lehitvake'akh	להתווכח
arm	zro'a	זרוע
to arrive	lehagi'a	להגיע
arrivals	haga'ot	הגעות
art	omanut	אמנות
art gallery	galeria	גלריה
artist	oman	אמן
artwork	yetsirat omanut	יצירת אמנות
ashtray	ma'afera	מאפרה
to ask (for something)	levakesh (mashehu)	לבקש (משהו)
to ask (a question)	lish'ol (she'ela)	לשאול (שאלה)
aspirin	aspirin	אספירין
asthmatic	asmati	אסמתי
atmosphere	avira	אווירה
aunt	doda	דודה
automatic teller (ATM)	kaspomat	כספומט
autumn	stav	סתיו
avenue	shdera	שדרה
awful	nora	נורא

B

baby	tinok	תינוק
baby food	okhel tinokot	אוכל תינוקות

English	Transliteration	Hebrew
baby powder	avkat tinokot	אבקת תינוקות
babysitter	shmartaf	שמרטף
back (body)	gav	גב
at the back (behind)	me'akhor	מאחור
backpack	tarmil gav	תרמיל גב
bad	ra	רע
bag	tik	תיק
baggage	mit'an	מטען
baggage claim	mizvadot	מזוודות
bakery	ma'afiya	מאפיה
balcony	mirpeset	מרפסת
ball	kadur	כדור
ballet	balet	בלט
band (music)	lehaka	להקה
bandage	takhboshet	תחבושת
bank	bank	בנק
banknotes	shtarot kesef	שטרות כסף
baptism	tvila	טבילה
bar; café	bar; bet kafe	באר, בית קפה
basket	sal	סל
bath	ambatiya	אמבטיה
bathing suit	beged yam	בגד ים
bathroom	khadar ambatiya	חדר אמבטיה
battery	solela	סוללה
to be	liheyot	להיות
beach	khof yam	חוף ים
beautiful	yafe	יפה
because	ki	כי
bed	mita	מיטה
bedroom	khadar shena	חדר שינה
before	lifnei	לפני
beggar	mekabets nedavot	מקבץ נדבות
begin	lehatkhil	להתחיל

English	Transliteration	Hebrew
behind	me'akhor	מאחור
below	mitakhat	מתחת
beside	leyad	ליד
best	hatov beyoter	הטוב ביותר
a bet	himur	הימור
between	bein	בין
the Bible	haTanakh	התנ"ך
bicycle	ofana'im	אופניים
big	gadol	גדול
to bike	lirkav al ...	לרכב על ...
bill	kheshbon	חשבון
binoculars	mishkefet	משקפפתי
biography	biografiya	ביוגרפיה
bird	tsipor	ציפור
birth certificate	te'udat leida	תעודת לידה
birthday	yom huledet	יום הולדת
birthday cake	ugat yom-huledet	עוגת יום-הולדת
bite (dog)	neshikha	נשיכה
bite (insect)	akitsa	עקיצה
black	shakhor	שחור
B&W (film)	seret shakhor lavan	סרט שחור לבן
blanket	smikha	שמיכה
to bleed	ledamem	לדמם
to bless	levarekh	לברך
Bless you! (when sneezing) labri'ut!		לבריאות!
blind	iver	עיוור
blood	dam	דם
blood group	sug dam	סוג דם
blood pressure	lakhats dam	לחץ דם
blood test	bdikat dam	בדיקת דם
blue	kakhol	כחול
to board (ship, etc)	la'alot (la'oniya)	לעלות (לאוניה ...)
boarding pass	kartis aliya lamatos	כרטיס עליה למטוס

English	Transliteration	Hebrew
boat	oniya	אוניה
body	guf	גוף
Bon appétit!		
bete'avon!		בתאבון!
Bon voyage!		
derekh tslekha!		דרך צלחה!
bone	etsem	עצם
book	sefer	ספר
to book (make a booking)	lehazmin merosh	להזמין מראש
bookshop	khanut sfarim	חנות ספרים
boots	magafa'im	מגפים
border	gvul	גבול
bored	meshu'amam	משועמם
boring	mesha'amem	משעמם
to borrow	lish'ol	לשאול
both	shneihem	שניהם
bottle	bakbuk	בקבוק
bottle opener	potkhan bakbukim	פותחן בקבוקים
(at the) bottom	batakhtit	בתחתית
box	kufsa	קופסא
boxing	he'avkut	האבקות
boy	yeled	ילד
boyfriend	khaver	חבר
branch (bank etc)	snif	סניף
branch (tree)	anaf	ענף
brave	gibor	גיבור
bread	lekhem	לחם
to break	lishbor	לשבור
broken	shavur	שבור
breakfast	arukhat boker	ארוחת בוקר
to breathe	linshom	לנשום
a bribe	shokhad	שוחד
to bribe	leshakhed	לשחד

English	Transliteration	Hebrew
bridge	gesher	גשר
brilliant	mavrik	מבריק
to bring	lehavi	להביא
brother	akh	אח
brown	khum	חום
a bruise	maka	מכה
bucket	dli	דלי
Buddhist	buddhisti	בודהיסטי
bug	kherek	חרק
to build	livnot	לבנות
building	binyan	בניין
bus (city)	otobus (ironi)	אוטובוס (עירוני)
bus (intercity)	otobus (bein-ironi)	אוטובוס (בין-עירוני)
bus station	takhana merkazit	תחנה מרכזית
bus stop	takhanat otobus	תחנת אוטובוס
business	esek	עסק
business person	ish asakim	איש עסקים
busker	nagan rehov	נגן רחוב
busy	asuk	עסוק
but	aval	אבל
butterfly	parpar	פרפר
buttons	kaftorim	כפתורים
to buy	liknot	לקנות

I'd like to buy ...
ani rotse (rotsa) liknot ...

אני רוצה (רוצה) לקנות ...

Where can I buy a ticket?
eifo konim kartisim?

איפה קונים כרטיסים?

C

English	Transliteration	Hebrew
calendar	lu'akh shana	לוח שנה
camera	matslema	מצלמה

camera operator	tsalam	צלם
camera shop	khanut tsilum	חנות צילום
to camp	lehakim ohel	להקים אוהל

Can we camp here?

efshar lehakim kan ohel?

אפשר להקים כאן אוהל?

| campsite | makhane | מחנה |
| can (to be able) | efshar, yakhol | אפשר, יכול |

We can do it.

anakhnu yekholim la'asot zot.

אנחנו יכולים לעשות זאת.

I can't do it.

ani lo yakhol la'asot ze.

אני לא יכול לעשות את זה.

can (aluminium)	pakhit	פחית
can opener	potkhan kufsa'ot	פותחן קופסאות
to cancel	levatel	לבטל
candle	ner	נר
car	mekhonit	מכונית
car owner's title	te'udat ba'alut al hamkhonit	תעודת בעלות על המכונית
car registration	te'udat rishui	תעודת רישוי
to care (about)	ikhpat	אכפת
to care (for someone)	lid'og le	לדאוג ל
cards	klafim	קלפים

Careful!

zehirut!

זהירות!

| caring | do'eg | דואג |
| to carry | laset | לשאת |

carton	carton	קרטון
cartoons	sratim metsuyarim	סרטים מצויירים
cash register	kupa	קופה
cashier	kupa'i(t)	קופאי(ת)
cassette	kaletet	קלטת
castle	tira	טירה
cat	khatul	חתול
cathedral	katedrala	קתדרלה
Catholic	katoli	קתולי
caves	me'arot	מערות
CD	compakt disk	קומפקט דיסק
to celebrate	lakhagog	לחגוג
centimetre	centimetre	סנטימטר
ceramic	keramika	קרמיקה
certificate	te'uda	תעודה
chair	kise	כסא
champagne	shampanya	שמפניה
championship	alifut	אליפות
chance	hizdamnut	הזדמנות
to change	lehakhlif	להחליף
change (coins)	kesef katan	כסף קטן
changing room	khadar halbasha	חדר הלבשה
charming	maksim	מקסים
to chat up	lefatpet	לפטפט
cheap hotel	malon zol	מלון זול
a cheat	hona'a	הונאה

Cheat!

rama'i!

רמאי!

| to check | livdok | לבדוק |
| check-in (desk) | delpak rishum | דלפק רישום |

Checkmate!

shakhmat

שחמט

| checkpoint | takhanat bikoret | תחנת ביקורת |

C

English	Translit	Hebrew
cheese	gvina	גבינה
chemist	roke'akh	רוקח
chess	shakh	שח
chess board	lu'akh shakhmat	לוח שחמט
chest	khaze	חזה
chewing gum	mastik	מסטיק
chicken	of	עוף
child	yeled	ילד
childminding	ma'on yeladim	מעון ילדים
children	yeladim	ילדים
chocolate	shokolad	שוקולד
to choose	livkhor	לבחור
Christian	notsri	נוצרי
christian name	shem prati	שם פרטי
Christmas Day	khag hamolad	חג המולד
Christmas Eve	erev khag hamolad	ערב חג המולד
church	knesiya	כנסיה
cigarette papers	neyar sigariyot	נייר סיגריות
cigarettes	sigariyot	סיגריות
cinema	kolno'a	קולנוע
circus	kirkas	קרקס
citizenship	ezrakhut	אזרחות
city	ir	עיר
city centre	merkaz ha'ir	מרכז העיר
city walls	khomot ha'ir	חומות העיר
class	kita	כיתה
class system	ma'amadot	מעמדות
classical art	omanut klassit	אמנות קלסית
classical theatre	teatron klassi	תיאטרון קלסי
clean	naki	נקי
clean hotel	malon naki	מלון נקי
cleaning	nikayon	ניקיון
client	lako'akh	לקוח

English	Translit	Hebrew
cliff	matsok	מצוק
to climb	letapes	לטפס
cloak	glima	גלימה
cloakroom	meltakha	מלתחה
clock	sha'on	שעון
to close	lisgor	לסגור
closed	sagur	סגור
clothing	bgadim	בגדים
clothing store	khanut bgadim	חנות בגדים
cloud	anan	ענן
cloudy	me'unan	מעונן
clown	leitsan	ליצן
coast	khof	חוף
coat	me'il	מעיל
cocaine	cocaine	קוקאין
coins	matbe'ot	מטבעות
a cold	tsinun	צינון
cold (adj)	kar	קר
It's cold. kar		קר.
I have a cold. ani metsunan		אני מצונן.
cold water	mayim karim	מים קרים
colleague	kolega	קולגה
college	college	קולג'
colour	tseva	צבע
comb	masrek	מסרק
to come	lavo	לבוא
to come (arrive)	lehagi'a	להגיע
comedy	komedia	קומדיה
comfortable	no'akh	נוח
comics	khovrot metsuyarot	חוברות מצויירות
communion	akhilat lekhem hakodesh	אכילת לחם הקודש

D I C T I O N A R Y

communion	akhilat	אכילת
	lekhem	לחם
	hakodesh	הקודש
communist	komunisti	קומוניסטי
companion	khaver	חבר
company	khevra	חברה
compass	matspen	מצפן
computer	miskhakei	משחקי מחשב
games	makhshev	
concert	concert	קונצרט
confession	vidui	וידוי
(religious)		
to confirm	le'asher	לאשר
(a booking)		

Congratulations!
mazal tov!
מזל טוב!

conservative	shamran	שמרן
to be	lisbol	לסבול
constipated	me'atsirut	מעצירות
constipation	atsirut	עצירות
construction	avodot	עבודות
work	bniya	בניה
consulate	konsuliya	קונסוליה
contact lenses	adshot maga	עדשות מגע
contraception	meni'at	מניעת
	herayon	הריון
contraceptives	emtsa'ei	אמצעי
	meni'a	מניעה
contract	khoze	חוזה
convent	minzr nashim	מנזר נשים
to cook	levashel	לבשל
cool (colloquial)	kef	כיף
corner	pina	פינה
corrupt	mushkhat	מושחת
to cost	la'alot	לעלות

How much is it to go to ...?
kama ole linso'a le ...?

כמה עולה לנסוע ל ...?

It costs a lot.		
ze ole hamon		זה עולה המון.
cotton	kutna	כותנה
country	erets	מדינה
countryside	ezor kafri	אזור כפרי
a cough	shi'ul	שיעול
to count	lispor	לספור
coupon	tlush	שובר
court (legal)	bet mishpat	בית משפט
court (tennis)	migrash	מגרש
	(tennis)	(טניס)
cow	para	פרה
crafts	omanuyot	אומנויות
crafty	armumi	ערמומי
crag; wall of	kir sla'im	קיר סלעים
rock		
crazy	meshuga	משוגע
credit card	kartis ashra'i	כרטיס אשראי
creep (slang)	sherets	שרץ
cricket	miskhak	משחק
	kriket	קריקט
cross	tslav	צלב
(religious)		
cross (angry)	ko'es	כועס
a cuddle	khibuk	חיבוק
cup	sefel	ספל
cupboard	aron	ארון
curator	otser	אוצר
current	inyanei	ענייני
affairs	hasha'a	השעה
customs	mekhes	מכס
to cut	lakhatokh	לחתוך
to cycle	lirkav	לרכב על אופניים
cycling	rekhiva al	רכיבה על
	ofna'im	אופניים
cyclist	rokhev	רוכב
	ofna'im	אופנים
cystitis	daleket	דלקת
	shalpukhit	שלפוחית
	hasheten	השתן

D

dad	aba	אבא
daily	yomi	יומי
dairy products	mutsarei khalav	מוצרי חלב
to dance	lirkod	לרקוד
dancing	rikudim	ריקוד
dangerous	mesukan	מסוכן
dark	khashukh	חושך
date (appointment)	pgisha	פגישה
date (time)	ta'arikh	תאריך
to date (someone)	latset im	לצאת עם
date of birth	ta'arikh leida	תאריך לידה
daughter	bat	בת
dawn	shakhar	שחר
day	yom	יום
day after tomorrow	mokhrota'im	מחרתיים
day before yesterday	shilshom	שלשום
in (six) days	be'od (shisha) yamim	בעוד (שישה) ימים
dead	met	מת
deaf	kheresh	חרש
to deal in	la'asok be	לעסוק ב
death	mavet	מוות
to decide	lehakhlit	להחליט
deck (of cards)	khafisat klafim	חפיסת קלפים
deep	amok	עמוק
deer	tsvi	צבי
deforestation	be'ur ye'arot	ביעור יערות
degree	to'ar	תואר
delay	ekhur	איחור
delicatessen	ma'adaniya	מעדניה
delirious	hoze	הוזה

democracy	demokratiya	דמוקרטיה
demonstration	hafgana	הפגנה
dental floss	khut leniku'i shina'im	חוט לניקוי שיניים
dentist	rofe shina'im	רופא שניים
to deny	lehak'khish	להכחיש
deodorant	deodorant	דאודורנט
to depart (leave)	lehipared	להיפרד
department store	khanut kolbo	חנות כלבו
departure	yetsi'a	יציאה
descendent	tse'etsa	צאצא
desert	midbar	מדבר
design	tokhnit	תוכנית
destination	ya'ad	יעד
to destroy	laharos	להרוס
detail	prat	פרט
diabetic	khole sakeret	חולה סכרת
dial tone	tslil khiyug	צליל חיוג
diarrhoea	shilshul	שלשול
diary	yoman	יומן
dice	kubiyot miskhak	קוביות משחק
dictionary	milon	מילון
to die	lamut	למות
different	shone/akher	שונה/אחר
difficult	kashe	קשה
dining car	kron mis'ada	קרון מסעדה
dinner	arukhat erev	ארוחת ערב
direct	yashir	ישיר
director	menahel	מנהל
dirty	melukhlakh	מלוכלך
disabled	nekhe	נכה
disadvantage	khisaron	חסרון
discount	hanakha	הנחה
to discover	legalot	לגלות
discrimination	aflaya	אפליה

E

disease	makhala	מחלה
dismissal	bitul	ביטול
distributor	mefits	מפיץ
diving	tslila	צלילה
diving equipment	tsiyud tslila	ציוד צלילה
(I'm) dizzy. yesh li skharkhoret.		יש לי סחרחורת.
to do	la'asot	לעשות
What are you doing? ma ata ose?		מה אתה עושה?
I didn't do it. lo asiti et ze		לא עשיתי את זה.
doctor	rofe	רופא
documentary	seret ti'udi	סרט תיעודי
dog	kelev	כלב
dole	dmei avtala	דמי אבטלה
dolls	bubot	בובות
door	delet	דלת
dope (drugs)	khashish	חשיש
double	kaful	כפול
a double bed	mita kfula	מיטה כפולה
a double room	kheder lishna'im	חדר לשניים
a dozen	treisar	תריסר
drama	drama	דרמה
dramatic	dramati	דרמטי
to dream	lakhalom	לחלום
dress	simla	שמלה
a drink	mashke	משקה
to drink	lishtot	לשתות
to drive	linhog	לנהוג
driver's licence	rishyon nehiga	רשיון נהיגה
drug	sam	סם
drug addiction	hitmakrut lesamim	התמכרות לסמים

drug dealer	sokher samim	סוחר סמים
drugs	samim	סמים
drums	tupim	תופים
to be drunk	liheyot shatui	להיות שתוי
to dry (clothes)	leyabesh	לייבש
dummy (pacifier)	motsets	מוצץ

E

each	kol ekhad	כל אחד
ear	ozen	אוזן
early	mukdam	מוקדם
It's early. ze mukdam		זה מוקדם.
to earn	leharvi'akh	להרוויח
earrings	agilim	עגילים
ears	ozna'im	אוזניים
Earth	kadur ha'arets	כדור הארץ
earth (soil)	adama	אדמה
earthquake	re'idat adama	רעידת אדמה
east	mizrakh	מזרח
Easter	khag hapaskha	חג הפסחא
easy	kal	קל
to eat	le'ekhol	לאכול
economy	kalkala	כלכלה
editor	orekh	עורך
education	khinukh	חינוך
elections	bkhirot	בחירות
electorate	tsibur bokharim	ציבור בוחרים
electricity	khashmal	חשמל
elevator	ma'alit	מעלית
embarassed	navokh	נבוך
embarassment	mevukha	מבוכה
embassy	shagrirut	שגרירות

E

D
I
C
T
I
O
N
A
R
Y

F

English	Transliteration	Hebrew
emergency	kherum	חירום
employee	sakhir	שכיר
employer	ma'asik	מעסיק
empty	rek	ריק
end	sof	סוף
to end	lesayem	לסיים
endangered	zanim	זנים
species	nik'khadim	נכחדים
engagement	erusim	אירוסים
engine	mano'a	מנוע
engineer	mehandes	מהנדס
engineering	handasa	הנדסה
English	anglit	אנגלית
to enjoy	levalot	לבלות
(oneself)		
enough	maspik	מספיק
Enough!		
dai!		די!
to enter	lehikanes	להכנס
entertaining	mesha'ashe'a	משעשע
envelope	ma'atafa	מעטפה
environment	sviva	סביבה
epileptic	khole	חולה
	bemakhalat	במחלת
	hanefila	הנפילה
equal	hizdamnuyot	הזדמנויות
opportunity	shavot	שוות
equality	shivyon	שיוויון
equipment	tsiyud	ציוד
European	erope'i	אירופאי
euthanasia	hamatat	המתת חסד
	khesed	
evening	erev	ערב
every day	kol yom	כל יום
example	dugma	דוגמא
For example, ...		
lemashal, ...		למשל, ...
excellent	metsuyan	מצוין

English	Transliteration	Hebrew
exchange	khilufim	חילופים
to exchange	lehakhlif	להחליף
exchange	sha'ar	שער
rate	khalifin	חליפין
excluded	mutsa min	מוצא מן
	haklal	הכלל
Excuse me.		
slikha		סליחה.
to exhibit	lehatsig	להציג
exhibition	ta'arukha	תערוכה
exit	yetsi'a	יציאה
expensive	yakar	יקר
exploitation	nitsul	ניצול
express	express	אקספרס
express mail	do'ar	דואר
	express	אקספרס
eye	a'in	עין

F

English	Transliteration	Hebrew
face	panim	פנים
factory	bet kharoshet	בית חרושת
factory worker	po'el	פועל
fall (autumn)	stav	סתיו
family	mishpakha	משפחה
famous	mefursam	מפורסם
fan	menifa	מניפה
(hand-held)		
fan (machine)	me'avrer	מאוורר
fans (of	ohadim	אוהדים
a team)		
far	rakhok	רחוק
farm	khava	חווה
farmer	ikar	איכר
fast	maher	מהר
fat	shamen	שמן
father	aba	אבא
father-in-law	khoten	חותן

English	Transliteration	Hebrew
fault (someone's)	ashma	אשמה
faulty	pagum	פגום
fear	pakhad	פחד
to feel	lehargish	להרגיש
feelings	regashot	רגשות
fence	gader	גדר
fencing (with swords)	siyuf	סיוף
festival	festival	פסטיבל
fever	khom	חום
few	akhadim	אחדים
fiancé(e)	arus(a)	ארוס(ה)
fiction	siporet	סיפורת
field	sade	שדה
fight	krav	קרב
to fight	lehilakhem	להלחם
figures	dmuyot	דמויות
to fill	lemale	למלא
a film (negatives)	seret tsilum	סרט צילום
film (cinema)	seret kolno'a	סרט קולנוע
film (for camera)	film	פילם
film speed	mehirut film	מהירות פילם
films (movies)	kolno'a	קולנוע
filtered	mesunan	מסונן
to find	limtso	למצוא
a fine	knas	קנס
finger	etsba	אצבע
fir	ashu'akh	אשוח
fire	esh	אש
firewood	atsei hasaka	עצי הסקה
first	rishon	ראשון
first-aid kit	tik ezra rishona	תיק עזרה ראשונה
fish (alive)	dag	דג
fish (as food)	dag	דג
fish shop	khanut dagim	חנות דגים

English	Transliteration	Hebrew
flag	degel	דגל
flat (land, etc)	shatu'akh	שטוח
flea	pishpeshim	פשפשים
flashlight	panas	פנס
flight	tisa	טיסה
floor	ritspa	ריצפה
floor (storey)	koma	קומה
flour	kemakh	קמח
flower	perakh	פרח
flower seller	mokher prakhim	מוכר פרחים
fly	zvuv	זבוב

It's foggy.
yesh arafel.
יש ערפל.

English	Transliteration	Hebrew
to follow	lalekhet be'ikvot	ללכת בעקבות
food	okhel	אוכל
foot	regel	רגל
football (soccer)	kaduregel	כדורגל
footpath	mish'ol	משעול
foreign	zar	זר
forest	ya'ar	יער
forever	letamid	לתמיד
to forget	lishko'akh	לשכוח

I forget.
shakhakhti.
שכחתי.

Forget about it, don't worry.
shkhakh mize, iheye beseder.
שכח מזה, יהיה בסדר.

English	Transliteration	Hebrew
to forgive	lislo'akh	לסלוח
fortnight	shvu'a'im	שבועיים
fortune teller	magid atidot	מגיד עתידות
foyer	ulam knisa	אולם כניסה
free (not bound)	khofshi	חופשי
free (of charge)	bekhinam	בחינם

G

English	Transliteration	Hebrew
to freeze	likpo	לקפוא
Friday	yom shishi	יום שישי
friend	khaver(a)	חבר(ה)
frozen foods	okhel kafu	אוכל קפוא
fruit picking	katif perot	קטיף פירות
full	male	מלא
fun	bidur	בידור
for fun	bitskhok	בצחוק
to have fun	levalot	לבלות
to make fun of	litskhok me	לצחוק מ
funeral	halvaya	הלוויה
future	atid	עתיד

G

English	Transliteration	Hebrew
game (games)	miskhak	משחק
game (sport)	miskhak	משחק
a game show	takharut	תחרות
garage	musakh	מוסך
garbage	zevel	זבל
gardening	ginun	גינון
gardens	ganim	גנים
gas cartridge	meikhal gaz	מיכל גז
gate	sha'ar	שער
gay	homosexual	הומוסקסואל
general	klali	כללי

Get lost!
lekh lekol harukhot! לך לכל הרוחות!

English	Transliteration	Hebrew
gift	matana	מתנה
gig	hofa'a	הופעה
girl	yalda	ילדה
girlfriend	khavera	חברה
to give	latet	לתת

Could you give me ...?
ata yakhol latet li ...? אתה יכול לתת לי ...?

English	Transliteration	Hebrew
glass	z'khukhit	זכוכית

English	Transliteration	Hebrew
to go	lalekhet	ללכת

Let's go.
bo'u nelekh בואו נלך.

We'd like to go to ...
anakhnu rotsim lalekhet le ... אנחנו רוצים ללכת ל ...

Go straight ahead.
lekh yashar kadima לך ישר קדימה.

English	Transliteration	Hebrew
to go out with	latset im	לצאת עם
goal	gol	גול
goalkeeper	sho'er	שוער
goat	ez	עז
God	Elohim	אלוהים
of gold	mizahav	מזהב
good	tov	טוב

Good evening.
erev tov ערב טוב.

Good night.
layla tov לילה טוב.

English	Transliteration	Hebrew
good hotel	malon tov	מלון טוב

Good luck!
be'hatslakha! בהצלחה!

Good morning.
boker tov בוקר טוב.

Goodbye.
lehitra'ot להתראות.

English	Transliteration	Hebrew
government	memshala	ממשלה
gram	gram	גראם
grandchild	nekhed(a)	נכד(ה)
grandfather	saba	סבא
grandmother	savta	סבתא
grapes	anavim	ענבים
graphic art	grafika	גראפיקה
grass	deshe	דשא
grave	kever	קבר

great	gadol	גדול
Great! nehedar, nifla!		נהדר, נפלא!
green	yarok	ירוק
greengrocer	yarkan	ירקן
grey	afor	אפור
to guess	lenakhesh	לנחש
guide (person)	madrikh	מדריך
guide (audio)	kaletet mesaperet	קלטת מספרת
guidebook	madrikh	מדריך
guidedog	kelev hankhaya	כלב הנחייה
guided trek	maslul munkhe	מסלול מונחה
guinea pig	shfan nisayon	שפן ניסיון
guitar	gitara	גיטרה
gym	ulam hit'amlut	אולם התעמלות
gymnastics	hit'amlut	התעמלות

H

hair	se'ar	שיער
hairbrush	mivreshet se'ar	מברשת שיער
half	khatsi	חצי
half a litre	khatsi liter	חצי ליטר
to hallucinate	lahazot	להזות
ham	hem	הם
hammer	patish	פטיש
hammock	arsal	ערסל
hand	yad	יד
handbag	tik yad	תיק יד
handicrafts	melakhot yad	מלאכות יד
handmade	avodat yad	עבודת יד
handsome	yafe	יפה
happy	same'akh	שמח

Happy birthday! yom huledet same'akh!		יום הולדת שמח!
harbour	namal	נמל
hard	kashe	קשה
harness	resen	רסן
harrassment	hatrada	הטרדה
hash	nafas	נאפאס
to have	yesh	יש
Do you have ...? yesh lekha ...?		יש לך ...?
I have ... yesh li ...		יש לי ...
hayfever	kadakhat hashakhat	קדחת השחת
he	hu	הוא
head	rosh	ראש
a headache	ke'ev rosh	כאב ראש
health	bri'ut	בריאות
to hear	lishmo'a	לשמוע
hearing aid	makhshir shmi'a	מכשיר שמיעה
heart	lev	לב
heat	khom	חום
heater	tanur khimum	תנור חימום
heavy	kaved	כבד
Hello. hi		הי.
Hello! (answering telephone) halo!		הלו!
helmet	kasda	קסדה
Help!	hatsilu!	הצילו!
to help	la'azor	לעזור
herbs	asabim	עשבים
herbalist	metapel be'isbei marpe	מטפל בעשבי מרפא

I

here	po	פה
heroin	heroin	הרואין
heroin addict	makhur le'heroin	מכור להרואין
high	gavoha	גבוה
high school	bet sefer tikhon	בית ספר תיכון
to hike	latset lemasa	לצאת למסע
hiking	masa	מסע
hiking boots	na'alei masa	נעלי מסע
hiking routes	maslulei halikha	מסלולי הליכה
hill	giv'a	גבעה
Hindu	hindu	הינדו
to hire	liskor	לשכור
to hitchhike	linso'a bitrempim	לנסוע בטרמפים
HIV positive	nasa virus HIV	נשא וירוס HIV
holiday	khag	חג
holidays	khagim	חגים
Holy Week	shavu'a kadosh	שבוע קדוש
homeless	homeless	הומלס
homeopathy	homeopatia	הומאופתיה
homosexual	homosexual	הומוסקסואל
honey	dvash	דבש
honeymoon	yerakh devash	ירח דבש
horrible	nora	נורא
horse	sus	סוס
horse riding	rekhiva al sus	רכיבה על סוס
hospital	bet kholim	בית חולים
hot	kham	חם

It's hot.
kham חם.

to be hot	kham li	חם לי
hot water	ma'im khamim	מים חמים

house	ba'it	בית
housework	melakhot ba'it	מלאכות בית
how	eikh	איך

How do I get to ...?
eikh magi'im le ...? ?... איך מגיעים ל
How do you say ...?
eikh omrim ...? ?... איך אומרים

hug	khibuk	חיבוק
human rights	zkhuyot adam	זכויות אדם
a hundred	me'a	מאה
to be hungry	liheyot ra'ev	להיות רעב
husband	ba'al	בעל

I

I	ani	אני
ice	kerakh	קרח
ice axe	garzen kerakh	גרזן קרח
icecream	glida	גלידה
identification	zihuy	זיהוי
identification card	te'udat zehut	תעודת זהות
idiot	idiot	אידיוט
if	im	אם
ill	khole	חולה
immigration	hagira	הגירה
important	khashuv	חשוב

It's important.
ze khashuv זה חשוב.
It's not important.
ze lo khashuv זה לא חשוב.

in a hurry	bimhirut	במהירות
in front of	lifnei	לפני
included	kalul	כלול
income tax	mas hakhnasa	מס הכנסה
incomprehensible	bilti muvan	בלתי מובן

indicator	siman heker	סימן הכר
indigestion	kilkul keiva	קלקול קיבה
industry	ta'asia	תעשיה
inequality	yi-shivyon	אי-שיוויון
to inject	lehazrik	להזריק
injection	zrika	זריקה
injury	ptsi'a	פציעה
inside	bifnim	בפנים
instructor	madrikh	מדריך
insurance	bitu'akh	ביטוח
intense	intensivi	אינטנסיבי
interesting	me'anyen	מעניין
intermission	hafsaka	הפסקה
international	beinle'umi	בינלאומי
interview	re'ayon	ראיון
island	yi	אי
itch	gerud	גרוד
itinerary	maslul	מסלול

J

jail	bet sohar	בית סוהר
jar	kad	כד
jealous	kanai	קנאי
jeans	jeans	ג'ינס
jeep	jeep	ג'יפ
jewellery	takhshitim	תכשיטים
Jewish	yehudi	יהודי
job	avoda	עבודה
job advertise-	moda'ot	מודעות
ment	drushim	דרושים
job centre	merkaz	מרכז
	ta'asuka	תעסוקה
job	te'ur	תאור
description	ha'avoda	העבודה
jockey	jockey	ג'וקי
joke	bdikha	בדיחה
to joke	lehitbade'akh	להתבדח
journalist	itona'i	עיתונאי

journey	masa	מסע
judge	shofet	שופט
juice	mits	מיץ
to jump	likpots	לקפוץ
jumper	sveder	סוודר
(sweater)		
justice	tsedek	צדק

K

key	mafte'akh	מפתח
keyboard	mikledet	מקלדת
kick	be'ita	בעיטה
kick off	be'itat ptikha	בעיטת פתיחה
to kill	laharog	להרוג
kilogram	kilo	קילו
kilometre	kilometer	קילומטר
kind	adiv	אדיב
kindergarten	gan yeladim	גן ילדים
king	melekh	מלך
kiss	neshika	נשיקה
to kiss	lenashek	לנשק
kitchen	mitbakh	מטבח
kitten	khataltul	חתלתול
knapsack	yalkut gav	ילקוס גב
knee	berekh	ברך
knife	sakin	סכין
to know	lehakir	להכיר
(someone)		
to know	lada'at	לדעת
(something)		

I don't know.
ani lo yode'a (yoda'at)

אני לא יודע (יודעת).

L

lace	takhara	תחרה
lake	agam	אגם
land	yabasha	יבשה

English	Transliteration	Hebrew
languages	safot	שפות
large	rakhav	רחב
last	akharon	אחרון
last month	hakhodesh she'avar	החודש שעבר
last night	emesh	אמש
last week	shavu'a she'avar	שבוע שעבר
last year	shana she'avra	שנה שעברה
late	me'ukhar	מאוחר
laugh	tskhok	צחוק
launderette	mikhbesa lesherut atsmi	מכבסה לשרות עצמי
law	khok	חוק
lawyer	orekh din	עורך דין
laxatives	khomer meshalshel	חומר משלשל
lazy	atslan	עצלן
leaded (petrol/gas)	im oferet	עם עופרת
leader	manhig	מנהיג
to learn	lilmod	ללמוד
leather	or	עור
leathergoods	mutsarei or	מוצרי עור
ledge	eden khalon	אדן חלון
to leave (behind)	lehash'ir	להשאיר
left (not right)	smol	שמאל
left luggage	shmirat khafatsim	שמירת חפצים
left-wing	smolani	שמאלני
leg	regel	רגל
leg (in race)	shalav	שלב
legalisation	ma'arekhet khukim	מערכת חוקים
legislation	khuka	חוקה
lens	adasha	עדשה

English	Transliteration	Hebrew
Lent	tsom halent	צום הלנט
lesbian	lesbit	לסבית
less	pakhot	פחות
letter	mikhtav	מכתב
liar	shakran	שקרן
library	sifriya	ספריה
lice	kinim	כינים
to lie	leshaker	לשקר
life	kha'im	חיים
lift (elevator)	ma'alit	מעלית
light (sun/lamp)	or	אור
light (adj)	kal	קל
light (clear)	barur	ברור
light bulb	nura	נורה
light meter	mad or	מד-אור
lighter	matsit	מצית
to like	lekhabev	לחבב
line	shura	שורה
lips	sfata'im	שפתיים
lipstick	sfaton	שפתון
to listen	lehakshiv	להקשיב
little (small)	katan	קטן
a little (amount)	me'at	מעט
a little bit	ktsat	קצת
to live (life)	likhyot	לחיות
to live (somewhere)	lagur be ...	לגור ב ...
Long live ...	yekhi ...	... יחי
local	mekomi	מקומי
local/city bus	otobus ironi	אוטובוס עירוני
location	mikum	מיקום
lock	man'ul	מנעול
to lock	lin'ol	לנעול
long	arokh	ארוך

long distance	litvakh arokh	לטווח ארוך
long-distance bus	otobus bein ironi	אוטובוס בין-עירוני
to look	lehistakel	להסתכל
to look after	lishmor al	לשמור על
to look for	lekhapes	לחפש
loose change	kesef katan	כסף קטן
to lose	le'abed/ lehafsid	לאבד/ להפסיד
loser	mafsidan	מפסידן
loss	aveda	אבידה
a lot	hamon	המון
loud	bekol ram	בקול רם
to love	le'ehov	לאהוב
lover	me'ahev	מאהב
low	namukh	נמוך
low/high blood	lakhats dam namukh/ gavoha	לחץ דם נמוך/ גבוה
loyal	ne'eman	נאמן
luck	mazal	מזל
lucky	bar-mazal	בר-מזל
luggage	mit'an	מטען
luggage lockers	lokerim	לוקרים
lump	gush	גוש
lunch	arukhat tsohora'im	ארוחת צהריים
lunchtime	tsohora'im	צהריים
luxury	motarot	מותרות

M

machine	mekhona	מכונה
mad	meshuga	משוגע
made (of)	asui me	עשוי מ
magazine	magazine	מגזין
magician	kosem	קוסם
mail	do'ar	דואר

mailbox	tevat do'ar	תיבת דואר
main road	derekh rashit	דרך ראשית
main square	kikar rashit	כיכר ראשית
majority	rov	רוב
to make	la'asot	לעשות
make-up	ipur	איפור
man	ish	איש
manager	menahel	מנהל
manual worker	po'el	פועל
many	harbe	הרבה

Many happy returns!
ad me'a ve'esrim!   עד מאה ועשרים!

map	mapa	מפה

Can you show me on the map?
ata yakhol lehar'ot li al hamapa?
אתה יכול להראות לי על המפה?

marijuana	marijuana	מריחואנה
marital status	matsav mishpakhti	מצב משפחתי
market	shuk	שוק
marriage	nisu'im	נישואים
to marry	lehitkhaten	להתחתן
marvellous	nifla	נפלא
mass (Catholic)	misa	מיסה
massage	isu'i	עיסוי
mat	shati'akh	שטיח
match	gafrur	גפרור
matches	gafrurim	גפרורים

It doesn't matter.
lo meshane.   לא משנה.
What's the matter?
ma kara?   מה קרה?

mattress	mizron	מזרון
maybe	ula'i	אולי
mayor	rosh ir	ראש עיר

English	Transliteration	Hebrew
mechanic	mekhona'i	מכונאי
medal	medalya	מדליה
medicine	trufa	תרופה
meditation	meditatsia	מדיטציה
to meet	lifgosh	לפגוש
member	khaver	חבר
menstruation	veset	וסת
menthol (cigarettes)	mentol	מנתול
menu	tafrit	תפריט
message	hoda'a	הודעה
metal	matekhet	מתכת
meteor	meteor	מטאור
metre	meter	מטר
midnight	khatsot	חצות
migraine	migrena	מיגרנה
military service	sherut tsva'i	שירות צבאי
milk	khalav	חלב
millimetre	millimetre	מילימטר
million	million	מיליון
mind	toda'a	תודעה
mineral water	mayim minerali'im	מים מינרליים
a minute	daka	דקה

Just a minute.
rak rega
רק רגע

in (five) minutes
be'od (khamesh) dakot

בעוד (חמש) דקות

English	Transliteration	Hebrew
mirror	mar'a	מראה
miscarriage	hapala	הפלה
to miss (someone)	lehitga'age'a	להתגעגע
mistake	ta'ut	טעות
to mix	le'arbev	לערבב

English	Transliteration	Hebrew
mobile phone	telephone nayad	טלפון נייד
modem	modem	מודם
moisturising cream	krem lakhut	קרם לחות
monastery	minzar	מנזר
money	kesef	כסף
monk	nazir	נזיר
month	khodesh	חודש
this month	hakhodesh	החודש
monument	yad	יד
moon	yare'akh	ירח
more	od	עוד
morning (6am - 1pm)	boker	בוקר
mosque	misgad	מסגד
mother	ima	אמא
mother-in-law	khotenet	חותנת
motorboat	sirat mano'a	סירת מנוע
motorcycle	ofno'a	אופנוע
motorway	kvish mahir	כביש מהיר
mountain	har	הר
mountain bike	ofnei harim	אופני הרים
mountain hut	biktat harim	בקתת הרים
mountain path	shvil harim	שביל הרים
mountain range	rekhes harim	רכס הרים
mountaineering	tipus harim	טיפוס הרים
mouse	akhbar	עכבר
mouth	pe	פה
movie	seret	סרט
mud	bots	בוץ
muscle	shrir	שריר
museum	muze'on	מוזיאון
music	musika	מוסיקה
musician	nagan	נגן
Muslim	muslemi	מוסלמי
mute	ilem	אילם

N

English	Transliteration	Hebrew
name	shem	שם
nappy	khitul	חיתול
nappy rash	gerui or tinokot	גרוי עור תינוקות
national park	shmurat teva	שמורת טבע
nationality	le'om	לאום
nature	teva	טבע
naturopath	ohev teva	אוהב טבע
nausea	bkhila	בחילה
near	karov	קרוב
nearby hotel	malon basviva	מלון בסביבה
necessary	nakhuts	נחוץ
necklace	sharsheret	שרשרת
to need	lehits'tarekh	להצטרך
needle (sewing)	makhat	מחט
needle (syringe)	mazrek	מזרק
neither	lo ze velo ze	לא זה ולא זה
net	reshet	רשת
never	af pa'am	אף פעם
new	khadash	חדש
news	khadashot	חדשות
newsagency	sokhnut khadashot	סוכנות חדשות
newspaper	iton	עיתון
newspapers	itonim	עיתונים
New Year's Day	rosh hashana	ראש השנה
New Year's Eve	erev rosh hashana	ערב ראש השנה
New Zealand	New Zealand	ניו-זילנד
next	haba	הבא
next month	hakhodesh haba	החודש הבא
next to	karov le	קרוב ל
next week	hashavu'a haba	השבוע הבא

English	Transliteration	Hebrew
next year	hashana haba'a	השנה הבאה
nice	nekhmad	נחמד
nickname	kinui khiba	כינוי חיבה
night	layla	לילה
no	lo	לא
noise	ra'ash	רעש
noisy	mar'ish	מרעיש
non-direct	akif	עקיף
none	af lo ekhad	אף לא אחד
noon	tsohora'im	צהריים
north	tsafon	צפון
nose	af	אף
notebook	makhberet	מחברת
nothing	shum davar	שום דבר
not yet	ada'in lo	עדיין לא
novel (book)	roman	רומן
now	akhshav	עכשיו
nuclear energy	energia atomit	אנרגיה אטומית
nuclear testing	nisui atomi	ניסוי אטומי
nun	nezira	נזירה
nurse	akhot	אחות

O

obvious	barur	ברור
ocean	oki'anus	אוקיאנוס
offence	avera	עבירה
office	misrad	משרד
office work	avodat misrad	עבודת משרד
office worker	pakid	פקיד
offside	nivdal	נבדל
often	le'itim krovot	לעיתים קרובות
oil (cooking)	shemen	שמן
oil (crude)	neft	נפט
OK	beseder	בסדר

English	Transliteration	Hebrew
old (people)	zaken	זקן
old (objects)	yashan	ישן
old city	ir atika	עיר עתיקה
olive oil	shemen za'it	שמן זית
olives	zeitim	זיתים
Olympic Games	hamis-khakim ha'olimpi'im	המשחקים האולימפיים
on	al	על
on time	bazman	בזמן
once; one time	pa'am; pa'am akhat	פעם; פעם אחת
one-way ticket	kartis halokh	כרטיס הלוך
only	rak	רק
open	patu'akh	פתוח
to open	lifto'akh	לפתוח
opening	petakh	פתח
opera	opera	אופרה
opera house	bet ha'opera	בית האופרה
operation	mivtsa	מבצע
operator	merkazan	מרכזן
opinion	de'a	דעה
opposite	hahefekh	ההיפך
or	o	או
oral	be'al pe	בעל פה
orange (colour)	katom	כתום
orchestra	tizmoret	תזמורת
order	seder	סדר
to order	lehazmin	להזמין
ordinary	ragil	רגיל
organise	le'argen	לארגן
orgasm	orgazma	אורגזמה
original	mekori	מקורי
other	akher	אחר
outgoing	khevruti	חברותי
outside	bakhuts	בחוץ
over	me'al	מעל

English	Transliteration	Hebrew
overcoat	me'il	מעיל
overdose	menat yeter	מנת יתר
to owe	liheyot khayav	להיות חייב
owner	be'alim	בעלים
oxygen	khamtsan	חמצן
ozone layer	shikhvat ha'ozone	שכבת האוזון

P

English	Transliteration	Hebrew
pacifier (dummy)	motsets	מוצץ
package	khavila	חבילה
packet (cigarette)	khafisat sigaryot	חפיסת סיגריות
padlock	man'ul	מנעול
page	daf	דף
a pain	ke'ev	כאב
painful	ko'ev	כואב
pain in the neck	ke'ev batsavar	כאב בצוואר
painkillers	kadurim neged ke'evim	כדורים נגד כאבים
to paint	litsbo'a	לצבוע
painter	tsaba	צבע
painting (the art)	tsiyur	ציור
paintings	tsiyurim	ציורים
pair (a couple)	zug	זוג
palace	armon	ארמון
pan	makhvat	מחבת
pap smear	pap smear	פאפ סמיר
paper	neyar	נייר
paraplegic	meshutak	משותק
parcel	khavila	חבילה
parents	horim	הורים
a park	park	פארק

to park	lakhanot	לחנות
parliament	parlament	פרלמנט
part	khelek	חלק
party (fiesta)	mesiba	מסיבה
party (politics)	miflaga	מפלגה
pass	rishyon ma'avar	רישיון מעבר
passenger	nose'a	נוסע
passive	savil	סביל
passport	darkon	דרכון
passport number	mispar darkon	מספר דרכון
past	avar	עבר
path	shvil	שביל
patient (adj)	savlani	סבלני
to pay	leshalem	לשלם
payment	tashlum	תשלום
peace	shalom	שלום
peak	pisga	פסגה
pedestrian	holekh regel	הולך רגל
pen (ballpoint)	et (kaduri)	עט (כדורי)
pencil	iparon	עפרון
penis	pin	פין
penknife	olar	אולר
pensioner	gimla'i	גימלאי
people	am	עם
pepper	pilpel	פלפל
percent	akhuz	אחוז
performance	hatsaga	הצגה
performance art	omanuyot bama	אמנויות במה
period pain	ke'evei makhzor	כאבי מחזור
permanent	kavu'a	קבוע
permanent collection	ta'arukha kvu'a	תערוכה קבועה
permission	reshut	רשות
permit	ishur	אישור
person	adam	אדם

personality	ishiyut	אישיות
to perspire	lehazi'a	להזיע
petition	atsuma	עצומה
petrol	delek	דלק
pharmacy	bet mirkakhat	בית מרקחת
phone book	sefer telefon	ספר טלפון
phone box	ta telefon	תא טלפון
phonecard	kartis telefon	כרטיס טלפון
photo	tmuna	תמונה

Can I take a photo?
efshar letsalem?

אפשר לצלם?

photographer	tsalam	צלם
photography	tsilum	צילום
pick/pickaxe	makosh	מכוש
to pick up	leharim	להרים
pie	pashtida	פשטידה
piece	khatikha	חתיכה
pig	khazir	חזיר
pill	kadur	כדור
the Pill	haglula	הגלולה
pillow	kar	כר
pillowcase	tsipit	ציפית
pinball	pinball	פינבול
pine	oren	אורן
pink	varod	ורוד
pipe	mikteret	מקטרת
place	makom	מקום
place of birth	mekom leida	מקום לידה
plain	mishor	מישור
plane	aviron	אווירון
planet	kokhav lekhet	כוכב לכת
plant	tsemakh	צמח
to plant	linto'a	לנטוע
plastic	plastic	פלסטיק
plate	tsalakhat	צלחת
plateau	rama	רמה

P

English	Transliteration	Hebrew
platform	bama	במה
play (theatre)	lesakhek	לשחק
to play (a game)	lesakhek	לשחק
to play (music)	lenagen	לנגן
player (sports)	sakhkan	שחקן
playing cards	klafim	קלפים
to play cards	lesakhek klafim	לשחק קלפים
plug (bath)	pkak	פקק
plug (electricity)	teka	תקע
pocket	kis	כיס
poetry	shira	שירה
to point	lehatsbi'a al	להצביע על
poker	poker	פוקר
police	mishtara	משטרה
politics	politika	פוליטיקה
political speech	ne'um politi	נאום פוליטי
politicians	politika'im	פוליטיקאים
pollen	avkat prakhim	אבקת פרחים
polls	bkhirot	בחירות
pollution	zihum avir	זיהום אוויר
pool (swimming)	brekhat skhiya	בריכת שחיה
pool (game)	billiard	ביליארד
poor	ani	עני
popular	populari	פופולארי
port	namal	נמל
portrait sketcher	tsayar portretim	צייר פורטרטים
possible	efshari	אפשרי

It's (not) possible.
ze (bilti) efshari. זה (בלתי) אפשרי.

postcard	gluya	גלויה
post code	mikud	מיקוד
postage	dmei do'ar	דמי דואר
poster	poster	פוסטר
post office	misrad do'ar	משרד דואר
pot (ceramic)	tsintsenet	צנצנת
pot (dope)	khashish	חשיש
pottery	klei kheres	כלי חרס
poverty	oni	עוני
power	ko'akh	כוח
prayer	tfila	תפילה
prayer book	sefer tfila	ספר תפילה
to prefer	leha'adif	להעדיף
pregnant	beherayon	בהריון
prehistoric art	omanut pre-historit	אמנות פרה-היסטורית
pre-menstrual tension	metakh nafshi shelifnei haveset	מתח נפשי שלפני הוסת
to prepare	lehakhin	להכין
present (gift)	matana	מתנה
present (time)	hove	הווה
presentation	hatsaga	הצגה
presenter (TV, etc)	mankhe	מנחה
president	nasi	נשיא
pressure	lakhats	לחץ
pretty	na'e	נאה
prevent	limno'a	למנוע
price	mekhir	מחיר
pride	ga'ava	גאווה
priest	komer	כומר
prime minister	rosh memshala	ראש ממשלה
print (artwork)	hedpes	הדפס
prison	bet sohar	בית סוהר
prisoner	asir	אסיר
private	prati	פרטי
private hospital	bet kholim prati	בית חולים פרטי

English	Transliteration	Hebrew
privatisation	hafrata	הפרטה
to produce	leyatser	לייצר
producer	yatsran	יצרן
profession	miktso'a	מקצוע
profit	revakh	רווח
profitability	rivkhiyut	ריווחיות
program	tokhnit	תוכנית
projector	makren	מקרן
promise	havtakha	הבטחה
proposal	hatsa'a	הצעה
to protect	lehagen	להגן
protected forest	ya'ar mugan	יער מוגן
protected species	zanim muganim	זנים מוגנים
protest	mekha'a	מחאה
to protest	limkhot	למחות
public toilet	sherutim tsiburi'im	שירותים ציבוריים
to pull	limshokh	למשוך
pump	mash'eva	משאבה
puncture	pancher	פנצ'ר
to punish	leha'anish	להעניש
puppy	klavlav	כלבלב
pure	tahor	טהור
purple	sagol	סגול
to push	lidkhof	לדחוף
to put	lasim	לשים

Q

qualifications	kishurim	כישורים
quality	eikhut	איכות
quarantine	bidud	בידוד
quarrel	meriva	מריבה
quarter	rova	רובע
queen	malka	מלכה
question	she'ela	שאלה
to question	lehatil safek	להטיל ספק
question (topic)	nose	נושא
queue	tor	תור
quick	mahir	מהיר
quiet (adj)	shaket	שקט
to quit	la'azov	לעזוב

R

rabbit	arnav	ארנב
race (breed)	geza	גזע
race (sport)	merots	מרוץ
racing bike	ofanei merots	אופני מירוץ
racism	gaz'anut	גזענות
racquet	makhbet	מחבט
radiator	radi'ator	רדיאטור
railroad	mesilat barzel	מסילת ברזל
railway station	takhanat rakevet	תחנת רכבת
rain	geshem	גשם

It's raining.
yored geshem יורד גשם.

English	Transliteration	Hebrew
rally	atseret	עצרת
rape	ones	אונס
rare	nadir	נדיר
a rash	prikha	פריחה
rat	akhbarosh	עכברוש
rate of pay	ta'arif	תעריף
raw (meat)	na	נא
razor	mekhonat gilu'akh	מכונת גילוח
razor blades	sakin gilu'akh	סכין גילוח
to read	likro	לקרוא
ready	mukhan	מוכן
to realise (attain)	lehagshim	להגשים
reason (cause)	siba	סיבה

English	Transliteration	Hebrew
receipt	kabala	קבלה
to receive	lekabel	לקבל
recent	ba'et ha'akharona	בעת האחרונה
recently	la'akharona	לאחרונה
to recognise	lehakir	להכיר
to recommend	lehamlits	להמליץ
recording	haklata	הקלטה
recyclable	nitan lemikhzur	ניתן למיחזור
recycling	mikhzur	מיחזור
red	adom	אדום
referee	shofet	שופט
reference	izkur	איזכור
reflection (mirror)	hishtakfut	השתקפות
reflection (thinking)	khashiva	חשיבה
refrigerator	frijider	פריג'ידר
refugee	palit	פליט
refund	hekhzer	החזר
to refund	lehakhzir et hakesef	להחזיר את הכסף
to refuse	lesarev	לסרב
regional	ezori	אזורי
registered mail	do'ar rashum	דואר רשום
to regret	lehitkharet	להתחרט
relationship	ma'arekhet yekhasim	מערכת יחסים
to relax	leheraga	להרגע
religion	dat	דת
religious	dati	דתי
to remember	lizkor	לזכור
remote	rakhok	רחוק
remote control	shlat rakhok	שלט רחוק
rent	skhar dira	שכר דירה
to rent	lehaskir	להשכיר
to repeat	lakhazor al	לחזור על
republic	republika	רפובליקה

English	Transliteration	Hebrew
reservation	hazmana merosh	הזמנה מראש
to reserve	lehazmin merosh	להזמין מראש
resignation	hitpatrut	התפטרות
respect	kavod	כבוד
rest (relaxation)	menukha	מנוחה
rest (what's left)	she'erit	שארית
to rest	lanu'akh	לנוח
restaurant	mis'ada	מסעדה
resumé	korot kha'im	קורות חיים
retired	begimla'ot	בגימלאות
to return	lakhazor	לחזור
return (ticket)	kartis halokh vashov	כרטיס הלוך ושוב
review	skira	סקירה
rhythm	ketsev	קצב
rich (wealthy)	ashir	עשיר
rich (food)	atir kaloriyot	עתיר קלוריות
to ride (a horse)	lirkav (al sus)	לרכב (על סוס)
right (correct)	nakhon	נכון
right (not left)	yamin	ימין
to be right	liheyot tsodek	להיות צודק
You're right. ata tsodek		אתה צודק.
civil rights	zkhuyot ezrakh	זכויות אזרח
right now	berega ze	ברגע זה
right-wing	yemani	ימני
ring (on finger)	taba'at	טבעת
ring (of phone)	tsiltsul	צלצול

I'll give you a ring.
etkasher itkha אתקשר איתך.

ring (sound)	tsiltsul	צלצול
rip-off	gzela	גזילה
risk	sikun	סיכון
river	nahar	נהר
road (main)	derekh (rashit)	דרך (ראשית)
road map	mapat drakhim	מפת דרכים
to rob	lishdod	לשדוד
rock	sela	סלע
rock climbing	tipus al tsukim	טיפוס על צוקים
(wall of) rock	matsok	מצוק
rock group	lehakat rok	להקת רוק
rolling	mitgalgel	מתגלגל
romance	parashat ahavim	פרשת אהבים
room	kheder	חדר
room number	mispar kheder	מספר חדר
rope	khevel	חבל
round	agol	עגול
(at the) roundabout	bisvivot	בסביבות
rowing	khatira	חתירה
rubbish	ashpa	אשפה
rug	shati'akh	שטיח
ruins	harisot	הריסות
rules	klalim	כללים
to run	laruts	לרוץ

S

sad	atsuv	עצוב
safe (adj)	batu'akh	בטוח
safe (n)	kasefet	כספת
safe sex	min batu'akh	מין בטוח
saint	kadosh	קדוש

salary	maskoret	משכורת
(on) sale	limkhira	למכירה
sales department	makhleket mekhirot	מחלקת מכירות
salt	melakh	מלח
same	oto davar	אותו דבר
sand	khol	חול
sanitary napkins	takhboshot higyeniyot	תחבושות היגיניות
Saturday	shabat	שבת
to save	lehatsil	להציל
to say	lomar	לאמר
to scale (climb)	leha'apil	להעפיל
scarves	tse'ifim	צעיפים
school	bet sefer	בית ספר
science	mada	מדע
scientist	mad'an	מדען
scissors	mispara'im	מספריים
to score	lizkot binkudot	לזכות בנקודות
scoreboard	lu'akh totsa'ot	לוח תוצאות
screen	masakh	מסך
sculpture	pisul	פיסול
sea	yam	ים
seasick	khole bemakhalat yam	חולה במחלת ים
seaside	khof yam	חוף ים
seat	moshav	מושב
seatbelt	khagorat moshav	חגורת מושב
second (n)	shniya	שנייה
second	sheni	שני
secretary	mazkir(a)	מזכיר(ה)
to see	lir'ot	לראות

We'll see!
nir'e! נראה!

English	Transliteration	Hebrew
I see. (understand)		
hevanti		הבנתי.
See you later.		
lehitra'ot		להתראות.
See you tomorrow.		
lehitra'ot makhar		להתראות מחר.
self-employed	atsma'i	עצמאי
selfish	anokhi	אנוכי
self-service	sherut atsmi	שירות עצמי
to sell	limkor	למכור
to send	lishlo'akh	לשלוח
sensible	hegyoni	הגיוני
sentence (words)	mishpat	משפט
sentence (prison)	psak din	פסק דין
to separate	lehafrid	להפריד
series	sidra	סדרה
serious	retsini	רציני
service (assistance)	sherut	שירות
service (religious)	tfila	תפילה
several	akhadim	אחדים
to sew	litpor	לתפור
sex	min	מין
sexism	aflaya minit	אפליה מינית
sexy	sexy	סקסי
shade/ shadow	tsel	צל
shampoo	shampoo	שמפו
shape	tsura	צורה
to share (with)	lehitkhalek im	להתחלק עם
to share a dorm	lehitkhalek bekheder	להתחלק בחדר
to shave	lehitgale'akh	להתגלח
she	hi	היא

English	Transliteration	Hebrew
sheep	kvasim	כבשים
sheet (bed)	sadin	סדין
sheet (of paper)	daf neyar	דף נייר
shell	klipa	קליפה
shelves	itstab'ot	אצטבאות
ship	oniya	אונייה
to ship	lishlo'akh	לשלוח
shirt	khultsa	חולצה
shoe shop	khanut na'ala'im	חנות נעלים
shoes	na'ala'im	נעלים
to shoot	lirot	לירות
shop	khanut	חנות
to go shopping	la'asot kniyot	לעשות קניות
short (length)	katsar	קצר
short (height)	namukh	נמוך
short films	sratim ktsarim	סרטים קצרים
short stories	sipurim ktsarim	סיפורים קצרים
shortage	khoser	חוסר
shorts	mikhnasa'im ktsarim	מכנסים קצרים
shoulders	ktefa'im	כתפים
to shout	lits'ok	לצעוק
a show	hatsaga	הצגה
to show	lehar'ot	להראות

Can you show me on the map?
ata yakhol lehar'ot li al hamapa?
אתה יכול להראות לי על המפה?

English	Transliteration	Hebrew
shower	miklakhat	מקלחת
shrine	mikdash	מקדש
to shut	lisgor	לסגור
shy	bayshan	ביישן
sick	khole	חולה
a sickness	makhala	מחלה

S

side	tsad	צד
a sign	shelet	שלט
to sign	lakhatom	לחתום
signature	khatima	חתימה
silk	meshi	משי
of silver	mikesef	מכסף
similar	dome	דומה
simple	pashut	פשוט
sin	khet	חטא
since (May)	me'az (Mai)	מאז (מאי)
to sing	lashir	לשיר
singer	zamar	זמר
singer-songwriter	zamar-kotev shirim	זמר-כותב שירים
single (person)	ravak	רווק
single (unique)	yakhid	יחיד
single room	kheder leyakhid	חדר ליחיד
sister	akhot	אחות
to sit	lashevet	לשבת
size (of anything)	godel	גודל
size (clothes)	mida	מידה
size (shoes)	mida	מידה
skiing	ski	סקי
to ski	la'asot ski	לעשות סקי
skin	or	עור
sky	shama'im	שמיים
to sleep	lishon	לישון
sleeping bag	sak shena	שק שינה
sleeping car	kron shena	קרון שינה
sleeping pills	kadurei shena	כדורי שינה
sleepy	menumnam	מנומנם
slide (film)	shikufit	שיקופית
slow	iti	איטי
slowly	le'at	לאט
small	katan	קטן

a smell	re'akh	ריח
to smell	lehari'akh	להריח
to smile	lekhayekh	לחייך
to smoke	le'ashen	לעשן
soap	sabon	סבון
soap opera	operat sabon	אופרת סבון
soccer	kaduregel amerikani	כדורגל אמריקני
social-democratic	sotsyal demokrati	סוציאל דמוקרטי
social sciences	mad'ei hakhevra	מדעי החברה
social security	bitu'akh le'umi	ביטוח לאומי
social welfare	sa'ad	סעד
socialist	sotsialisti	סוציאליסטי
solid	mutsak	מוצק
some	kama	כמה
somebody/someone	mishehu	מישהו
something	mashehu	משהו
sometimes	lif'amim	לפעמים
son	ben	בן
song	shir	שיר
soon	bekarov	בקרוב
I'm sorry. ani mitsta'er		אני מצטער.
sound	tslil	צליל
south	darom	דרום
souvenir	mazkeret	מזכרת
souvenir shop	khanut mazkarot	חנות מזכרות
space	khalal	חלל
to speak	ledaber	לדבר
special	meyukhad	מיוחד
specialist	mumkhe	מומחה

English	Transliteration	Hebrew
speed	mehirut	מהירות
speed limit	mehirut muteret	מהירות מותרת
spicy (hot)	kharif	חריף
sport	sport	ספורט
sportsperson	sporta'i	ספורטאי
a sprain	neka	נקע
spring (season)	aviv	אביב
spring (coil)	kfits	קפיץ
square (shape)	meruba	מרובע
square (in town)	kikar	כיכר
stadium	itstadyon	אצטדיון
stage	bama	במה
stairway	khadar madregot	חדר מדרגות
stamps	bulim	בולים
standard (usual)	tikni	תיקני
standard of living	ramat kha'im	רמת חיים
stars	kokhavim	כוכבים
to start	lehatkhil	להתחיל
station	takhana	תחנה
stationer's	khanut lemutsarei ktiva	חנות למוצרי כתיבה
statue	pesel	פסל
to stay (remain)	lehisha'er	להישאר
to stay (somewhere)	lish'hot be ...	לשהות ב ...
to steal	lignov	לגנוב
steam	edim	אדים
steep	talul	תלול
step	madrega	מדרגה
stomach	keiva	קיבה
stomachache	ke'ev beten	כאב בטן

English	Transliteration	Hebrew
stone	even	אבן
stoned (drugged)	mesumam	מסומם
stop	takhana	תחנה
to stop	la'atsor	לעצור
Stop!	atsor!	עצור!
stork	khasida	חסידה
storm	se'ara	סערה
story	sipur	סיפור
stove	tanur	תנור
straight	yashar	ישר
strange	muzar	מוזר
stranger	zar	זר
stream	nakhal	נחל
street	rekhov	רחוב
strength	ko'akh	כוח
a strike	shvita	שביתה
on strike	bishvita	בשביתה
string	khut	חוט
stroll	tiyul	טיול
strong	khazak	חזק
stubborn	akshan	עקשן
student	student	סטודנט
studio	studio	סטודיו
stupid	tipesh	טיפש
style	signon	סגנון
subtitles	kituviyot	כיתוביות
suburb	parvar	פרבר
suburbs of	parvarei	פרברי
subway station	takhanat rakevet takhtit	תחנת רכבת תחתית
success	hatslakha	הצלחה
to suffer	lisbol	לסבול
sugar	sukar	סוכר
suitcase	mizvada	מזוודה
summer	ka'its	קיץ
sun	shemesh	שמש

T

sunblock	krem shizuf	קרם שיזוף
sunburn	makat shemesh	מכת שמש
sunglasses	mishkefei shemesh	משקפי שמש
sunny	mutsaf shemesh	מוצף שמש
sunrise	zrikhat hashemesh	זריחת השמש
sunset	shki'at hashemesh	שקיעת השמש
Sure.	betakh	בטח.
surface mail	do'ar yam	דואר ים
surfboard	galshan	גלשן
surname	shem mishpakha	שם משפחה
a surprise	hafta'a	הפתעה
to survive	lisrod	לשרוד
sweet	matok	מתוק
to swim	liskhot	לשחות
swimming	skhiya	שחיה
swimming pool	brekhat skhiya	בריכת שחיה
swimsuit	beged yam	בגד ים
sword	kherev	חרב
sympathetic	simpati	סימפטי
synagogue	bet kneset	בית כנסת
synthetic	sinteti	סינטטי
syringe	mazrek	מזרק

T

table	shulkhan	שולחן
table tennis	shulkan tenis	שולחן טניס
tail	zanav	זנב
to take (away)	lakakhat	לקחת

to take (food)	take away	טייק אווי
to take (the train)	linso'a barakevet	לנסוע ברכבת
to take photographs	letsalem	לצלם
to talk	ledaber	לדבר
tall	gavoha	גבוה
tampons	tamponim	טמפונים
tasty	ta'im	טעים
tax	mas	מס
taxi stand	takhanat moniyot	תחנת מוניות
teacher	more	מורה
teaching	hora'a	הוראה
team	tsevet	צוות
tear (crying)	dim'a	דימעה
technique	tekhnika	טכניקה
teeth	shen	שן
telegram	mivrak	מברק
telephone	telphone	טלפון
to telephone	letalpen	לטלפן
telephone operator	merkazan	מרכזן
telescope	telescope	טלסקופ
television	televizia	טלוויזיה
to tell	lesaper	לספר
temperature (fever)	khom	חום
temperature (weather)	ma'alot	מעלות
temple	mikdash	מקדש
tennis	tennis	טניס
tennis court	migrash tennis	מגרש טניס
tent	ohel	אוהל
tent pegs	yetedot	יתדות
tenth	asiri	עשירי
term of office	tkufat kehuna	תקופת כהונה
terrible	ayom	איום

D I C T I O N A R Y

test	mivkhan	מבחן	tobacco	khanut	חנות
to thank	lehodot	להודות	kiosk	tabak	טבק
Thank you.				vesigariyot	וסיגריות
toda		תודה.	today	hayom	היום
			together	beyakhad	ביחד
theatre	te'atron	תיאטרון	toilet paper	neyar twalet	נייר טואלט
they	hem	הם	toilets	sherutim	שירותים
thick	ave	עבה	tomorrow	makhar	מחר
thief	ganav	גנב	tomorrow	makhar akhar	מחר אחר
thin	raze	רזה	afternoon	hatsohora'im	הצהריים
to think	lakhashov	לחשוב	tomorrow	makhar	מחר
third	shlishi	שלישי	evening	baerev	בערב
thirsty	tsame	צמא	tomorrow	makhar	מחר
this (one)	haze	הזה	morning	baboker	בבוקר
thought	makhshava	מחשבה	tonight	halayla	הלילה
throat	garon	גרון	too (as well)	gam	גם
ticket	kartis	כרטיס	too expensive	yakar midai	יקר מידי
ticket collector	kartisan	כרטיסן	too much/	yoter midai	יותר מידי
ticket	otomat	אוטומט	many		
machine	kartisim	כרטיסים	tooth	shen	שן
ticket office	misrad	משרד	tooth (wisdom)	shen bina	שן בינה
	kartisim	כרטיסים	toothache	ke'ev	כאב
tide	ge'ut	גאות		shina'im	שיניים
tight	haduk	הדוק	toothbrush	mivreshet	מברשת
time	zman	זמן		shina'im	שיניים
timetable	lu'akh zmanim	לוח זמנים	toothpaste	mishkhat	משחת
tin (can of	pakhit	פחית		shina'im	שיניים
drink)			torch	panas	פנס
tin (can of	kufsat	קופסת	(flashlight)		
food)	shimurim	שימורים	to touch	laga'at	לגעת
tin opener	potkhan	פותחן	tour	tiyul	טיול
	kufsa'ot	קופסאות	tourist	tayar	תייר
tip (gratuity)	tip	טיפ	tourist inform-	modi'in	מודיעין
tired	ayef	עייף	ation office	tayarim	תיירים
tissues	mimkhatot	ממחטות	towards	le'ever	לעבר
	neyar	נייר	towel	magevet	מגבת
toad	karpada	קרפדה	tower	migdal	מגדל
toast	toast	טוסט	toxic waste	psolet ra'alit	פסולת רעלית
tobacco	tabak	טבק	track	maslul	מסלול
			(car-racing)		

track (footprints)	akevot	עקבות
track (sports)	maslul	מסלול
track (path)	shvil	שביל
trade union	igud ovdim	איגוד עובדים
traffic	tnu'a	תנועה
traffic lights	ramzor	רמזור
trail (route)	shvil	שביל
train	rakevet	רכבת
train station	takhanat rakevet	תחנת רכבת
tram	khashmalit	חשמלית
transit lounge	ulam nos'im	אולם נוסעים
to translate	letargem	לתרגם
to travel	letayel	לטייל
travel agency	misrad nesi'ot	משרד נסיעות
travel sickness	bkhila binsi'a	בחילה בנסיעה
travel (books)	madrikh	מדריך
travellers cheques	hamkha'ot nos'im	המחאות נוסעים
tree	ets	עץ
trek	masa ragli	מסע רגלי
trendy (person)	ofnati	אופנתי
trip	masa; tiyul	מסע, טיול
trousers	mikhnasa'im	מכנסיים
truck	masa'it	משאית
It's true.	ze nakhon	זה נכון.
trust	emun	אמון
to trust	livto'akh be	לבטוח ב
truth	emet	אמת
to try on	limdod	למדוד
to try (attempt)	lenasot	לנסות
T-shirt	khultsat ti	חולצת טי

tune	mangina	מנגינה
Turn left.	pne smola	פנה שמאלה.
Turn right.	pne yamina	פנה ימינה.
TV	televisia	טלוויזיה
TV set	makhshir televisia	מכשיר טלוויזיה.
twice	pa'ama'im	פעמיים
twin beds	mita kfula	מיטה כפולה
twins	te'omim	תאומים
to type	lehadpis	להדפיס
typical	ofyani	אופייני
tyres	tsmigim	צמיגים

U

umbrella	mitriya	מטרייה
to understand	lehavin	להבין
unemployed	muvtal	מובטל
unemployment	avtala	אבטלה
unions	igudim	איגודים
universe	olam	עולם
university	universita	אוניברסיטה
unleaded	netul oferet	נטול עופרת
unsafe	lo batu'akh	לא בטוח
until (June)	ad (yuni)	עד (יוני)
unusual	lo ragil	לא רגיל
up	lema'ala	למעלה
uphill	ma'ale hahar	מעלה ההר
urgent	dakhuf	דחוף
useful	shimushi	שימושי

V

vacant	rek	ריק
vacation	khufsha	חופשה
vaccination	khisun	חיסון
valley	emek	עמק
valuable	yekar erekh	יקר ערך
value (price)	mekhir	מחיר
van	tender	טנדר

English	Transliteration	Hebrew
vegetable	yerek	ירק
vegetarian	tsimkhoni	צמחוני
I'm vegetarian.	ani tsimkhoni(t)	אני צמחוני(ת).
vegetation	tsimkhiya	צמחיה
vein	vrid	וריד
venereal disease	makhalat min	מחלת מין
venue	atar eru'im	אתר אירועים
very	me'od	מאוד
video tape	kaletet	קלטת
view	nof	נוף
village	kfar	כפר
vine	gefen	גפן
vineyard	kerem	כרם
virus	virus	וירוס
visa	visa	ויזה
to visit	levaker	לבקר
vitamins	vitaminim	ויטמינים
voice	kol	קול
volume	nefakh	נפח
to vote	lehatsbi'a	להצביע

W

Wait!	khake!	חכה!
waiter	meltsar	מלצר
waiting room	khadar hamtana	חדר המתנה
to walk	lalekhet	ללכת
wall (inside)	kir	קיר
wall (outside)	khoma	חומה
to want	lirtsot	לרצות
war	milkhama	מלחמה
wardrobe	meltakha	מלתחה
warm	khamim	חמים
to warn	lehazhir	להזהיר

English	Transliteration	Hebrew
to wash (something)	lirkhots	לרחוץ
to wash (oneself)	lehitrakhets	להתרחץ
washing machine	mekhonat kvisa	מכונת כביסה
watch	sha'on	שעון
to watch	litspot	לצפות
water	ma'im	מים
mineral water	ma'im minerali'im	מים מינרליים
water bottle	bakbuk ma'im	בקבוק מים
waterfall	mapal	מפל
wave	gal	גל
way	derekh	דרך

Please tell me the way to ...
slikha, ma haderekh le ...
סליחה, מה הדרך ל ...

Which way?
eizo derekh?
איזו דרך?

Way Out.
yetsi'a
יציאה.

English	Transliteration	Hebrew
we	anakhnu	אנחנו
weak	khalash	חלש
wealthy	ashir	עשיר
to wear	lilbosh	ללבוש
weather	mezeg avir	מזג אוויר
wedding	khatuna	חתונה
wedding cake	ugat khatuna	עוגת חתונה
wedding present	matnat khatuna	מתנת חתונה
week	shavu'a	שבוע
this week	hashavu'a	השבוע
weekend	sofshavu'a	סופשבוע
to weigh	lishkol	לשקול
weight	mishkal	משקל
welcome	barukh haba	ברוך הבא
welfare	sa'ad	סעד

English	Transliteration	Hebrew
well	tov	טוב
west	ma'arav	מערב
wet	ratuv	רטוב
what	ma	מה

What's he saying?
ma hu omer? מה הוא אומר?

What time is it?
ma hasha'a? מה השעה?

wheel	galgal	גלגל
wheelchair	kise galgalim	כסא גלגלים
when	matai	מתי

When does it leave?
matai hu yotse? מתי הוא יוצא?

| where | eifo | איפה |

Where's the bank?
eifo habank? איפה הבנק?

| white | lavan | לבן |
| who | mi | מי |

Who is it?
mi ze? מי זה?

Who are they?
mi hem? מי הם?

| whole | shalem | שלם |
| why | lama | למה |

Why is the museum closed?
lama hamuzeon sagur?
למה המוזיאון סגור?

wide	rakhav	רחב
wife	isha	אישה
wild animal	khayat pere	חית פרא
to win	lizkot	לזכות
wind	ru'akh	רוח
window	khalon	חלון

English	Transliteration	Hebrew
to go window-shopping	lehitbonen bekhalonot ra'ava	להתבונן בחלונות ראווה
windscreen	shimsha kidmit	שמשה קידמית
wine	ya'in	יין
winery	yekev	יקב
wings	knafa'im	כנפיים
winner	menatse'akh	מנצח
winter	khoref	חורף
wire	khut barzel	חוט ברזל
wise	khakham	חכם
to wish	le'akhel	לאחל
with	im	עם
within	betokh	בתוך
within an hour	betokh sha'a	בתוך שעה
without	bli	בלי
without filter	bli filter	בלי פילטר
woman	isha	אישה
wonderful	nifla	נפלא
wood	ets	עץ
wool	tsemer	צמר
word	mila	מילה
work	avoda	עבודה
to work	la'avod	לעבוד
workout	imun kosher	אימון כושר
work permit	rishyon avoda	רישיון עבודה
workshop	sadna	סדנה
world	olam	עולם
World Cup	gvi'a olam	גביע עולם
worms	tola'im	תולעים
worried	mud'ag	מודאג
worship	avodat elohim	עבודת אלוהים
worth	shovi	שווי
wound	petsa	פצע
to write	likhtov	לכתוב

Y

writer	sofer	סופר
wrong	lo nakhon	לא נכון

I'm wrong. (my fault)
ta'iti
טעיתי.

I'm wrong. (not right)
ani lo tsodek(et)
אני לא צודק(ת).

Y

year	shana	שנה
this year	hashana	השנה
yellow	tsahov	צהוב
yesterday	etmol	אתמול
yesterday afternoon/ evening	etmol akhar hatsohora'im/ ba'erev	אתמול אחר הצהריים/ בערב

yesterday morning	etmol baboker	אתמול בבוקר
yet	ada'in	עדיין
you (pol)	ata (at)	אתה (את)
young	tsa'ir	צעיר
youth (collective)	no'ar	נוער
youth hostel	akhsaniyat no'ar	אכסניית נוער

Z

zebra	zebra	זברה
zodiac	galgal hamazalot	גלגל המזלות
zoo	gan khayot	גן חיות

The following legend is intended to help you find the right sound for the transliteration.

Vowels
a   as the 'a' in 'after'
e   as the 'e' in 'egg'
i   as the 'i' in 'mistake'
o   as the 'o' in 'north'
u   as the 'u' in 'flute'

Diphthongs
ei   as the 'ay' in 'day'

Consonants
g   as the 'g' in 'go'
kh as the 'ch' in 'Bach'
s   as the 's' in 'see', never as the 's' in 'pleasure'
ts as the 'ts' in 'its'
y   as the 'y' in 'yellow'

A

aba	father	אבא
ad (yuni)	until (June)	עד (יוני)
ada'in lo	not yet	עדיין לא
ada'in	yet	עדיין
adam	person	אדם
adama	earth (soil)	אדמה
adasha	lens	עדשה
adiv	kind	אדיב
adom	red	אדום
adshot maga	contact lenses	עדשות מגע
af	nose	אף
af lo ekhad	none	אף לא אחד
af pa'am	never	אף פעם
aflaya minit	sexism	אפליה מינית
aflaya	discrimination	אפליה
afor	grey	אפור

agam	lake	אגם
agilim	earrings	עגילים
agol	round	עגול
aids	AIDS	איידס
a'in	eye	עין
akevot	track (footprints)	עקבות
akh	brother	אח
akhadim	few	אחדים
akhadim	several	אחדים
akhar hatsohora'im	afternoon	אחר הצהרים
akharon	last	אחרון
akhbar	mouse	עכבר
akhbarosh	rat	עכברוש
akher	other	אחר
akhilat lekhem hakodesh	communion	אכילת לחם הקודש

A

akhot	nurse/sister	אחות
akhrei	after	אחרי
akhsaniyat no'ar	youth hostel	אכסניית נוער
akhshav	now	עכשיו
akhuz	percent	אחוז
akif	non-direct	עקיף
akitsa	bite (insect)	עקיצה
akshan	stubborn	עקשן
al	on	על
alergya	an allergy	אלרגיה
alifut	championship	אליפות
am	people	עם
ambatiya	bath	אמבטיה
amok	deep	עמוק
anaf	branch (tree)	ענף
anakhnu	we	אנחנו
anan	cloud	ענן
anavim	grapes	ענבים
anglit	English	אנגלית
ani	I	אני
ani	poor	עני
anokhi	selfish	אנוכי
antibiotika	antibiotics	אנטיביוטיקה
anti-gar'ini	antinuclear	אנטי-גרעיני
arkhe'ologi	archaeological	ארכיאולוגי
arkhitekt	architect	ארכיטקט
arkhitektura	architecture	ארכיטקטורה
armon	palace	ארמון
armumi	crafty	ערמומי
arnav	rabbit	ארנב
arokh	long	ארוך
aron	cupboard	ארון
arsal	hammock	ערסל
arukhat boker	breakfast	ארוחת-בוקר
arukhat erev	dinner	ארוחת ערב
arukhat tsohora'im	lunch	ארוחת צהריים

arus(a)	fiancé(e)	ארוס/ה
asabim	herbs	עשבים
ashir	rich (wealthy)	עשיר
ashir	wealthy	עשיר
ashma	fault (someone's)	אשמה
ashpa	rubbish	אשפה
ashu'akh	fir	אשוח
asir	prisoner	אסיר
asiri	tenth	עשירי
asmati	asthmatic	אסמטי
aspirin	aspirin	אספירין
asui me	made of	עשוי מ
asuk	busy	עסוק
at	you (f)	את
ata	you (m)	אתה
atar eru'im	venue	אתר ארועים
atem	you (m, pl)	אתם
aten	you (f, pl)	אתן
atid	future	עתיד
atik	ancient	עתיק
atikot	antiques	עתיקות
atir kaloriyot	rich (food)	עתיר קלוריות
atsei hasaka	firewood	עצי הסקה
atseret	rally	עצרת
atsirut	constipation	עצירות
atslan	lazy	עצלן
atsma'i	self-employed	עצמאי
atsor! Stop!		עצור!
atsuma	petition	עצומה
atsuv	sad	עצוב
aval	but	אבל
avar	past	עבר
ave	thick	עבה
aveda	loss	אבידה
avera	offence	עבירה

224

B

avir	air	אוויר
avira	atmosphere	אווירה
aviron	plane	אווירון
aviv	spring (season)	אביב
avkat prakhim	pollen	אבקת פרחים
avkat tinokot	baby powder	אבקת תינוקות
avoda	job/work	עבודה
avodat elohim	worship	עבודת אלוהים
avodat misrad	office work	עבודת משרד
avodat yad	handmade	עבודת יד
avodot bniya	construction work	עבודות בניה
avtala	unemployment	אבטלה
ayef	tired	עייף
ayom	terrible	איום

B

ba'al	husband	בעל
ba'et ha'akharona	recent	בעת האחרונה
ba'it	house	בית
bakbuk ma'im	water bottle	בקבוק מים
bakbuk	bottle	בקבוק
bakhuts	outside	בחוץ
balet	ballet	בלט
bama	platform/ stage	במה
bar-mazal	lucky	בר-מזל
barukh haba	welcome	ברוך הבא
barur	clear/obvious	ברור
bat	daughter	בת
batakhtit	at the bottom	בתחתית

batu'akh	safe (adj)	בטוח
bayshan	shy	ביישן
bazman	on time	בזמן
bdikat dam	blood test	בדיקת דם
bdikha	joke	בדיחה
be	aboard	ב
be'al pe	oral	בעל פה
be'alim	owner	בעלים
beged yam	swimsuit	בגד ים
begimla'ot	retired	בגימלאות
be'hatslakha! Good luck!		בהצלחה!
beherayon	pregnant	בהריון
bein	among/ between	בין
beinle'umi	international	בינלאומי
be'ita	kick	בעיטה
be'itat ptikha	kick off	בעיטת פתיחה
bekarov	soon	בקרוב
bekhinam	free (of charge)	בחינם
bekol ram	loud	בקול רם
ben	son	בן
berega ze	right now	ברגע זה
berekh	knee	ברך
beseder	OK	בסדר
bet ha'opera	opera house	בית האופרה
bet kafe	café	בית קפה
bet kharoshet	factory	בית חרושת
bet kholim	hospital	בית חולים
bet kholim prati	private hospital	בית חולים פרטי
bet kneset	synagogue	בית כנסת
bet mirkakhat	chemist (pharmacy)	בית מרקחת
bet mishpat	court (legal)	בית משפט
bet sefer	school	בית ספר

bet sefer tikhon	high school	בית ספר תיכון
bet sohar	jail/prison	בית סוהר
betakh	Sure.	בטח.
bete'avon!	Bon appétit!	בתאבון!
betokh	within	בתוך
betokh sha'a	within an hour	בתוך שעה
be'ur ye'arot	deforestation	ביעור יערות
beyakhad	together	ביחד
bgadim	clothing	בגדים
bidud	quarantine	בידוד
bidur	fun	בידור
bifnim	inside	בפנים
biktat harim	mountain hut	בקתת הרים
bilti muvan	incompre-hensible	בלתי מובן
bimhirut	in a hurry	במהירות
binyan	building	בניין
biografiya	biography	ביוגרפיה
bishvita	on strike	בשביתה
bisvivot	roundabout	בסביבות
bitskhok	for fun	בצחוק
bitu'akh	insurance	ביטוח
bitu'akh le'umi	social security	ביטוח לאומי
bitul	dismissal	ביטול
bkhila	travel sickness	בחילה
binsi'a		בנסיעה
bkhila	nausea	בחילה
bkhirot	elections/polls	בחירות
bli	without	בלי
bli filter	without filter	בלי פילטר
boger	adult	בוגר
boker	morning	בוקר

boker tov Good morning.		בוקר טוב.
bots	mud	בוץ
brekhat skhiya	swimming pool	בריכת שחייה
bri'ut	health	בריאות
bubot	dolls	בובות
buddhisti	Buddhist	בודהיסטי
bulim	stamps	בולים

D

daf	page	דף
daf neyar	sheet (of paper)	דף נייר
dag	fish	דג
dai! Enough!		די!
daka	a minute	דקה
dakhuf	urgent	דחוף
daleket shalpukhit hasheten	cystitis	דלקת שלפוחית השתן
dam	blood	דם
darkon	passport	דרכון
darom	south	דרום
dat	religion	דת
dati	religious	דתי
de'a	opinion	דעה
degel	flag	דגל
delek	petrol	דלק
delet	door	דלת
delpak rishum	check-in (desk)	דלפק רישום
demokratiya	democracy	דמוקרטיה
deodorant	deodorant	דאודורנט
derekh	way/road	דרך
derekh rashit	main road	דרך ראשית

E

derekh tslekha!	Bon voyage!	דרך צלחה!
deshe	grass	דשא
dim'a	tear (crying)	דימעה
diyur	accommodation	דיור
dli	bucket	דלי
dmei avtala	dole	דמי אבטלה
dmei do'ar	postage	דמי דואר
dmei knisa	admission (to a museum)	דמי כניסה
dmuyot	figures	דמויות
do'ar ...	... mail	דואר ...
avir	air	דואר אוויר
ekspres	express	דואר אקספרס
rashum	registered	דואר רשום
yam	surface	דואר ים
doda	aunt	דודה
do'eg	caring	דואג
dome	similar	דומה
drama	drama	דרמה
dramati	dramatic	דרמטי
dugma	example	דוגמא
dvash	honey	דבש

E

edim	steam	אדים
eden khalon	ledge	אדן חלון
efshar	allowed	אפשר
efshar yakhol	can (to be able)	אפשר יכול
efshari	possible	אפשרי
eifo	where	איפה
eikh	how	איך
eikhut	quality	איכות
ekhur	delay	איחור
elohim	God	אלוהים
emek	valley	עמק

emesh	last night	אמש
emet	truth	אמת
emtsa'ei meni'a	contraceptives	אמצעי מניעה
emun	trust	אמון
energia atomit	nuclear energy	אנרגיה אטומית
erets	country	מדינה
erev	evening	ערב
erev khag hamolad	Christmas Eve	ערב חג המולד
erev rosh hashana	New Year's Eve	ערב ראש השנה
erev tov	Good evening.	ערב טוב.
erope'i	European	אירופאי
erusim	engagement	אירוסים
esek	business	עסק
esh	fire	אש
et (kaduri)	pen (ballpoint)	עט (כדורי)
etkasher itkha	I'll give you a ring.	אתקשר איתך.
etmol	yesterday	אתמול
ets	tree/wood	עץ
etsa	advice	עצה
etsba	finger	אצבע
etsem	bone	עצם
even	stone	אבן
ez	goat	עז
ezor kafri	countryside	אזור כפרי
ezori	regional	אזורי
ezra	aid (help)	עזרה
ezrakhut	citizenship	אזרחות

F

frijider	refrigerator	ידר'פריג

G

ga'ava	pride	גאווה
gader	fence	גדר
gadol	big/great	גדול
gafrur	match	גפרור
gafrurim	matches	גפרורים
gal	wave	גל
galeria	art gallery	גלריה
galgal	wheel	גלגל
galgal hamazalot	zodiac	גלגל המזלות
galshan	surfboard	גלשן
gam	also/too	גם
gan khayot	zoo	גן חיות
gan yeladim	kindergarten	גן ילדים
ganav	thief	גנב
ganim	gardens	גנים
garon	throat	גרון
garzen kerakh	ice axe	גרזן קרח
gav	back (of body)	גב
gavoha	high/tall	גבוה
gaz'anut	racism	גזענות
gefen	vine	גפן
gerud	itch	גירוד
gerui or tinokot	nappy rash	גרוי עור תינוקות
geshem	rain	גשם
gesher	bridge	גשר
ge'ut	tide	גאות
geza	race (breed)	גזע
gibor	brave	גיבור
gil	age	גיל
gimla'i	pensioner	גימלאי
ginun	gardening	גינון
gitara	guitar	גיטרה
giv'a	hill	גבעה
glida	icecream	גלידה
glima	cloak	גלימה
gluya	postcard	גלויה
godel	size (of anything)	גודל
gol	goal	גול
gova	altitude	גובה
grafika	graphic art	גראפיקה
gram	gram	גראם
guf	body	גוף
gush	lump	גוש
gvi'a olam	World Cup	גביע עולם
gvina	cheese	גבינה
gvul	border	גבול
gzela	rip-off	גזילה

H

haba	next	הבא
haduk	tight	הדוק
hafgana	demonstration	הפגנה
hafrata	privatisation	הפרטה
hafsaka	intermission	הפסקה
hafta'a	a surprise	הפתעה
haga'ot	arrivals	הגעות
hagira	immigration	הגירה
haglula	the Pill	הגלולה
hahefekh	opposite	ההיפך
hakhodesh haba	next month	החודש הבא
hakhodesh she'avar	last month	החודש שעבר
hakhodesh	this month	החודש
haklata	recording	הקלטה
hakol	all	הכל
halayla	tonight	הלילה
halvaya	funeral	הלוויה
hamatat khesed	euthanasia	המתת חסד
hamiskhakim ha'olimpi'im	Olympic Games	המשחקים האולימפיים

I

hamkha'ot nos'im	travellers cheques	המחאות נוסעים
hamon	a lot	המון
hanakha	discount	הנחה
handasa	engineering	הנדסה
hapala	abortion	הפלה
hapala tiv'it	miscarriage	הפלה טבעית
har	mountain	הר
harbe	many	הרבה
harisot	ruins	הריסות
hashana	this year	השנה
hashana haba'a	next year	השנה הבאה
hashavu'a	this week	השבוע
hashavu'a haba	next week	השבוע הבא
hatanakh	the Bible	התנ"ך
hatov beyoter	best	הטוב ביותר
hatsa'a	proposal	הצעה
hatrada	harrassment	הטרדה
hatsaga	show/ performance/ presentation	הצגה
hatsilu! Help!	Help!	הצילו!
hatslakha	success	הצלחה
havtakha	promise	הבטחה
hayom akhar hatsohora'im	this afternoon	היום אחר הצהריים
hayom	today	היום
haze	this one	הזה
hazmana merosh	reservation	הזמנה מראש
he'avkut	boxing	האבקות
hedpes	a print (artwork)	הדפס
hegyoni	sensible	הגיוני
hekhzer	refund	החזר

hem	they	הם
hevanti I see. (understand)		הבנתי.
hi	she	היא
himur	a bet	הימור
hindu	Hindu	הינדו
hishtakfut	reflection (mirror)	השתקפות
hit'amlut	gymnastics	התעמלות
hitmakrut lesamim	drug addiction	התמכרות לסמים
hitmakrut	addiction	התמכרות
hitpatrut	resignation	התפטרות
hizdamnut	chance	הזדמנות
hizdamnuyot shavot	equal opportunity	הזדמנויות שוות
hoda'a	message	הודעה
hofa'a	gig	הופעה
holekh regel	pedestrian	הולך רגל
homeopatia	homeopathy	הומאופתיה
hona'a	a cheat	הונאה
hora'a	teaching	הוראה
horim	parents	הורים
hove	present (time)	הווה
hoze	delirious	הוזה
hu	he	הוא

I

igud ovdim	trade union	איגוד עובדים
igudim	unions	איגודים
ikar	farmer	איכר
ikhpat	to care (about)	אכפת
ilem	mute	אילם
im oferet	leaded (petrol)	עם עופרת
im	if	אם

im	with	עם
ima	mother	אמא
imun kosher	workout	אימון כושר
intensivi	intense	אינטנסיבי
inyanei	current	ענייני
hasha'a	affairs	השעה
iparon	pencil	עפרון
ipur	make-up	איפור
ir	city	עיר
ir atika	old city	עיר עתיקה
ish asakim	business person	איש עסקים
ish	man	איש
isha	woman/wife	אישה
ishiyut	personality	אישיות
ishur	permit	אישור
isu'i	massage	עיסוי
iti	slow	איטי
iton	newspaper	עיתון
itona'i	journalist	עיתונאי
itonim	newspapers	עיתונים
itstab'ot	shelves	אצטבאות
itstadyon	stadium	אצטדיון
iver	blind	עיוור
izkur	reference	איזכור

K

kabala	receipt	קבלה
kad	jar	כד
kadakhat hashakhat	hayfever	קדחת השחת
kadima	ahead	קדימה
kadosh	saint	קדוש
kadur	ball/pill	כדור
kadur ha'arets	planet earth	כדור הארץ
kaduregel	football (soccer)	כדורגל

kadurei shena	sleeping pills	כדורי שינה
kadurim neged ke'evim	painkillers	כדורים נגד כאבים
kaftorim	buttons	כפתורים
kaful	double	כפול
ka'its	summer	קיץ
kakhol	blue	כחול
kal	easy/light (adj)	קל
kaletet	cassette; video tape	קלטת
kaletet mesaperet	guide (audio)	קלטת מספרת
kalkala	economy	כלכלה
kalul	included	כלול
kama	some	כמה
kanai	jealous	קנאי
kar	pillow/ cold (adj)	כר
kar It's cold.		קר.
karov	near	קרוב
karov le	next to	קרוב ל
karpada	toad	קרפדה
kartis ...	... ticket	כרטיס ...
halokh	one-way	הלוך
halokh vashov	return	הלוך ושוב
kartis aliya lamatos	boarding pass	כרטיס עלייה למטוס
kartis ashra'i	credit card	כרטיס אשראי
kartis telefon	phonecard	כרטיס טלפון
kartisan	ticket collector	כרטיסן
kasda	helmet	קסדה
kasefet	safe (n)	כספת

230

kashe	difficult	קשה
kaspomat	automatic teller (ATM)	כספומט
katan	little/small	קטן
katedrala	cathedral	קתדרלה
katif perot	fruit picking	קטיף פירות
katoli	Catholic	קתולי
katom	orange (colour)	כתום
katsar	short (length)	קצר
kaved	heavy	כבד
kavod	respect	כבוד
kavu'a	permanent	קבוע
ke'ev	a pain	כאב
ke'ev batsavar	pain in the neck	כאב בצוואר
ke'ev beten	stomachache	כאב בטן
ke'ev rosh	headache	כאב ראש
ke'ev shina'im	toothache	כאב שיניים
ke'evei makhzor	period pain	כאבי מחזור
kef	cool (colloquial)	כיף
keiva	stomach	קיבה
kelev	dog	כלב
kelev hankhaya	guidedog	כלב הנחייה
kemakh	flour	קמח
kerakh	ice	קרח
keramika	ceramic	קרמיקה
kerem	vineyard	כרם
kesef	money	כסף
kesef katan	loose change	כסף קטן
ketsev	rhythm	קצב
kever	grave	קבר
kfar	village	כפר
kfits	spring (coil)	קפיץ

khadar ...	... room	חדר ...
ambatiya	bath	אמבטיה
halbasha	changing	הלבשה
hamtana	waiting	המתנה
shena	bed	שינה
khadar madregot	stairway	חדר מדרגות
khadash	new	חדש
khadashot	news	חדשות
khafisat	deck	חפיסת
klafim	(of cards)	קלפים
khafisat	packet	חפיסת
sigaryot	(of cigarettes)	סיגריות
khag	holiday	חג
khag hamolad	Christmas Day	חג המולד
khag hapaskha	Easter	חג הפסחא
khagorat moshav	seatbelt	חגורת מושב
kha'im	life	חיים
khake!	Wait!	חכה!
khakham	wise	חכם
khakla'ut	agriculture	חקלאות
khalal	space	חלל
khalash	weak	חלש
khalav	milk	חלב
khalon	window	חלון
kham	hot	חם
kham li!	I'm hot!	חם לי!
khamim	warm	חמים
khamtsan	oxygen	חמצן
khanut ...	... shop	חנות ...
bgadim	clothes	בגדים
dagim	fish	דגים
mazkarot	souvenir	מזכרות

na'ala'im	shoe	נעלים	khazir	pig	חזיר
sfarim	book	ספרים	kheder ...	... room	חדר ...
tsilum	camera	צילום	leyakhid	single	ליחיד
khanut	department	חנות	lishna'im	double	לשניים
kolbo	store	כלבו	khelek	part	חלק
khanut	newsagency	חנות	kherek	bug	חרק
lemutsarei		למוצרי	kheresh	deaf	חרש
ktiva		כתיבה	kherev	sword	חרב
khanut tabak	tobacco	חנות טבק	kherum	emergency	חירום
vesigariyot	kiosk	וסיגריות	khesaron	disadvantage	חסרון
kharif	spicy (hot)	חריף	kheshbon	bill	חשבון
khashish	hash	חשיש	khet	sin	חטא
khashiva	reflection	חשיבה	khevel	rope	חבל
	(thought)		khevra	company	חברה
khashmal	electricity	חשמל	khevruti	outgoing	חברותי
khashmalit	tram	חשמלית	khgim	holidays	חגים
khashukh	dark	חושך, חשוך	khibuk	a cuddle/hug	חיבוק
khashuv	important	חשוב	khilufim	exchange	חילופים
khasida	stork	חסידה	khinukh	education	חינוך
khataltul	kitten	חתלתול	khisun	vaccination	חיסון
khatikha	piece	חתיכה	khitul	nappy	חיתול
khatima	signature	חתימה	khodesh	month	חודש
khatira	rowing	חתירה	khof	coast	חוף
khatsi liter	half a litre	חצי ליטר	khof yam	beach/seaside	חוף ים
khatsi	half	חצי	khofshi	free (not bound)	חופשי
khatsot	midnight	חצות	khok	law	חוק
khatul	cat	חתול	khol	sand	חול
khatuna	wedding	חתונה	khole	ill	חולה
khava	farm	חווה	khole	epileptic	חולה
khaver	boyfriend/	חבר	bemakhalat		במחלת
	friend/		hanefila		הנפילה
	member		khole	seasick	חולה
khavera	girlfriend/friend	חברה	bemakhalat		במחלת
	member		yam		ים
khavila	package/parcel	חבילה	khole sakeret	diabetic	חולה סכרת
khayat pere	wild animal	חית פרא	khom	heat/fever	חום
khayot	animals	חיות	khoma	exterior wall	חומה
khazak	strong	חזק	khomer	laxatives	חומר
khaze	chest	חזה	meshalshel		משלשל

khomot ha'ir	city walls	חומות העיר
khoref	winter	חורף
khoser	shortage	חוסר
khoten	father-in-law	חותן
khotenet	mother-in-law	חותנת
khovev	amateur	חובב
khovrot metsuyarot	comics	חוברות מצויירות
khoze	contract	חוזה
khufsha	vacation	חופשה
khuka	legislation	חוקה
khultsa	shirt	חולצה
khultsat ti	T-shirt	חולצת טי
khum	brown	חום
khut barzel	wire	חוט ברזל
khut leniku'i shina'im	dental floss	חוט לניקוי שיניים
khut	string	חוט
khuts la'arets	abroad	חוץ לארץ
ki	because	כי
kikar rashit	main square	כיכר ראשית
kikar	square (in town)	כיכר
kilkul keiva	indigestion	קלקול קיבה
kim'at	almost	כמעט
kinim	lice	כינים
kinui khiba	nickname	כינוי חיבה
kir sla'im	crag; wall of rock	קיר סלעים
kir	interior wall	קיר
kirkas	circus	קרקס
kis	pocket	כיס
kise	chair	כסא
kise galgalim	wheelchair	כסא גלגלים
kishurim	qualifications	כישורים
kita	class	כיתה
kituviyot	subtitles	כיתוביות
klafim	playing cards	קלפים
klali	general	כללי
klalim	rules	כללים
klavlav	puppy	כלבלב
klei kheres	pottery	כלי חרס
klipa	shell	קליפה
knafa'im	wings	כנפיים
knas	a fine	קנס
knesiya	church	כנסיה
ko'akh	power/strength	כוח
ko'es	angry	כועס
ko'ev	painful	כואב
kokhav lekhet	planet	כוכב לכת
kokhavim	stars	כוכבים
kol	voice	קול
kol ekhad	each	כל אחד
kol yom	every day	כל יום
kolega	colleague	קולגה
kolno'a	cinema/films	קולנוע
kolshehu	any	כלשהו
koma	floor (storey)	קומה
komedia	comedy	קומדיה
komer	priest	כומר
komunisti	communist	קומוניסטי
konsuliya	consulate	קונסוליה
kosem	magician	קוסם
krav	fight	קרב
krem lakhut	moisturiser	קרם לחות
krem shizuf	sunblock	קרם שיזוף
kron mis'ada	dining car	קרון מסעדה
korot kha'im	resumé	קורות חיים
kron shena	sleeping car	קרון שינה
ktefa'im	shoulders	כתפיים
ktovet	address	כתובת
ktsat	a little bit	קצת
kubiyot miskhak	dice	קוביות משחק
kufsa	box	קופסא

L

kufsat shimurim	tin/can (of food)	קופסת שימורים
kupa	cash register	קופה
kupa'i(t)	cashier	קופאי(ת)
kutna	cotton	כותנה
kvar	already	כבר
kvasim	sheep	כבשים
kvish mahir	motorway (tollway)	כביש מהיר

L

la'akharona	recently	לאחרונה
la'alot	to board (ship etc)	לעלות
la'alot	to cost	לעלות
la'anot	to answer	לענות
la'asok be	to deal in	לעסוק ב
la'asot	to do/make	לעשות
la'asot kniyot	to go shopping	לעשות קניות
la'asot ski	to ski	לעשות סקי
la'atsor	to stop	לעצור
la'avod	to work	לעבוד
la'azor	to help	לעזור
la'azov	to quit	לעזוב
labri'ut!	לבריאות!
Bless you! (when sneezing)		
labri'ut!	לבריאות!
Good health!; Cheers!		
lada'at	to know (something)	לדעת
laga'at	to touch	לגעת
lagur be	to live (somewhere)	לגור ב
laharog	to kill	להרוג
laharos	to destroy	להרוס
lahazot	to hallucinate	להזות

lakakhat	to take (away)	לקחת
lakhagog	to celebrate	לחגוג
lakhalom	to dream	לחלום
lakhanot	to park	לחנות
lakhashov	to think	לחשוב
lakhatokh	to cut	לחתוך
lakhatom	to sign	לחתום
lakhats	pressure	לחץ
lakhats dam	blood pressure	לחץ דם
lakhats dam namukh/gavoha	low/high blood pressure	לחץ דם נמוך/גבוה
lakhazor	to return	לחזור
lakhazor al	to repeat	לחזור על
lako'akh	client	לקוח
lalekhet be'ikvot	to follow	ללכת בעקבות
lalekhet	to go/walk	ללכת
lama	why	למה
lamut	to die	למות
lanu'akh	to rest	לנוח
laruts	to run	לרוץ
laset	to carry	לשאת
lashevet	to sit	לשבת
lashir	to sing	לשיר
lasim	to put	לשים
latet	to give	לתת
latset im	to date (someone)	לצאת עם
latset lemasa	to hike	לצאת למסע
lavan	white	לבן
lavo	to come	לבוא
layla	night	לילה
layla tov. Good night.	לילה טוב.
le'abed	to lose	לאבד
le'akhel	to wish	לאחל
le'arbev	to mix	לערבב

DICTIONARY

le'argen	organise	לארגן
le'ashen	to smoke	לעשן
le'asher	to confirm (a booking)	לאשר
le'at	slowly	לאט
ledaber	to speak	לדבר
ledamem	to bleed	לדמם
le'ehov	to love	לאהוב
le'ekhol	to eat	לאכול
le'ever	towards	לעבר
lefakhed me	to be afraid of	לפחד מ
legalot	to discover	לגלות
leha'adif	to prefer	להעדיף
leha'anish	to punish	להעניש
leha'apil	to scale/climb	להעפיל
leha'arits	to admire	להעריץ
lehadpis	to type	להדפיס
lehafrid	to separate	להפריד
lehafsid	to lose	להפסיד
lehagen	to protect	לגונן
lehagi'a	to come/arrive	להגיע
lehagshim	to realise (attain)	להגשים
lehaka	band (music)	להקה
lehakat rok	rock group	להקת רוק
lehakhin	to prepare	להכין
lehakhlif	to exchange	להחליף
lehakhlit	to decide	להחליט
lehakhzir et hakesef	to refund	להחזיר את הכסף
lehakim ohel	to camp	להקים אוהל
lehakir	to know/ recognise	להכיר
lehak'khish	to deny	להכחיש
lehakshiv	to listen	להקשיב
lehamlits	to recommend	להמליץ
lehari'akh	to smell	להריח
leharim	to pick up	להרים
lehar'ot	to show	להראות
leharshot	to allow	להרשות
leharvi'akh	to earn	להרוויח
lehash'ir	to leave behind	להשאיר
lehaskim	to accept/ agree	להסכים
lehaskir	to rent	להשכיר
lehatil safek	to question	להטיל ספק
lehatkhil	begin	להתחיל
lehatsbi'a al	to point	להצביע על
lehatsbi'a	to vote	להצביע
lehatsig	to exhibit	להציג
lefatpet	to chat up	לפטפט
lehargish	to feel	להרגיש
lehatsil	to save	להציל
lehavi	to bring	להביא
lehavin	to understand	להבין
lehazhir	to warn	להזהיר
lehazi'a	to perspire	להזיע
lehazmin merosh	to make a booking	להזמין מראש
lehazmin	to order	להזמין
lehazrik	to inject	להזריק
leheraga	to relax	להירגע
lehikanes	to enter	להכנס
lehilakhem	to fight	להלחם
lehipared	to depart	להיפרד
lehisha'er	to stay/remain	להישאר
lehistakel	to look	להסתכל
lehitbade'akh	to joke	להתבדח
lehitbonen bekhalonot ra'ava	to go window shopping	להתבונן בחלונות ראווה
lehitga'age'a	to miss someone	להתגעגע
lehitgale'akh	to shave	להתגלח
lehitkhalek bekheder	to share a dorm	להתחלק בחדר

lehitkhalek im	to share with	להתחלק עם
lehitkharet	to regret	להתחרט
lehitkhaten	to marry	להתחתן
lehitrakhets	to wash yourself	להתרחץ
lehitra'ot. Goodbye.		להתראות.
lehitra'ot. See you later.		להתראות.
lehits'tarekh	to need	להצטרך
lehitvake'akh	to argue	להתווכח
lehodot	to admit	להודות ב
lehodot	to thank	להודות
le'itim krovot	often	לעיתים קרובות
leitsan	clown	ליצן
lekabel	to receive	לקבל
lekhabev	to like	לחבב
lekhapes	to look for	לחפש
lekhayekh	to smile	לחייך
lekhem	bread	לחם
lema'ala	up	למעלה
lemale	to fill	למלא
lemashal	for example	למשל
lenagen	to play (music)	לנגן
lenakhesh	to guess	לנחש
lenashek	to kiss	לנשק
lenasot	to try (attempt)	לנסות
le'om	nationality	לאום
lesakhek klafim	to play cards	לשחק קלפים
lesakhek	play (theatre); to play (a game)	לשחק
lesaper	to tell	לספר
lesarev	to refuse	לסרב
lesayem	to end	לסיים
lesbit	lesbian	לסבית
leshaker	to lie	לשקר
leshakhed	to bribe	לשחד
leshalem	to pay	לשלם
letalpen	to telephone	לטלפן
letamid	forever	לתמיד
letapes	to climb	לטפס
letargem	to translate	לתרגם
letayel	to travel	לטייל
letsalem	to take photographs	לצלם
lev	heart	לב
levad	alone	לבד
levaker	to visit	לבקר
levakesh (mashehu)	to ask (for something)	לבקש (משהו)
levalot	to have fun	לבלות
levarekh	to bless	לברך
levashel	to cook	לבשל
levatel	to cancel	לבטל
leyabesh	to dry (clothes)	לייבש
leyad	beside	ליד
leyatser	to produce	לייצר
lidkhof	to push	לדחוף
lid'og le	to care (for someone)	לדאוג ל
lif'amim	sometimes	לפעמים
lifgosh	to meet	לפגוש
lifnei	before; in front of	לפני
lifnei zman ma	a while ago	לפני זמן מה
lifto'akh	to open	לפתוח
lignov	to steal	לגנוב
liheyot	to be	להיות
liheyot khayav	to owe	להיות חייב
liheyot ra'ev	to be hungry	להיות רעב
liheyot shatui	to be drunk	להיות שתוי

liheyot tsodek	to be right	להיות צודק
liheyot	to be able;	להיות
yakhol	can	יכול
likhtov	to write	לכתוב
likhyot	to live (life)	לחיות
liknot	to buy	לקנות
likpo	to freeze	לקפוא
likpots	to jump	לקפוץ
likro	to read	לקרוא
lilbosh	to wear	ללבוש
lilmod	to learn	ללמוד
limdod	to try on	למדוד
limkhira	on sale	למכירה
limkhot	to protest	למחות
limkor	to sell	למכור
limno'a	prevent	למנוע
limshokh	to pull	למשוך
limtso	to find	למצוא
linhog	to drive	לנהוג
lin'ol	to lock	לנעול
linshom	to breathe	לנשום
linso'a	to take the	לנסוע
barakevet	train	ברכבת
linso'a	to hitchhike	לנסוע
bitrempim		בטרמפים
linto'a	to plant	לנטוע
lirkav al	to cycle	לרכב על
ofana'im		אופניים
lirkav al sus	to ride a	לרכב על סוס
	horse	
lirkhots	to wash	לרחוץ
	(something)	
lirkod	to dance	לרקוד
lirot	to shoot	לירות
lir'ot	to see	לראות
lirtsot	to want	לרצות
lisbol	to be	לסבול
me'atsirut	constipated	מעצירות

lisbol	to suffer	לסבול
lisgor	to close	לסגור
lishbor	to break	לשבור
lishdod	to rob	לשדוד
lish'hot be	to stay	לשהות ב
lishko'akh	to forget	לשכוח
lishkol	to weigh	לשקול
lishlo'akh	to send/ship	לשלוח
lishmo'a	to hear	לשמוע
lishmor al	to look after	לשמור על
lish'ol	to borrow	לשאול
lish'ol	to ask	לשאול
(she'ela)	(a question)	(שאלה)
lishon	to sleep	לישון
lishtot	to drink	לשתות
liskhot	to swim	לשחות
liskor	to hire	לשכור
lislo'akh	to forgive	לסלוח
lispor	to count	לספור
lisrod	to survive	לשרוד
litpor	to sew	לתפור
litsbo'a	to paint	לצבוע
litskhok me	to make fun of	לצחוק מ
lits'ok	to shout	לצעוק
litspot	to watch	לצפת
litvakh arokh	long distance	לטווח ארוך
livdok	to check	לבדוק
livkhor	to choose	לבחור
livnot	to build	לבנות
livto'akh be	to trust	לבטוח ב
lizkor	to remember	לזכור
lizkot	to win	לזכות
lizkot	to score	לזכות
binkudot		בנקודות
lo	no	לא
lo batu'akh	unsafe	לא-בטוח
lo nakhon	wrong	לא נכון
lo ragil	unusual	לא רגיל
lo ze velo ze	neither ...	לא זה ולא זה
	nor ...	

lokerim	luggage lockers	לוקרים
lomar	to say	לאמר
lu'akh shakhmat	chess board	לוח שחמט
lu'akh shana	calendar	לוח שנה
lu'akh totsa'ot	scoreboard	לוח תוצאות
lu'akh zmanim	timetable	לוח זמנים

M

ma	what	מה
ma'adaniya	delicatessen	מעדניה
ma'afera	ashtray	מאפרה
ma'afiya	bakery	מאפייה
ma'ale hahar	uphill	מעלה ההר
ma'alit	lift (elevator)	מעלית
ma'alot	temperature	מעלות
ma'amadot	class system	מעמדות
ma'arav	west	מערב
ma'arekhet khukim	legalisation	מערכת חוקים
ma'arekhet 'yekhasim	relationship	מערכת יחסים
ma'asik	employer	מעסיק
ma'atafa	envelope	מעטפה
mad or	light meter	מד אור
mada	science	מדע
mad'an	scientist	מדען
mad'ei hakhevra	social sciences	מדעי החברה
madrega	step	מדרגה
madrikh	guide/ guidebook	מדריך
mafsidan	loser	מפסידן
mafte'akh	key	מפתח
magafa'im	boots	מגפיים

magevet	towel	מגבת
magid atidot	fortune teller	מגיד עתידות
maher	fast	מהר
mahir	quick	מהיר
ma'im khamim	hot water	מים חמים
maksim	charming	מקסים
ma'im	water	מים
ma'im minerali'im	mineral water	מים מינרליים
maka	a bruise	מכה
makat shemesh	sunburn	מכת שמש
makhala	sickness/ disease	מחלה
makhalat min	venereal disease	מחלת מין
makhane	campsite	מחנה
makhar	tomorrow	מחר
makhat	sewing needle	מחט
makhberet	notebook	מחברת
makhbet	racquet	מחבט
makhleket mekhirot	sales department	מחלקת מכירות
makhshava	thought	מחשבה
makhshir shmi'a	hearing aid	מכשיר שמיעה
makhshir televisia	TV set	מכשיר טלוויזיה
makhur le'heroin	heroin addict	מכור להרואין
makhvat	pan	מחבת
makom	place	מקום
makosh	pick/pickaxe	מכוש
makren	projector	מקרן
male	full	מלא
malka	queen	מלכה
malon ... basviva	... hotel nearby	מלון ... בסביבה

M

naki	clean	נקי
tov	good	טוב
zol	cheap	זול
mankhe	presenter (TV etc)	מנחה
mangina	tune	מנגינה
manhig	leader	מנהיג
mano'a	engine	מנוע
man'ul	padlock	מנעול
ma'on yeladim	childminding	מעון ילדים
mapa	map	מפה
mapal	waterfall	מפל
mapat drakhim	road map	מפת דרכים
mar'a	mirror	מראה
marijuana	marijuana	מריחואנה
mar'ish	noisy	מרעיש
mas	tax	מס
mas hakhnasa	income tax	מס הכנסה
mas namal	airport tax	מס נמל
masa	journey/hike	מסע
masa ragli	trek	מסע רגלי
masa'it	truck	משאית
masakh	screen	מסך
mashehu	something	משהו
mash'eva	pump	משאבה
mashke	a drink	משקה
maskoret	salary	משכורת
maslul mekhof el khof	cross-country trail	מסלול מחוף אל חוף
maslul munkhe	guided trek	מסלול מונחה
maslul	itinerary; sports track; car-racing track	מסלול
maslulei halikha	hiking routes	מסלולי הליכה

maspik	enough	מספיק
masrek	comb	מסרק
mastik	chewing gum	מסטיק
matai	when	מתי
matana	present/gift	מתנה
matbe'ot	coins	מטבעות
matekhet	metal	מתכת
matnat khatuna	wedding present	מתנת חתונה
matok	sweet	מתוק
matos	aeroplane	מטוס
matsav mishpakhti	marital status	מצב משפחתי
matsit	lighter	מצית
matslema	camera	מצלמה
matsok	cliff; wall of rock	מצוק
matspen	compass	מצפן
mavet	death	מוות
mavrik	brilliant	מבריק
mazal	luck	מזל
mazal tov! Congratulations!		מזל טוב!
mazkeret	souvenir	מזכרת
mazkir(a)	secretary	מזכיר(ה)
mazrek	syringe	מזרק
me'a	a hundred	מאה
me'ahev	lover	מאהב
me'akhor	at the back; behind	מאחור
me'al	above/over	מעל
me'anyen	interesting	מעניין
me'arot	caves	מערות
me'at	a little	מעט
me'avrer	electric fan	מאוורר
me'az (Mai)	since (May)	מאז (מאי)
medalya	medal	מדליה
meditatsia	meditation	מדיטציה

me'ever	across	מעבר
mefits	distributor	מפיץ
mefursam	famous	מפורסם
mehandes	engineer	מהנדס
mehirut	speed	מהירות
mehirut film	film speed	מהירות פילם
mehirut muteret	speed limit	מהירות מותרת
meikhal gaz	gas cartridge	מיכל גז
me'il	overcoat	מעיל
mekabets nedavot	beggar	מקבץ נדבות
mekha'a	protest	מחאה
mekhate	antiseptic	מחטא
mekhes	customs	מכס
mekhir	price/value	מחיר
mekhona	machine	מכונה
mekhona'i	mechanic	מכונאי
mekhonat gilu'akh	razor	מכונת גילוח
mekhonat kvisa	washing machine	מכונת כביסה
mekhonit	car	מכונית
mekom leida	place of birth	מקום לידה
mekomi	local	מקומי
mekori	original	מקורי
melakh	salt	מלח
melakhot ba'it	housework	מלאכות בית
melakhot yad	handicrafts	מלאכות יד
melekh	king	מלך
meltakha	cloakroom/ wardrobe	מלתחה
meltsar	waiter	מלצר
melukhlakh	dirty	מלוכלך
memshala	government	ממשלה
menahel	director/ manager	מנהל

menat yeter	overdose	מנת יתר
menatse'akh	winner	מנצח
meni'at herayon	contraception	מניעת הריון
menifa	fan (hand-held)	מניפה
menukha	rest (relaxation)	מנוחה
menumnam	sleepy	מנומנם
me'od	very	מאוד
meriva	quarrel	מריבה
merkaz ha'ir	city centre	מרכז העיר
merkaz ta'asuka	job centre	מרכז תעסוקה
merkazan	telephone operator	מרכזן
merots	race (sport)	מרוץ
meruba	square (shape)	מרובע
mesha'amem	boring	משעמם
mesha'ashe'a	entertaining	משעשע
meshi	silk	משי
meshu'amam	bored	משועמם
meshuga	crazy/mad	משוגע
meshutak	paraplegic	משותק
mesiba	party (fiesta)	מסיבה
mesilat barzel	railroad	מסילת ברזל
mesof mizvadot	baggage claim	מסוף מזוודות
mesukan	dangerous	מסוכן
mesumam	stoned (drugged)	מסומם
mesunan	filtered	מסונן
met	dead	מת
metakh nafshi shelifnei haveset	pre-menstrual tension	מתח נפשי שלפני הווסת

metapel be'isbei	herbalist	מטפל בעשבי
marpe		מרפא
metsuyan	excellent	מצוין
me'ukhar	late	מאוחר
me'unan	cloudy	מעונן
mevukha	embarrassment	מבוכה
meyukhad	special	מיוחד
mezeg avir	weather	מזג אוויר
mi	who	מי
mida	size (clothes/ shoes)	מידה
midbar	desert	מדבר
miflaga	party (politics)	מפלגה
migdal	tower	מגדל
migrash (tennis)	court (tennis)	מגרש (טניס)
migrena	migraine	מיגרנה
mikdash	shrine/temple	מקדש
mikesef	of silver	מכסף
mikhbesa lesherut atsmi	launderette	מכבסה לשרות עצמי
mikhnasa'im ktsarim	shorts	מכנסיים קצרים
mikhnasa'im	trousers	מכנסיים
mikhtav	letter	מכתב
mikhzur	recycling	מיחזור
miklakhat	shower	מקלחת
mikledet	keyboard	מקלדת
mikteret	pipe	מקטרת
miktso'a	profession	מקצוע
mikud	post code	מיקוד
mikum	location	מיקום
mila	word	מילה
milkhama	war	מלחמה
millimetre	millimetre	מילימטר
million	million	מיליון
milon	dictionary	מילון
mimkhatot	tissues	ממחטות
neyar		נייר
min batu'akh	safe sex	מין בטוח
min	sex	מין
minzar	monastery	מנזר
minzar nashim	convent	מנזר נשים
mirpeset	balcony	מרפסת
misa	mass (Catholic)	מיסה
mis'ada	restaurant	מסעדה
misgad	mosque	מסגד
mishehu	somebody/ someone	מישהו
mishkal	weight	משקל
mishkefei shemesh	sunglasses	משקפי שמש
mishkefet	binoculars	משקפת
mishkhat shina'im	toothpaste	משחת שיניים
mish'ol	footpath	משעול
mishor	plain	מישור
mishpakha	family	משפחה
mishpat	sentence (words)	משפט
mishtara	police	משטרה
miskhak	game	משחק
miskhak kriket	cricket	משחק קריקט
miskhakei makhshev	computer games	משחקי מחשב
mispar darkon	passport number	מספר דרכון
mispar kheder	room number	מספר חדר
mispara'im	scissors	מספריים
misrad	office	משרד
misrad do'ar	post office	משרד דואר
misrad kartisim	ticket office	משרד כרטיסים
misrad nesi'ot	travel agency	משרד נסיעות
mita	bed	מיטה

mita kfula	double bed	מיטה כפולה
mitakhat	below	מתחת
mit'an	luggage	מטען
mitbakh	kitchen	מטבח
mitgalgel	rolling	מתגלגל
mitriya	umbrella	מטרייה
mits	juice	מיץ
mivkhan	test	מבחן
mivrak	telegram	מברק
mivreshet se'ar	hairbrush	מברשת שיער
mivreshet shina'im	toothbrush	מברשת שיניים
mivtsa	operation	מבצע
mizahav	of gold	מזהב
mizrakh	east	מזרח
mizron	mattress	מזרון
mizug avir	air-conditioned	מיזוג אוויר
mizvada	suitcase	מזוודה
moda'ot drushim	job advertisement	מודעות דרושים
modi'in tayarim	tourist information office	מודיעין תיירים
mokher prakhim	flower seller	מוכר פרחים
more	teacher	מורה
moshav	seat	מושב
motarot	luxury	מותרות
motsets	dummy (pacifier)	מוצץ
mud'ag	worried	מודאג
mukdam	early	מוקדם
mukhan	ready	מוכן
mumkhe	specialist	מומחה
musakh	garage	מוסך
mushkhat	corrupt	מושחת
musika	music	מוסיקה
muskam! Agreed!		מוסכם!

muslemi	Muslim	מוסלמי
mutsa min haklal	excluded	מוצא מן הכלל
mutsaf shemesh	sunny	מוצף שמש
mutsak	solid	מוצק
mutsarei khalav	dairy products	מוצרי חלב
mutsarei or	leathergoods	מוצרי עור
muvtal	unemployed	מובטל
muzar	strange	מוזר
muze'on	museum	מוזיאון

N

na	raw (meat)	נא
na'ala'im	shoes	נעלים
na'alei masa	hiking boots	נעלי מסע
nadir	rare	נדיר
na'e	pretty	נאה
nafas	hash	נאפאס
nagan	musician	נגן
nagan rehov	busker	נגן רחוב
nahar	river	נהר
nakhal	stream	נחל
nakhon	right (correct)	נכון
nakhuts	necessary	נחוץ
naki	clean	נקי
namal	harbour/port	נמל
namukh	low/short	נמוך
nasa virus HIV	HIV positive	נשא וירוס HIV
nasi	president	נשיא
navokh	embarassed	נבוך
nazir	monk	נזיר
ne'eman	loyal	נאמן
nefakh	volume	נפח
neft	oil (crude)	נפט
neged	against	נגד

nehedar! Great!		נהדר!
neka	a sprain	נקע
nekhe	disabled	נכה
nekhed(a)	grandchild	נכד(ה)
nekhmad	nice	נחמד
nemala	ant	נמלה
ner	candle	נר
neshika	kiss	נשיקה
neshikha	bite (dog)	נשיכה
netul oferet	unleaded	נטול עופרת
ne'um politi	political speech	נאום פוליטי
neyar	paper	נייר
neyar sigariyot	cigarette papers	נייר סיגריות
neyar twalet	toilet paper	נייר טואלט
nezira	nun	נזירה
nifla	wonderful/great	נפלא
nikayon	cleaning	ניקיון
nir'e! We'll see!		נראה!
nisui atomi	nuclear testing	ניסוי אטומי
nisu'im	marriage	נישואים
nitan lemikhzur	recyclable	ניתן למיחזור
nitsul	exploitation	ניצול
nitu'akh	surgery	ניתוח
nivdal	offside	נבדל
no'akh	comfortable	נוח
no'ar	youth (collective)	נוער
nof	view	נוף
nora	horrible	נורא
nose	question (topic)	נושא
nose'a	passenger	נוסע
notsri	Christian	נוצרי
nura	light bulb	נורה

O

o	or	או
od	more	עוד
of	chicken	עוף
ofana'im	bicycle	אופניים
ofnati	trendy (person)	אופנתי
ofnei harim	mountain bike	אופני הרים
ofnei merots	racing bike	אופני מירוץ
ofno'a	motorcycle	אופנוע
ofyani	typical	אופייני
ohadim	fans (of a team)	אוהדים
ohel	tent	אוהל
ohev teva	naturopath	אוהב טבע
okhel	food	אוכל
okhel kafu	frozen food	אוכל קפוא
okhel tinokot	baby food	אוכל תינוקות
oki'anus	ocean	אוקיאנוס
olam	universe/ world	עולם
olar	penknife	אולר
oman	artist	אמן
omanut ...	... art	אמנות ...
klassit	classical	אמנות קלסית
pre-historit	prehistoric	אמנות פרה-היסטורית
omanuyot	crafts	אומנויות
omanuyot bama	performance art	אמנויות במה
ones	rape	אונס
oni	poverty	עוני
oniya	boat/ship	אוניה
operat sabon	soap opera	אופרת סבון
or	skin/leather/ bright light	עור
orekh	editor	עורך
orekh din	lawyer	עורך-דין

oren	pine	אורן
orgazma	orgasm	אורגזמה
oto davar	same	אותו דבר
otobus ...	... bus	אוטובוס ...
bein-ironi	intercity	בין-עירוני
ironi	city/local	עירוני
otomat	ticket	אוטומט
kartisim	machine	כרטיסים
otser	curator	אוצר
ozen	ear	אוזן
ozna'im	ears	אוזניים

P

pa'am	once	פעם
pa'am akhat	one time	פעם אחת
pa'ama'im	twice	פעמיים
pakhad	fear	פחד
pagum	faulty	פגום
pa'il	activist	פעיל
pakhit	can (aluminium)	פחית
pakhot	less	פחות
pakid	office worker	פקיד
palit	refugee	פליט
panas	torch (flashlight)	פנס
panim	face	פנים
pancher	puncture	פנצ'ר
para	cow	פרה
parashat	romance	פרשת
ahavim		אהבים
park	a park	פארק
parpar	butterfly	פרפר
parvar	suburb	פרבר
parvarei ...	suburbs of ...	פרברי ...
pashtida	pie	פשטידה
pashut	simple	פשוט
patish	hammer	פטיש
patu'akh	open	פתוח

pe	mouth	פה
perakh	flower	פרח
pesel	statue	פסל
petakh	opening	פתח
petsa	wound	פצע
pgisha	date/ appointment	פגישה
pilpel	pepper	פלפל
pin	penis	פין
pina	corner	פינה
pisga	peak	פסגה
pishpeshim	flea	פשפשים
pisul	sculpture	פיסול
pkak	plug (bath)	פקק
plastik	plastic	פלסטיק
pne smola Turn left.		פנה שמאלה.
pne yamina Turn right.		פנה ימינה.
po	here	פה
po'el	manual worker	פועל
politika	politics	פוליטיקה
politika'im	politicians	פוליטיקאים
populari	popular	פופולארי
poster	poster	פוסטר
potkhan	bottle	פותחן
bakbukim	opener	בקבוקים
potkhan	can/tin	פותחן
kufsa'ot	opener	קופסאות
prat	detail	פרט
prati	private	פרטי
prikha	a rash	פריחה
psak din	sentence (prison)	פסק דין
psolet ra'alit	toxic waste	פסולת רעלית
ptsia	injury	פציעה

R

ra	bad	רע
ra'ash	noise	רעש
radi'ator	radiator	רדיאטור
ragil	ordinary	רגיל
rak	only	רק
rakevet	train	רכבת
rakhav	large/wide	רחב
rakhok	far/remote	רחוק
rama	plateau	רמה
rama'i! Cheat!		!רמאי
ramat kha'im	standard of living	רמת חיים
ramzor	traffic lights	רמזור
ratuv	wet	רטוב
ravak	single (person)	רווק
raze	thin	רזה
re'akh	a smell	ריח
re'ayon	interview	ראיון
regashot	feelings	רגשות
regel	foot/leg	רגל
re'idat adama	earthquake	רעידת אדמה
rek	empty/vacant	ריק
rekhes harim	mountain range	רכס הרים
rekhiva al ofna'im	cycling	רכיבה על אופניים
rekhiva al sus	horse riding	רכיבה על סוס
rekhov	street	רחוב
republika	republic	רפובליקה
resen	harness	רסן
reshet	net	רשת
reshut	permission	רשות
retsini	serious	רציני
revakh	profit	רווח
rikudim	dancing	ריקוד

rishon	first	ראשון
rishyon avoda	work permit	עבודהרשיון
rishyon ma'avar	pass	רשיון מעבר
rishyon nehiga	driver's licence	רשיון נהיגה
ritspa	floor	ריצפה
rivkhiyut	profitability	ריווחיות
rofe shina'im	dentist	רופא שינים
rofe	doctor	רופא
roke'akh	chemist	רוקח
rokhev ofna'im	cyclist	רוכב אופניים
roman	novel (book)	רומן
rosh	head	ראש
rosh hashana	New Year's Day	ראש השנה
rosh ir	mayor	ראש עיר
rosh memshala	prime minister	ראש ממשלה
rov	majority	רוב
rova	quarter	רובע
ru'akh	wind	רוח

S

sa'ad	social welfare	סעד
saba	grandfather	סבא
sabon	soap	סבון
sade	field	שדה
sadin	bedsheet	סדין
sadna	workshop	סדנה
safot	languages	שפות
sagol	purple	סגול
sagur	closed	סגור
sak shena	sleeping bag	שק שינה
sakhir	employee	שכיר
sakhkan	player (sports)	שחקן
sakin	knife	סכין

sakin gilu'akh	razor blade	סכין גילוח
sal	basket	סל
sam	drug	סם
same'akh	happy	שמח
samim	drugs	סמים
savil	passive	סביל
savlani	patient (adj)	סבלני
savta	grandmother	סבתא
sde te'ufa	airport	שדה-תעופה
se'ar	hair	שיער
se'ara	storm	סערה
sefel	cup	ספל
sefer	book	ספר
sefer telefon	phone book	ספר טלפון
sefer tfila	prayer book	ספר תפילה
seder	order	סדר
sela	rock	סלע
seret	movie	סרט
seret kolno'a	film (cinema)	סרט קולנוע
seret shakhor lavan	B&W film	סרט שחור לבן
seret ti'udi	documentary	סרט תיעודי
seret tsilum	film (negatives)	סרט צילום
sfata'im	lips	שפתיים
sfaton	lipstick	שפתון
sha'ar	gate	שער
sha'ar khalifin	exchange rate	שער חליפין
shabat	Saturday	שבת
shagrir	ambassador	שגריר
shagrirut	embassy	שגרירות
shaket	quiet (adj)	שקט
shakh	chess	שח
shakhar	dawn	שחר
shakhmat! Checkmate!		שחמט!
shakhor	black	שחור

shakran	liar	שקרן
shalav	leg (in race)	שלב
shalem	whole	שלם
shalom	peace	שלום
shama'im	sky	שמיים
shamen	fat	שמן
shampanya	champagne	שמפניה
shamran	conservative	שמרן
shana she'avra	last year	שנה שעברה
shana	year	שנה
sha'on	clock/watch	שעון
sha'on me'orer	alarm clock	שעון מעורר
sharsheret	necklace	שרשרת
shati'akh	mat/rug	שטיח
shatu'akh	flat (land, etc)	שטוח
shavu'a	week	שבוע
shavu'a kadosh	Holy Week	שבוע קדוש
shavu'a she'avar	last week	שבוע שעבר
shavur	broken	שבור
shdera	avenue	שדרה
she'ela	question	שאלה
she'erit	rest (what's left)	שארית
shelet	a sign	שלט
shem	name	שם
shem mishpakha	surname	שם משפחה
shem prati	christian name	שם פרטי
shemen	oil (cooking)	שמן
shemen za'it	olive oil	שמן זית
shemesh	sun	שמש
shen	tooth/teeth	שן
shen bina	wisdom tooth	שן בינה
sheni	second	שני
sherets	creep (slang)	שרץ
sherut	service (assistance)	שירות

sherut atsmi	self-service	שירות עצמי
sherut tsva'i	military service	שירות צבאי
sherutim	toilets	שירותים
sherutim tsiburi'im	public toilet	שירותים ציבוריים
shfan nisayon	guinea pig	שפן ניסיון
shikhvat ha'ozone	ozone layer	שכבת האוזון
shikufit	slide (film)	שיקופית
shilshul	diarrhoea	שלשול
shimsha kidmit	windscreen	שימשה קידמית
shimushi	useful	שימושי
shir	song	שיר
shira	poetry	שירה
shi'ul	a cough	שיעול
shivyon	equality	שיוויון
shki'at hashemesh	sunset	שקיעת השמש
shlat rakhok	remote control	שלט-רחוק
shlishi	third	שלישי
shmartaf	babysitter	שמרטף
shmirat khafatsim	left luggage	שמירת חפצים
shmurat teva	national park	שמורת טבע
shnati	annual	שנתי
shneihem	both	שניהם
shniya	second (n)	שנייה
sho'er	goalkeeper	שוער
shofet	judge/referee	שופט
shokhad	a bribe	שוחד
shokolad	chocolate	שוקולד
shone	different	שונה
shovar	coupon	שובר
shovi	worth	שווי
shrir	muscle	שריר
shtarot kesef	banknotes	שטרות כסף
shuk	market	שוק

shulkan tenis	table tennis	שולחן טניס
shulkhan	table	שולחן
shum davar	nothing	שום דבר
shura	line	שורה
shuv	again	שוב
shvil	track/path/trail	שביל
shvil harimn	mountain path	שביל הרים
shvita	a strike	שביתה
shvu'a'im	fortnight	שבועיים
siba	reason (cause)	סיבה
sidra	series	סדרה
sifriya	library	ספריה
sigariyot	cigarettes	סיגריות
signon	style	סגנון
sikun	risk	סיכון
siman heker	indicator	סימן הכר
simla	dress	שמלה
simpati	sympathetic	סימפטי
sinteti	synthetic	סינטטי
siporet	fiction	סיפורת
sipur	story	סיפור
sipurim ktsarim	short stories	סיפורים קצרים
sirat mano'a	motorboat	סירת מנוע
siyuf	fencing (with foils)	סיוף
skhar dira	rent	שכר-דירה
skhiya	swimming	שחייה
ski	skiing	סקי
skira	review	סקירה
slikha	Excuse me.	סליחה.
smikha	blanket	שמיכה
smol	left (not right)	שמאל
smolani	left-wing	שמאלני

snif	branch (bank etc)	סניף
sof	end	סוף
sofer	writer	סופר
sofshavu'a	weekend	סופשבוע
sokher samim	drug dealer	סוחר סמים
sokhnut khadashot	newsagency	סוכנות חדשות
solela	battery	סוללה
sotsialisti	socialist	סוציאליסטי
sotsyal demokrati	social-democratic	סוציאל-דמוקרטי
sport	sport	ספורט
sporta'i	sportsperson	ספורטאי
sratim ktsarim	short films	סרטים קצרים
sratim metsuyarim	cartoons	סרטים מצויירים
sreifa	fire	שריפה
stav	autumn (fall)	סתיו
studio	studio	סטודיו
sug dam	blood group	סוג דם
sukar	sugar	סוכר
sus	horse	סוס
sveder	jumper (sweater)	סוודר
sviva	environment	סביבה

T

ta telefon	phone box	תא טלפון
ta'arif	rate of pay	תעריף
ta'arikh	date (time)	תאריך
ta'arikh leida	date of birth	תאריך לידה
ta'arukha	exhibition	תערוכה
ta'arukha kvu'a	permanent collection	תערוכה קבועה
ta'asia	industry	תעשיה
taba'at	ring (on finger)	טבעת
tabak	tobacco	טבק
tafrit	menu	תפריט
tahor	pure	טהור
ta'im	tasty	טעים
takhana	stop	תחנה
takhana merkazit	bus station	תחנה מרכזית
takhanat ...		תחנת ...
bikoret	checkpoint	ביקורת
moniyot	taxi stand	מוניות
otobus	bus stop	אוטובוס
rakevet	train station	רכבת
rakevet takhtit	subway station	רכבת תחתית
takhara	lace	תחרה
takharut	a game show	תחרות
takhboshet	bandage	תחבושת
takhboshot higyeniyot	sanitary napkins	תחבושות היגייניות
takhshitim	jewellery	תכשיטים
talul	steep	תלול
tamid	always	תמיד
tamponim	tampons	טמפונים
tanur	stove	תנור
tanur khimum	heater	תנור חימום
tarmil gav	backpack	תרמיל גב
tashlum	payment	תשלום
ta'ut	mistake	טעות
tayar	tourist	תייר
te'atron	theatre	תיאטרון
teatron klassi	classical theatre	תיאטרון קלסי
teka	plug (electric)	תקע
tekhnika	technique	טכניקה
telephone nayad	mobile phone	טלפון נייד
televizia	television	טלוויזיה

248

tender	van	טנדר
te'omim	twins	תאומים
te'uda	certificate	תעודה
te'udat ba'alut al hamkhonit	car owner's title	תעודת בעלות על המכונית
te'udat leida	birth certificate	תעודת-לידה
te'udat rishui	car registration	תעודת רישוי
te'udat zehut	identification card	תעודת זהות
te'una	accident	תאונה
te'ur ha'avoda	job description	תאור העבודה
teva	nature	טבע
tevat do'ar	mailbox	תיבת דואר
tfila	prayer/service (religious)	תפילה
tik ezra rishona	first-aid kit	תיק עזרה ראשונה
tik	bag	תיק
tik yad	handbag	תיק יד
tikni	standard (usual)	תיקני
tinok	baby	תינוק
tip	tip (gratuity)	טיפ
tipesh	stupid	טיפש
tipus al tsukim	rock climbing	טיפוס על צוקים
tipus harim	mountaineering	טיפוס הרים
tira	castle	טירה
tisa	flight	טיסה
tiyul	walk/tour	טיול
tizmoret	orchestra	תזמורת
tkufat kehuna	term of office	תקופת כהונה
tmuna	photo	תמונה

tnu'a	traffic	תנועה
to'ar	degree	תואר
toast	toast	טוסט
toda	Thank you.	תודה.
toda'a	mind	תודעה
tokhnit	design/ program	תוכנית
tokpani	aggressive	תוקפני
tola'im	worms	תולעים
tor	queue	תור
tov	well	טוב
treisar	a dozen	תריסר
trufa	medicine	תרופה
tsaba	painter	צבע
tsad	side	צד
tsafon	north	צפון
tsahov	yellow	צהוב
tsa'ir	young	צעיר
tsalakhat	plate	צלחת
tsalam	photographer	צלם
tsame	thirsty	צמא
tsayar portretim	portrait sketcher	צייר פורטרטים
tsedek	justice	צדק
tse'etsa	descendent	צאצא
tse'ifim	scarves	צעיפים
tsel	shade/ shadow	צל
tsemakh	plant	צמח
tsemer	wool	צמר
tseva	colour	צבע
tsevet	team	צוות
tshuva	answer	תשובה
tsibur bokharim	electorate	ציבור בוחרים
tsiltsul	ring (of phone)	צלצול
tsiltsul	ring (sound)	צלצול

tsilum	photography	צילום
tsimkhiya	vegetation	צמחיה
tsimkhoni	vegetarian	צמחוני
tsintsenet	pot (ceramic)	צנצנת
tsinun	a cold	צינון
tsipit	pillowcase	ציפית
tsipor	bird	ציפור
tsiyud tslila	diving equipment	ציוד צלילה
tsiyud	equipment	ציוד
tsiyur	painting (the art)	ציור
tsiyurim	paintings	ציורים
tskhok	laugh	צחוק
tslav	cross (religious)	צלב
tslil	sound	צליל
tslil khiyug	dial tone	צליל חיוג
tslila	diving	צלילה
tsmigim	tyres	צמיגים
tsohora'im	lunchtime/noon	צהריים
tsom halent	Lent	צום הלנט
tsura	shape	צורה
tsvi	deer	צבי
tupim	drums	תופים
tvila	baptism	טבילה

U

ugat khatuna	wedding cake	עוגת חתונה
ugat yom-huledet	birthday cake	עוגת יום-הולדת
ula'i	maybe	אולי
ulam hit'amlut	gym	אולם התעמלות
ulam knisa	foyer	אולם כניסה
ulam nos'im	transit lounge	אולם נוסעים
universita	university	אוניברסיטה

V

varod	pink	ורוד
ve	and	ו
veset	menstruation	וסת
vidui	confession (religious)	וידוי
visa	visa	ויזה
vitaminim	vitamins	ויטמינים
vrid	vein	וריד

Y

ya'ad	destination	יעד
ya'ar mugan	protected forest	יער מוגן
ya'ar	forest	יער
yabasha	land	יבשה
yad	hand/monument	יד
yafe	beautiful/handsome	יפה
ya'in	wine	יין
yakar	expensive	יקר
yakar midai	too expensive	יקר מידי
yakhid	single (unique)	יחיד
yalda	girl	ילדה
yalkut gav	knapsack	ילקוט גב
yam	sea	ים
yamin	right (not left)	ימין
yare'akh	moon	ירח
yarkan	greengrocer	ירקן
yarok	green	ירוק
yashan	old (objects)	ישן
yashar	straight	ישר
yashir	direct	ישיר
yatsran	producer	יצרן
yehudi	Jewish	יהודי
yekar erekh	valuable	יקר ערך
yekev	winery	יקב
yekhi ...!	Long live ...!	!... יחי

yeladim	children	ילדים
yeled	child/boy	ילד
yemani	right-wing	ימני
yerakh devash	honeymoon	ירח דבש
yerek	vegetable	ירק
yesh	to have	יש
yetedot	tent pegs	יתדות
yetsi'a	departure/exit	יציאה
yetsirat omanut	artwork	יצירת אמנות
yi	island	אי
yi efshar		אי אפשר.
It's not allowed.		
yi-shivyon	inequality	אי-שיוויון
yitaron	advantage	יתרון
yom	day	יום
yoman	diary	יומן
yom huledet	birthday	יום-הולדת
yom huledet same'akh!		יום הולדת שמח!
Happy birthday!		
yomi	daily	יומי
yom shishi	Friday	יום שישי
yored geshem		יורד גשם.
It's raining.		
yoter midai	too much; many	יותר מידי

zaken	old (people)	זקן
zamar	singer	זמר
zanav	tail	זנב
zanim muganim	protected species	זנים מוגנים
zanim nik'khadim	endangered species	זנים נכחדים
zar	foreign/stranger	זר
ze mukdam		זה מוקדם.
It's early.		
ze nakhon		זה נכון.
It's true.		
zehirut!		זהירות!
Careful!		
zeitim	olives	זיתים
zevel	garbage	זבל
zihum avir	pollution	זיהום אוויר
zihuy	identification	זיהוי
z'khukhit	glass	זכוכית
zkhuyot adam	human rights	זכויות אדם
zkhuyot ezrakh	civil rights	זכויות אזרח
zman	time	זמן
zrika	injection	זריקה
zrikhat hashemesh	sunrise	זריחת השמש
zro'a	arm	זרוע
zug	pair (a couple)	זוג
zvuv	fly	זבוב

INDEX

HEBREW FINDER